A LATE HARVEST

Reflections on the Old Testament

William McKane

St Mary's College, St Andrews

T&T CLARK
EDINBURGH

T&T CLARK LTD
59 GEORGE STREET
EDINBURGH EH2 2LQ
SCOTLAND

First published 1995

ISBN 0 567 09727 7

British Library Cataloguing-in-Publication Data
A catalogue record for this book is available from the British Library

Typeset by Fakenham Photosetting Ltd, Fakenham, Norfolk
Printed and bound in Great Britain by Hartnolls Limited, Bodmin, Cornwall

CONTENTS

PREFACE

My 'Reflections' have a relation to the transactions of the Honours seminar on Old Testament Theology which I conducted at St Mary's College for the most part of my tenure of the Chair of Hebrew and Oriental Languages in the University of St Andrews and as such they are a concatenated description of my own Odyssey. The relation is not an exact one and the account which is given is far from comprehensive, but the nature of the enquiry should be clear. The students who participated were sometimes perplexed, but I should like to think that they were aware of the rigour and seriousness of the quest. It will be seen that I have tended to resist the fashions of Old Testament scholarship and that I have usually been swimming against the current.

In Glasgow I had been locking horns with Eichrodt and von Rad, and I was especially absorbed in the latter. This phase continued for some time at St Andrews from 1968 on and chapter 8 partly represents it. I was never greatly taken by Eichrodt, but I discerned, especially in his first volume, a reaction against an Old Testament theology which was too theoretical, too anaemic, and which he clothed in flesh and blood by employing the concept of 'covenant' and by crediting it with the power to generate and integrate the religious institutions of Israelite religion. It was the marriage of von Rad's theology of traditions with his own and Noth's biblical criticism which had a special attraction for me and a comparison between von Rad's hermeneutical treatment of Old Testament credal traditions and Schökel's book was suggested by my reading of *The Inspired Word* some years after my arrival in St Andrews. Both von Rad and Schökel are confronting a fixed, historical-critical exegesis with a view that the Old Testament texts have a hermeneutical thrust and that their exegesis is open to the future. There are fundamental differences between them and these are explored in chapter 8 and elsewhere. Von Rad begins with credal traditions and Schökel with Old Testament literature, especially poetry. Schökel supposes that literary inspiration, a subject which he enriches with an analysis of different kinds of Old Testament literature, is a stepping-stone to the ecclesiastical doctrine of the 'inspiration' of the Bible which he affirms. Von Rad's theology of the traditions of the Old Testament is a hermeneutical method through and through, and its goal is to legitimize the exegesis of Old Testament texts in the light of the New Testament.

I could not stomach von Rad's contention that New Testament meanings should be found in Old Testament texts by an exegesis done in the freedom of the Holy Spirit and my respect for the solid virtues of

viii

A Late Harvest

historical-critical exegesis and for the justice of its claims to a kind of objectivity were revived. My interest had become concentrated on the canonical prophets, especially Jeremiah, and I had become convinced that the important questions to ask were, What kind of men were they? How are they to be interpreted in their historical setting? The nature of my exegetical curiosity, text-critical, higher-critical, lexicographical, grammatical and semantic, inclined me to a historical-critical exegesis.

It was in these connections that I encountered the challenge of Engnell (see chapters 4 and 6) and those similarly minded that such a historical reconstruction as I have indicated had a fatal flaw: that we had not been been recovering ancient men and establishing that their mental organization and human traits joined them to us in a common humanity. Rather we had been recreating them in our own image and making them into modern men. I considered the implications of this and weighed the consequences of turning the ancients into such strange creatures, so differently constituted to us, that we would make them inaccessible.

My dissatisfaction with the old doctrines of 'revelation' and 'inspiration', which Schökel had affirmed, was another factor and I had noticed that the Renaissance scholarship (see chapter 3) which was evident in Fulke, Calvin and Zwingli did not go beyond the lexicographical rigour and linguistic competence which they demanded in order to turn the Hebrew Bible and the Greek New Testament into vernacular languages. In perceiving that translation was the foundation of exegesis and that it must be done by specialists who could use the tools of scholarship their instinct was sure, but their critical awareness was only skin-deep and they supposed that the Scriptures could then be entrusted to the theologians as a reliable foundation for Christian doctrine. Zwingli, at the Zurich disputation of 1523, declared his confidence in the judgement of Christian hearts who, with the help of the Holy Spirit, could tell which side rightly and which side wrongly interpreted Scripture. In the seventeenth century Simon effected a much deeper penetration which aimed to secure autonomy for Old Testament critical scholarship, but which reposed in ecclesiastical theologians the sole right and responsiblility for formulating Christian dogma.

With regard to the doctrines of 'inspiration' and 'revelation', it was largely Maimonides (see chapters 1 and 2) who impressed on me the limits of our knowledge of God, the need for reserve and the unwisdom of giving a literal sense to the statement 'God speaks' and so to the term 'word of God'. It will be observed that throughout my book there is a steady resistance to the portraying of the canonical prophets as the 'mouthpieces of God', as if they supplied their vocal chords to enable the Almighty to speak. This is particularly evident in my reaction to the spookiness of Farrar's portrayal. The subject is a treacherous sea and there are hidden perils on which we can make shipwreck, but a docetic account of the canonical prophets, the destruction of their authentic humanity, is the worst of all options. To avoid this the prophet who has an inner voice which is identified with the voice of God is an assumption which should be dispensed with.

It was the focusing of my interest on the exceptional human dimensions of the canonical prophets which directed me to Kuenen and Wellhausen (see chapter 4). A similar kind of concentration is found in Robertson Smith (see chapter 5), in whom there is a special emphasis on their cool deliberation and reasonableness, but who appeals finally to the Holy Spirit as the witness that they spoke the word of God. Duhm's account is like that of Kuenen in that it eschews a supernatural explanation of prophecy and also in the circumstance that its orientation is theological, or, if you like, non-theological but ideological. Theological questions were a matter of small moment to Wellhausen and he concluded that Kuenen's ideological fixation and his long polemic against supernaturalism were wearisome, and distorted the shape of his book on the prophets. Wellhausen's vocabulary is different; his language is humanist and his models are literary: the canonical prophets were giants among the pygmies and they are heroes of tragic stature.

The dichotomy created by the connection of the prophetic activity of a canonical prophet with temporary, abnormal states troubled me. According to this view he was from time to time a prophet, but otherwise a normal human being. This thought was developed particularly by connecting accounts of visionary experience with a condition of ecstatic excitation and in Gunkel and Lindblom (see chapters 6 and 7) it co-existed with the view that a diminution of such psychological excitement and the advent of a cooler deliberation is evident in the canonical prophets. It was to preserve the wholeness of man and prophet that I coined the dictum, 'the prophet is always both a man and a prophet', a conclusion to which Duhm had leaned in the case of Jeremiah. I have noticed that the saying of Maimonides 'nor can a man not be a prophet on a certain evening and a prophet on the following morning' does not achieve this, since it is consistent with Maimonides' view that when the prophetic state overtakes him then, and only then, does he become a superman to whom God 'reveals' his knowledge. The word 'reveal' has no supernatural implications, since a man is born with the chemistry which makes him a prophet.

The trend which makes the canonical prophets into spell-binders or practitioners of a kind of sympathetic magic is another aspect of the diminution of their humanity. I have illustrated the former by examining the 'word-concept' which is formed for *dābār* by the employment of an illegitimate lexicography and the latter by the fixing of the sense of *māšāl* as 'sovereign word' instead of 'likeness'. When they are uttering oracles the canonical prophets, it is alleged, are not merely predicting

the future but creating it, and the *māšāl* which they act is not a simu-
lation of the shape of the future but a foreclosure of it. The argument
that they were overwhelmed by a divine compulsion in carrying out
their vocation and did not enjoy a normal freedom is a further distanc-
ing of them from the human condition.

Gunkel and Lindblom investigate the psychological states of the
canonical prophets which they correlate with the prophet's utterance of
the 'word of God'. The question which they are asking is, What kind of
men were the canonical prophets? and they are not themselves confess-
ing their belief in a doctrine of 'revelation', certainly not Gunkel. They
are asserting that when the canonical prophets prefaced their oracles
with 'These are the words of Yahweh' they were making the claim that
they had heard God speak. Auld, on the other hand (see chapter 4),
does not suppose that they were making this claim and holds that the
preface 'These are the words of Yahweh' or the like is the product of a
secondary literary elaboration motivated by the concerns of a 'canonical
theology'. This contention has been considered. It is at the other pole
from the assertion that the prefaces and the literary form of the oracles
as word of God settle the matter conclusively and that a further analysis
of the statement 'God speaks' is superfluous.

The switch of interest from the psychological experiences of the
canonical prophets to the prophetic literature is notable in Schökel (see
chapter 8). It is *The Inspired Word* about which he writes and he equates
this with Old Testament literature, especially poetry. His anecdote
discloses his point of view: 'A certain painter once said to his friend
Mallarmé, "I also am a poet; many thoughts come to me, however I
cannot find the words". Mallarmé answered him, "Poetry is made with
words".' Schökel concentrates on the literary product and is reticent
about the psychological experiences which precede it. He thus raises a
question about the relation between prophetic psychological states and
prophetic literature and calls in question the assumption that the literature is a transcript of the visions seen and the speech heard in states of
ecstasy. The reconstruction of abnormal psychology founded on literary accounts is problematic.

The conclusion which this adds up to is that the use of 'word of God'
in connection with prophetic utterances and as a term for the Scriptures
as a whole has had serious disadvantages. More may be said than I have
attempted about the mystery of the divine-human encounter, of the
converse between a prophet and God, and it may be urged that there is
human language which can capture it. My contention is that God does
not speak Hebrew, that the language of the Old Testament is human
language and that, with this in mind, it must be studied like any other
literature embedded in ancient documents.

I

THE GOD OF THE PHILOSOPHERS AND THE GOD OF THE BIBLE

I

Since a beginning has to be made somewhere let us make it with Moses ben Maimon, better known as Maimonides, of whom it was said by Jewish Rabbis of the later Middle Ages, 'From Moses (The biblical Moses) to Moses there is none like to Moses'. He was born in Cordoba in 1135 and he died in 1204; he may justly be regarded as the greatest mediaeval, philosophical exponent of Judaism and also as a celebrated exegete of the Torah. In his *Guide of the Perplexed* he repeats a dictum of earlier Jewish scholars to the effect that 'the Torah speaks in the language of the sons of man' and he comments on this with the help of a quotation from the Babylonian Talmud:

> Someone who came into the presence of Rabbi Haninah said (in prayer): God, the Great, the Valiant, the Terrible, the Mighty, the Strong, the Tremendous, the Powerful. Thereupon Rabbi Haninah said to him: Have you finished all the praises of your Master? Even as regards the first three epithets, we could not have uttered them if Moses, our Master, had not pronounced them in the Law and if the men of the great synagogue had not come and established their use (in prayer). Yet you come and say all this. What does this resemble? It is as if a mortal king who had millions of gold pieces were praised for possessing silver. Would not this be an offence to him? (Yebamoth 71a; Meṣi'a 31b)

The two authorities cited in Rabbi Haninah's comment are the Torah and the men of the Great Synagogue. The text of the Torah to which he refers is Deut. 10.17, 'For the Lord your God is God of gods and Lord of lords, the great, mighty and terrible God'. His point is that since these three attributes of God are given by the Torah they may be affirmed. The move from affirming them in a statement to using them in prayer when addressing God is a further significant step which would not be justified if it did not rest on the authority of the Men of the Great Synagogue. According to Jewish tradition they were a group of scholars who first conferred during the days of Ezra and who continued for two centuries after him to interpret existing laws and create new ones. The conclusion which arises most immediately out of Rabbi Haninah's

comment and his concluding parable is that a proliferation of God's
attributes in the language of prayer has the affect of demeaning and
cheapening him rather than ascribing glory to him. Maimonides sums
up:

> Accordingly we should not have mentioned these attributes (great,
> mighty and terrible) at all but for the first necessity (i.e., their
> appearance in the Torah); and but for the second necessity (i.e.,
> their use in prayer by the Men of the Great Synagogue), we should
> not have taken them out of their context and have had recourse to
> them in our prayers. As you continue it will become clear to you
> from this statement that we are not permitted in our prayers to use
> and cite all the attributes ascribed to God in the books of the
> prophets. (Pines' translation, I 59; pp. 140f)

There is a background to this which has to be explored. The Hebrew
bible is written in the language of the sons of man, that is to say, in
human language: in language which ordinary people use or which story-
tellers, historians, psalmists and prophets use when they are discours-
ing on God or describing his relations to his created order, especially
the human part of it. Maimonides is caught between his philosophical
rigour according to which no attributes can be ascribed to God and his
respect for the authority of the Torah and the Men of the Great Synagogue. We might suppose that his bow to authority is a matter of
expediency or circumspection, but he had written a commentary on the
Torah and had a serious exegetical interest in the Hebrew bible, so this
unevenness should be taken more seriously. What can be said with
more reason is that he is aware of the incompatibility between his
philosophical conclusions and the authority of the Torah and that he is
concerned to place a severe restriction on his waiving of philosophical
rigour.

This, however, would be only a partial explanation and to get to the
root of the matter we need to examine Maimonides' exegetical method
of reconciling the Torah (to which he accords a higher rank than the
prophetical books) and the other books of the Hebrew bible with the
rigorous *via negativa* of his philosophical approach to God: 'Know that
the description of God by means of negations is the right description – a
description that is not affected by an indulgence in facile language and
does not imply any deficiency with respect to God in general or in any
particular mode' (i, p. 134). With this corresponds his arcane interpretation of the Hebrew bible, and especially the Torah, which explains the
anthropomorphic language used of God in such a way that it does not
contradict his oneness and simplicity by adding attributes to him. Nor
does it represent him as hearing, seeing or speaking as a man, though
the language employed gives this appearance: The Torah speaks in the

language of the sons of man 'because it is presented in such a manner as to make it possible for the young, the women and the people to begin with it and to learn it. Now it is not within their power to understand these matters as they truly are' (i, p. 71). The Torah leads the mind 'toward the existence of the objects of these opinions and representations but not toward grasping their essence as it truly is' (i, p. 71). 'Accordingly it behooves us to believe with regard to the attributes figuring in the revealed books [the Torah?] or the books of the prophets that all of them are mentioned only to direct the mind toward nothing but his perfection or that they are all attributes referring to actions proceeding from him' (i, p. 147).

In short, the remoteness and inaccessibility of God is much more austere than appears from this biblical language and the description of his relation to the created world and to human beings is to be undertaken with the language of negation: by a denial of what he is not rather than an account of what he is. This severe economy is in accord with Maimonides' concept of 'overflow': the 'overflow' of God's surplus energy and benevolence on the world which he created is a representation of his relation to it and to his creatures which does not pretend to know too much, which does not pry into the unknowability of his essence and preserves the distance which makes him incomparable:

> For nothing is more fitting as a simile to the action of one that is separate from matter than this expression ... For we are not capable of finding the true reality of a term that would correspond to the true reality of the notion. For the mental representation of the action of one who is separate from matter is very difficult, in a way similar to the difficulty of the mental representation of the existence of one who is separate from matter. For just as the imagination cannot represent to itself an existent other than a body or a force in a body, the imagination cannot represent to itself an action taking place otherwise than through the immediate contact of an agent or at a certain distance and from one particular direction. (ii, pp. 279f)

One way of describing the language of the Hebrew bible from Maimonides' point of view is to say that it is 'imaginative', where 'imaginative' has a technical meaning within his philosophical system. The language is pictorial or imaginative and in Maimonides' scheme language derived from images given by the senses and grounded in our embodied existence – our corporeality – cannot express ultimate truth about God. This holds even for the Torah, to which Maimonides accords a higher form of truth than the remainder of the Hebrew bible. The Torah also is written in the language of the sons of man. The right conclusion is that Maimonides' concession to the Torah does not imply that the language of the Hebrew bible is anywhere capable of expressing ultimate truth about God, since ultimate truth about God, which is in any case in short supply, is expressed philosophically and not imaginatively and is characterized by negation rather than affirmation. Its tendency is to strip away erroneous affirmations and to demonstrate that hardly anything can be said about God in his essence.

Aquinas makes the same remarks about the limitation placed on the knowledge of God by the 'imaginative' character of language and about the unknowability of the essence of God:

> The essence of God is not seen by the imagination. What appears there is an image representing God according to some likeness, as is the way with the divine scriptures which describe God metaphorically by means of material things. (iii, p. 13)

> The knowledge that is natural to us has its source in the senses and extends just as far as it can be led by sensible things; from these, however, our understanding cannot reach to the divine essence. (iii, p. 41)

> It is impossible that any created mind should see the essence of God by its own natural powers. A thing is known by being present to the knower; how it is present depends on the way of being of the knower. Thus the way something knows depends on the way it exists. So if the way of being of the thing to be known were beyond that of the knower, knowledge of that thing would be beyond the natural power of the knower. (iii, p. 15)

With Maimonides' contention that subject and predicate affirmations about God should not be equated with descriptions of God's attributes but are rather a deduction from the created effects of a creator or first cause, should be compared, 'God is known to the natural reason through the images of his effects' (iii, p. 41). The name 'God' is used with reference to divine effects:

> But from divine effects we do not come to an understanding of what the divine nature is in itself, so we do not know of God what he is. We know of him only as transcending all creatures, as the cause of their perfections and as lacking in anything that is merely creaturely ... It is in this way that 'God' signifies the divine nature: it is used to mean something that is above all that is, and that is the source of all things and is distinct from them all. (iii, p. 81)

Attributes (so Maimonides) cannot be affirmed of God: to say that he is just, good, holy or mighty is to attach a predicate to him which implies that he is composite and this is to do violence to the unique simplicity or oneness of his being: 'It is not meet that belief in the corporeality of God or in his being provided with any concomitants of the bodies should be permitted to establish itself in anyone's mind any more than it is meet that belief should be established in the non-existence of the deity' (i, p. 81). Ascribing attributes to God is imaginative and anthropomorphic thinking:

> This imagination being pursued it was thought that He is similarly composed of various notions namely, His essence and the notions that are super-added to His essence. Several groups of people pursued the likening of God to other beings and believed Him to be a body endowed with attributes. Another group raised themselves above this consequence and denied His being a body but preserved the attributes. All this was rendered necessary by their keeping to the external sense of the revealed books. (i, p. 114)

God is one in all respects and no multiplicity should be posited of him; no attribute should be added to his essence: 'His essence is . . . one and simple, having no notion that is added to it in any respect. This essence has created everything that is created and knows it, but absolutely and not by virtue of a super-added notion' (i, pp. 122f).

Aquinas also holds that predicates affirmed of God do not signify that he has attributes, and are not inconsistent with his oneness and simplicity. What they do indicate is that God cannot be comprehended in his essence and that the creaturely context of language encounters limits which it cannot transcend when it tries to grasp him: 'God considered in himself is altogether one and simple, yet we think of him through a number of different concepts because we cannot see him as he is in himself. But although we think of him in these different ways, we also know that to each corresponds a single simplicity that is one and the same for all' (iii, p. 95).

No word used of God is appropriate to him as a signification of his essence. Our minds do not understand the simplicity of God and we treat him as if he were a subject to which predicates could be attached. We understand this oneness, which is superior to our mode of existence, in our own way, on the model of composite things; not that we suppose the simple things to be composite, but that the composition is involved in our understanding of them, so that our statements about God are composite and inadequate but not false. They are not false because we recognize the deficiency of our language and so do not suppose that God has attributes or aspects or accidents, but we can do no better and the alternative is defeat and dumbness (iii, p. 95, see further below). In talking about simple things we have to use as models the composite things from which our knowledge derives, so that the diversity implied by our speech is not to be attributed to God himself but to the imperfect way in which we conceive him (ii, pp. 29–31). 'God's effects resemble God as far as they can, but not perfectly. One of the defects in resemblance is that they reproduce only manifoldly what in itself is one and simple. As a result they are composite and cannot be identified with their natures' (ii, p. 31).

The conclusion to which Aquinas' discourse, like that of Maimonides, leads is that statements about God are not literal and his emphasis on the metaphorical or analogical character of such statements is in general accord with this: 'All words used metaphorically of God apply primarily to creatures and secondarily (analogically) to God. When used of God they signify merely a certain parallelism between God and the creation. The meaning of such words as applied to God depends on and is secondary to the meaning it has when applied to creatures' (iii, p. 69). He holds, however, and the element of perplexity associated with the claim has been acknowledged (iii, Appendix 3, pp. 104f), that there are literal statements which can be made about God. If all these non-metaphorical words did was to give expression to God's causality, if their basis was the inspection of the effects of that causality in a creaturely context, they would not transcend the limits of analogical language and would be secondary: 'If "God is good" meant "God is the cause of goodness in creatures", the word "good" as applied to God would have contained within its meaning the goodness of the creature and hence "good" would apply primarily to creatures and secondarily to God' (iii, p. 69). Aquinas argues that this is not the case and also that 'God is good' is not a variant of the *via negativa*, not a transformation of 'God is not evil'. The argument is difficult to conduct and is focused on God's perfections:

> So far as the perfections signified are concerned the words are used literally of God more appropriately than they are used of creatures, for these perfections belong primarily to God and only secondarily to others. But so far as the way of signifying these perfections is concerned the words are used inappropriately, for they have a way of signifying what is appropriate to creatures. (iii, p. 57)

Some words can be used of God only metaphorically such as 'Rock'; it is constituent of the meaning of 'rock' 'that it has part of its being merely in a material way' (iii, p. 59). 'There are other words, however, that simply mean certain perfections without any indication how these perfections are possessed – words, for example, like "being", "good", "living" and so on' (iii, p. 59). These words can be used literally of God, but 'what they signify does not belong to God in the way that they signify it, but in a higher way' (iii, p. 59). The question is whether 'imperfect signification' (cf. iii, pp. 104f) and literal language about God can march together, whether this is an intelligible synthesis or a combination of contradictories. To say that this language signifies God imperfectly is to say that it does not transcend the limitations of creaturely language, the language of the sons of man (Maimonides) and should it not then be classed as analogical and secondary? It refers primarily to creatures and secondarily to God.

For the most part this is Aquinas' conclusion about language: 'All words used metaphorically about God apply primarily to creatures and secondarily to God. When used of God they signify merely a certain parallelism between God and the creature' (iii, p. 69). Statements like 'God is good' have the defects of all creaturely language, but, according to Aquinas, they are literal and not metaphorical. He acknowledges that if 'God is good' were to be equated with 'God is the cause of goodness in creatures', the word 'good' would refer primarily to creatures and secondarily to God (iii, p. 69), but he argues that 'God is good' is to be analysed differently. We do not *mean* that God is composite by using a subject and predicate, but we encounter an impassable linguistic barrier in trying to *signify* what we mean. 'God is good' does not rest on the evidences of goodness in the world he created or in his creatures. He is good not because he causes goodness 'but rather goodness flows from him because he is good' (iii, p. 55); goodness pre-exists in God in a higher way than it does in his creatures. Many words used of God derive from his causal activity and are analogical language, but the words 'God is good' are literal: ' "God is living" does not mean the same as God causes life; the sentence is used to say that life pre-exists in the source of all things, though in a higher way than we can understand or signify' (iii, p. 55).

The limitations of metaphorical or analogical language used of God are associated with the circumstance 'that sensible creatures are effects of God which are less than typical of the power of their cause' (iii, p. 41) and Aquinas is concerned to establish that there is literal language about God which is not so derived. But he also has a positive view of analogical language which depends on God's causality: 'They are nevertheless effects depending on a cause, and so we can at least be led from them to know of God that he exists and that he has whatever must belong to the first cause of all things which is beyond what is caused' (iii, p. 41). This is seen also in his discussion of the name of God:

> But from divine effects we do not come to understand what the divine nature is in itself, so we do not know of God what he is. We know of him only as transcending all creatures, as the cause of their perfections and as lacking anything that is merely creaturely . . . It is in this way that the word 'God' signifies the divine nature: it is used to mean something that is above all that is, and that is the source of all things and is distinct from them all (iii, p. 81).

'God' refers to 'divine Providence, which is what makes us use this word in the first place' (iii, p. 81).

God exists necessarily as an Active Intellect who is the subject and object of his own thought (so Maimonides). Hence the Hebrew bible is incapable of expressing or disclosing 'revealed truth' as this term has been understood in connection with the theological concepts of 'inspiration' and 'revelation'. It should be observed that although Maimonides allows the three attributes of God which appear in the Torah in religious use, whether in credal affirmation or prayer, he does not allow the addition of further attributes on the basis of what is ascribed to God in the prophetic literature. It might be argued from suppositions which are different from his that there is more evidence of revealed truth in the prophetic literature than elsewhere, since the prophets claim it with such directness that they attribute the words which they speak to God himself. Maimonides' answer to this is bound up with his account of prophecy which will be considered later (see pp. 35–41).

Let us contemplate the great gap which has opened up between the God who emerges at the conclusion of Maimonides' philosophical rigour and the God of the Hebrew bible. It should be interpolated here that the bareness of Maimonides' philosophical God is not an isolated case, that his is not an unrepresentative God of the philosophers, though he cultivates assiduously the self-containment and unrelatedness of God. As we have seen, the greatest doctor of the mediaeval church, St Thomas Aquinas, also pursued a *via negativa* in his *Summa Theologicae* and reached conclusions about the limitations of imaginative language in relation to the Being of God similar, in important respects, to those of Maimonides. Aquinas has a section on theological language which is full of interest for the modern mind and the problems which beset it, a section in which a method of analogy is presented as a means of stretching language and overcoming what would otherwise be insuperable linguistic barriers to valid theological discourse.

If we turn to modern philosophical theologians, there is Paul Tillich's Ultimate Concern and Ground of Being, the first thought to be more promising than the second, whether it is a concern for truth or an ethical concern for justice. Both, it may be agreed should be constituents of a religious commitment. However, it is not clear that Ultimate Concern is a reinterpretation which captures God: it may be rather a summing-up of a profound and concerned kind of humanism, confronting the riddle of our existence with anguish and discernment. At any rate it is difficult to resist the conclusion that Paul van Buren's God is such a reduction, since it appears that there is no more to 'God' than a special way of using language in order to press to the frontiers of truth about our human existence (1972, p. 168). Van Buren makes no bones about having abandoned metaphysics. There is no transcendent being to whom the word 'God' refers when we work language to its furthest limits in order to win comprehension in the darkest, deepest and most inaccessible areas of our existence. The conclusion which is required is evidently that 'God' is no more than these linguistic endeavours and the concern to plumb the mysteries of life which sustains them. Van Buren acknowledges that this account 'is not a theistic interpretation of Christianity' which 'will hardly be as relevant to our culture as that of the form of Christianity we are considering. A religion that is not at its heart an acknowledgement of, and a participation in using, the edges of language can hardly be expected to stand against the positivistic pressures of the culture in which we live' (1972, p. 170).

John MacQuarrie's analysis of 'God talk' (1967) is significantly different from biblical language about God and how we are related to him. A trans-subjective validity is claimed for what are called 'affective intuitions', so that our being or existing in the world is a participation in God's being. This is an endeavour to give ontological status to the thoughts and feelings which lie too deep for tears, which are intuited as our most profound grasp of the mystery of our human existence.

Martin Buber's representation of an I-Thou relation between God and human creatures comes nearer to biblical forms of discourse than anything considered up till now and establishes that God is personal in a sense which is continuous with human personality, so that a relation between him and a human being might be asserted on the analogy of the relation between one human being and another. A relation of this kind could not be contemplated between the philosophical God of Maimonides and a human being. One is always asking the question whether Maimonides' God is a person in any sense or a non-personal entity – a He or an It.

A different attitude to the rational pursuit of God is discernible in Edwyn Bevan. He takes part in the chase and questions the grounds on which Thomas Aquinas holds that God is not to be conceived as having attributes, but he decides that the game is not worth the candle and his conclusion is influenced by Mansel's Bampton Lectures in the nineteenth century. Bevan is alive to the obstacles on the rational path to God and to the tendency in the methods of Maimonides and Aquinas to impoverish God until the concept is an empty one: 'If everything known as a characteristic or constituent of human personality was stripped from the mind of God, nothing would be left' (1938, p. 254). God would be a blank. It would not be worth your while saying that you believed in the existence of God at all, any more than that you believed in the existence of an unknown.

There is no path of reason which leads to God and natural or rational theology is an illusion (so Mansel and Karl Barth): 'We may have conducted the process of reasoning with flawless logical consistency all through, but we are operating all the time only with counters, not with the realities themselves' (1938, p. 324). The transfer from the language of the sons of man in the Bible to a process of reasoning is not an advance, because human reason cannot outreach human limits and does not have access to the mind of God. It is a mistake to think that we can reach anything more literally true concerning God than the anthropomorphic imagery of Scripture, even though the inconceivable reality is immensely different from the human imagery. Those who have attempted this formulate what seem to be philosophical statements about God but these are marked just as much by the essential limitations of the human mind as the anthropomorphic imagery of the Bible (1938, pp. 322f).

Mansel's case rested on the view that the Bible was revealed knowledge and that the anthropomorphic account of God which it contained was the best knowledge of God which we could have. Hence when he made his descent from metaphysics, having found nothing of value, he landed perfectly on a runway with sure foundations. Bevan does not embrace Mansel's doctrine of Scripture, his fundamentalism, but he argues that the anthropomorphic God of the Bible is the best access to him which we can have: 'While our best conceptions of God remain symbols of a Reality we cannot imagine, it is because these conceptions when acted upon produce a life of a certain quality as compared with other conceptions of the universe that the man who believes in God gains assurance that he does right in believing' (1938, p. 335). Bevan asks how this differs from the 'pragmatic' position which he has previously outlined and he replies:

> It differs because in religious faith there is an enduring reference all-through to a Reality believed to exist in absolute independence. As merely symbolic of the reality, it is to that extent unlike the Reality, but this does not rule out its being in some respects like the Reality. The Theist or Christian view is not merely pragmatic. It is not: Act as if there were a God who is a loving Father and you will find that certain desirable results follow. Rather: Act as if there were a God who is a loving Father and you will in so doing be making the right response to that which God really is. (1938, p. 335)

This is the closest approach which we can make to the reality of God and the accent is on guidance and a way of life rather than ratiocination. Thus if we seek God along the path of reason, if we tread that transcendental way, the outcome is agnosticism and we have to be content with the knowledge of God transmitted in the language of the sons of man.

C. A. Campbell's 1953–55 Gifford Lectures, *On Selfhood and God-*

hood (London, 1957) are a model of clarity and penetration. His book is marked by tolerance, courtesy, fairness, high moral seriousness and insight into the belief in a personal God to which, nevertheless, the logic and metaphysics of his idealist philosophy do not lead him. The approach to God through rational argument is the way to which he has a single-minded attachment and dedication. He has no other route in his sights and any other access to God which is claimed is not his business. If he had to descend from logic and metaphysics, he does not recognize any method of contriving a safe landing and of continuing the search for God on different terrain. He is impressed by the moral imperative, by the peculiar claim of duty on which he confers an objective significance: it is evidence that there is a Power making for righteousness, an 'ought-ness' which is not to be dissolved into a subjective feeling of compulsion. He is less confident about the validity of a metaphysic whose destination is the Being of God than he is about this moral reality. If there is such a metaphysic, it reaches a transcendental structure rather than grasping a personal God. He does not discover a God who communicates with human beings and has personal relations with them, who is addressed by them in the language of devotion and in prayer, who answers their prayers, guides them, corrects them and, in general, oversees their lives. The view that a God anthropomorphically conceived serves us better than the empty God of the philosophers is outside his sphere of interest and is not thought to be worthy of serious consideration. It does not belong to the method of pursuing the truth as he understands it. The earnestness and power of Campbell's idealist logic and metaphysics mark him off from those who dispense with metaphysics in their search for God.

II

In describing the language of the Hebrew bible as imaginative I was following the scale of a theory of knowledge found in both Maimonides and Aquinas, where the imaginative quality of language is a limiting factor in relation to its capacity to express truth. A less technical and broader way of viewing the language of the Hebrew bible, and a means of connecting it with the dictum that the Torah speaks in the language of the sons of man, would be to say that its tendency is to humanize God, to represent him and his activities in relation to human individuals and communities in such anthropomorphic and anthropopathic ways that, though there may be a concern to avoid undue familiarity and preserve distance or otherness, there is an assumption that God is a principal character and that he participates actively in the story of Israel which the Hebrew bible contains.

This is a generalization which is necessarily defective and which is incapable of doing justice to the different ways in which God and his activity are represented within the Hebrew bible. A God who walks in the garden of Eden in the cool of the evening (Gen. 3.8, 10) is integrated into the human scene, and it can be said of the more mythological representations of God that they have the effect of demolishing the distance between God and humans and of making his interventions natural and something to be expected. In *Studies in the Patriachal Narratives* I noticed that in the short, swift-moving and action-packed Abraham stories theophany was an essential part of the narrative machinery: that a God who is always present to act decisively in order to bring the narrative to a conclusion dominates the human participants. These short stories which move swiftly to a conclusion achieved by God, and which allow little scope for the development of human characters or for the conflict of human wills, contrast with the Joseph stories, where a psychological interest is more fully in evidence and where God is seen to achieve his ends despite the freedom which he allows human beings to express their characteristics, pursue their ambitions and engage in their conflicts. The God of the Joseph stories has been described by von Rad as a hidden God, because he is not manifestly present on the level of human interactions and conflicts and yet by a mysterious superintendence and overruling achieves his ends.

That God intervenes so as to shape the course of history and bring the nations to heel is a regular assumption of the historical narratives in the Hebrew bible and so Austin Farrar has remarked on the absence of God from the Succession or Court narrative (2 Sam. 11 – 2 Kgs 2) that we have 'a faint awareness that we are being allowed a holiday from the proper business of the Old Testament muse' (p. 124). The theocentric character of the prophetic literature has made a powerful impression on the same scholar, especially the circumstance that the prophets give out what they say as Yahweh's utterance and not their own. However, there is a sense in which God is also hidden in the prophetic literature, for his control of the movements of history set out by the prophets is not achieved by theophany but by an unexplained harmonizing of the imperial ambitions of nations with his design, though they have no awareness that they are serving his purposes or any care to do so.

The major pre-exilic prophets do not predict direct, supernatural interventions by God in order to achieve his historical ends. They look at the ordinary face of history and the movements of nations competing for power and empire, whether the Assyrians or the Babylonians, and they assert that what is fuelled by motives which have no relation to God's purposes will somehow be incorporated in his moral order. Yet when account is taken of all these differences in the representation of the presentness of God on the human scene in the Hebrew bible, even the remoteness of God in Ecclesiastes and a general tendency to set him at a greater distance from the world in the later literature, the generalization with which a beginning was made that the God of the Hebrew bible is humanized and portrayed anthropomorphically and anthropopathically should be allowed to stand.

There is still some unfinished business in connection with Maimonides' compromise and a suggestion can be offered why he made it, although this should be regarded as tentative and as probably only a partial answer. It may be viewed as a recognition on his part, influenced by his respect for the authority of the Torah, that the God of his philosophy is inadequate to meet the demands made by credal affirmation and liturgical practice. The striking aspect of Maimonides' philosophical definition is the utter self-containment of the deity. The implication of this is that any account of the relations between God and the created order must be undertaken with the greatest economy and caution.

The most that Maimonides can do if he is to preserve his philosophical integrity is to employ the idea of 'overflow' which marches with his emphasis on the incorporeality of God: 'The meaning of all this is that these actions are the actions of one who is not a body. And it is His action which is called overflow' (ii, p. 279). 'This term . . . is sometimes also applied in Hebrew to God with a view to likening Him to an overflowing spring of water' (ii, p. 279). It is legitimate to conclude that the universe is a consequence of the expression of God's volition; that it is an overflow of his creative energy informed by reason and benevolence. From the nature of the created order inferences can be made about the power, intellectual grasp and goodness which issue from God's will. The idea of 'overflow' suits an impersonal connection rather than a personal relationship; it is an excess of rational and moral energy; it provides meagre rations for the affirmation of religious belief or for a liturgy which would sustain religious devotion. It is difficult to believe that it would suffice for the language of prayer and worship. It should be noticed that the same metaphor is used by Aquinas in connection with what he claims are literal statements about God. Analysing 'God is good' he says, 'Thus God is not good because he causes goodness, but rather goodness flows from him because he is good: *sed potius e converso quia est bonus bonitatem rebus diffundit* (iii, pp. 54f).

Even if we should be right in supposing that there is a concession to perceived liturgical deficiency in Maimonides, the manner of his approach suggests that he is on the side of the philosophers. His sharpest concern is that the purity of his philosophical definition of God should not be contaminated by a riot of imagery. He is convinced that the attaching of prolix images to God and a general indiscipline in the choice of religious language is an emptying of God's majesty of a more

disastrous kind than the devotional deprivation imposed by his severe
regimen of negation.

III

The description of the language which the Hebrew bible uses to discourse about God as 'imaginative' was related to an intention to employ
the word 'imagination' in the context in which it appears in the theories
of knowledge associated with Maimonides and Thomas Aquinas. The
implication is that imagination is an inferior kind of cognition because
of its indissoluble corporeal connections and that only the rational
faculty severed from such connections has a capacity to grasp truth. A
true understanding can issue only from the rational faculty and valid
statements about God are expressions of it. It follows from this that a
theological concept of 'revelation' or 'revealed truth' in the sense of the
highest or most ultimate truth about God cannot be sustained by the
language of the Bible ('the language of the sons of man') nor be founded
on it. That is not to say that Maimonides and Aquinas dispense entirely
with the thought that a form of divine truth is communicated through
imaginative language, though Maimonides does not appear to have
anything corresponding to a biblical concept of revelation. Aquinas, on
the other hand, allows for it in one important respect which will be fully
considered later in connection with his exposition of prophecy.

An evaluation of biblical images, the reverse of the one which we
have been considering, which exalts imagination above reason and com-
plexes of images above rational discourse, appears in Austin Farrar.
The context is a New Testament one and the images in question are said
to communicate supernatural revelation. The dominant images are
listed: the Kingdom of God, Son of Man, Israel, the Trinity. Of Jesus it
is said that 'He displayed in the action of the Supper (the Last Supper)
the infinitively complex and fertile image of sacrifice and communion,
of expiation and covenant'. Farrar goes on:

> These tremendous images and others like them are not the whole
> of Christ's teaching, but they set forth the supernatural mystery
> which is at the heart of the teaching. Without them the teaching
> would not be supernatural revelation, but instruction in piety and
> morals. It is because the spiritual instruction is related to the great
> images that it becomes revealed truth. (*The Glass of Vision*, 1948,
> pp. 42ff)

These great images 'interpreted the events of Christ's ministry, death
and resurrection and the events interpreted the images; the interplay of
the two is revelation ... The events by themselves are not revelation,
for they do not by themselves reveal the Divine work which is accom-

plished in them' (1948, p. 43). Moving from the teaching of Jesus to the apostles, Farrar describes the apostolic mind 'in which God-given images lived, not statically but with an inexpressible creative force. The several distinct images grew together into fresh unities, opened out in detail, attracted to themselves and assimilated other image material; all this within the life of a generation. This is the way inspiration worked. The stuff of inspiration is living images' (1948, pp. 43f).

Some of this is profoundly puzzling and creates a sense of confusion. It might have been supposed that the images or constellations of images to which Farrar attributes such exclusive power of supernatural illumination would be startling in their newness, but the examples which he offers do not bear this out. They are largely reinterpretations or developments of material from the Hebrew bible: Israel is reinterpreted as the society of the people of God, the Church, of which the twelve apostles are the founders just as the twelve sons of Jacob were the founders of the old Israel. These are cases of exegetical development and do not seem to require the supernatural dignity and miraculous power which Farrar confers on them. They do not fall out of heaven in order to give supernatural truth in the manner which his treatment of them suggests.

Again it appears that 'images' in Farrar's use can comprehend a great deal and that the images which are said to communicate Christian truth are difficult to distinguish from statements of Christian doctrine. What, for example are we to make of the so-called 'images' of sacrifice, communion and expiation associated with 'the action of the Supper'? (1948, p. 42). And how are we to understand the following complicated account of how the natural body, functioning as a parable, commmunicates revealed truth about Christ's mystical body? The text from which Farrar sets out is 1 Cor. 12.12, 'As the body is one and has many organs, yet all the organs of the body being many are one body, so is Christ'. He continues:

> I am taught the mystery of Christ's mystical body in terms of physical organism. But there is no real and causal relation between natural organisms and Christ's mystical body: bodies, by being bodies, do not really participate in the mystery of saving incorporation. I do in fact participate in Christ's mystical body, but not by being a natural bodily creature: I participate in Christ's body by a supernatural and imperceptible gift; and this gift is no part of the figure by which revelation teaches about the body of Christ. On the contrary, I need the revealed figures just as much to teach me about my supernatural gift as I need them to teach about the divine body in which, by reason of the gift, I partake. Only the figures are revealed and the figures are simply parables. (1948, p. 95)

Here the supernatural images are connected not only with the appropriation of divine truth but with the gift of divine grace and it becomes
increasingly difficult to distinguish between the special kind of illumination conveyed through supernatural images and statements of Christian doctrine. All the more so since we learn that the image itself does
not contain the divine revelation: it is a parable and as with all parables
we have to make an intuitive leap from the parable to the truth which it
figures. But if this is the state of affairs with regard to these so-called
supernatural images would it not be more economical to regard them as
parables of an ordinary kind and perhaps even to view some of them as
an imaginative attempt to project Christian doctrine which had been
already formulated?

Farrar has an answer to this, namely, that these supernatural images
are irreducible and cannot be translated into alternative forms of expression: 'We must be content to refer to the reality by understanding
what the images tell us' (1948, p. 94). Given Farrar's presuppositions
this makes sense if it means that there is no access to Christian truth
except through these supernatural images and that the illumination
which they provide cannot be transformed into the discourse of a
rational theology. The chapter in which the passage occurs supplies a
context which lends support to such an interpretation of it. Since,
however, Farrar has described the images as parables and since they will
only work as parables if an intuitive leap is made to the truth which is
imaged, we arrive at conclusions about the supernatural images which
are irreconcilable. A correction which Farrar might impose on what has
been said would have the form of a rebuttal of the suggestion that some
of his images may be secondary rather than primary expressions of
Christian truth. This would arise from an insistence that the primal
communication of Christian truth has a parabolic form and that the
indirectness and allusiveness of this mode of communication, which
points to the truth rather than containing it cannot be transcended.

Schökel's contention (1967, p. 162) that the language of Scripture is
literary rather than 'intellectual' has some affinity with the position of
Farrar but does not coincide with it (see further pp. 163–7). Schökel is
urging that we are not entitled to go back to a supposed previous
conceptual stage of development which the biblical author has subsequently clothed in literary language. The Bible is literature, not theology, and its literary language comes before concepts, notions and
terms. Its meaning cannot be obtained by a distillation of its literary
qualities into theology.

The point which Farrar is making is not quite the same as Bevan's
distinction between two different kind of symbols (1938, pp. 256f), a
symbol 'unimaginable in the life of God', for example, 'the love of
God', 'the will of God', and a symbol behind which we can see, which

has a reference to an idea, for example, the Virgin Birth as a symbol of the union of the divine and human nature in Jesus Christ: 'Being able to contemplate both the symbolic picture and the reality behind it, he could compare one with the other and definitely see that the symbol was only a symbol, that is, how it was *unlike* the reality' (1938, p. 257). On the other hand, the first kind of symbol is untranslatable, those which we use 'to represent the life of God, . . . have only analogical and not literal truth' (1938, p. 257). They are elements in the life of man taken to symbolize something unimaginable in the life of God: 'We cannot see behind the symbol: we cannot have any discernment of the reality better and truer than the symbolical idea, we cannot compare the symbol with the reality as it is more truly apprehended and see how they differ. The symbol is the nearest we can get to the reality' (1938, p. 257).

The circumstance that Farrar's 'images' are supernatural integrates them with theology, with a doctrine of revelation, rather than with literature. In so far as they can be considered in relation to literature, a tendency to regard them in abstraction from it is discernible: they are given a kind of photographic definition before they have received literary expression, as if they conferred illumination different from that supplied by words and by reading, a more memorable kind of perception. Schökel (1967, p. 160) writes: 'A certain painter once said to his friend Mallarmé, "I also am a poet, many thoughts come to me, however I cannot find the words." Mallarmé answered him, "Poetry is made with words."' Schökel remarks:

> The error of many writers who treat of inspiration is found in the fact that they envisage the poem or the work to be written as already existing before it is given verbal form . . . In poetry and in literature, more generally, the work only exists in its verbal expression, the central intuition becomes objective and communicable only in its literary realization and the activity by which this existence is conferred characterizes a literary author or poet. (1967, p. 190)

The alleged supernatural character of Farrar's images is a further complication. Van Buren (1972, p. 169) holds that 'poetry, humor and human love is behaviour logically similar to that of religion' and urges that 'there is no such entity as religious language' (1972, p. 170). There is only human language. With this should be associated Maimonides' dictum that the language of the Hebrew bible is that of the sons of man and the assumption of general linguists that speaking and writing is a human activity and that 'divine language' or 'supernatural (literary) images' is a contradiction in terms. If God does not speak or write, language is necessarily human and 'Word of God' as used of the Scriptures is metaphorical or analogical language and is anthropomorphic. Whatever sense is found for 'revelation' it is not that God speaks or writes. Nor do those who are 'inspired' hear the voice of God, whether sounding in their ears or as an extraordinary inner voice.

There are two respects in which Aquinas connects knowledge with special divine assistance, the first through grace and the second, which recalls Farrar more particularly, through revelation. Both are associated with 'images': 'By grace we have a more perfect knowledge of God than we have by the natural reason. The latter depends on two things: images derived from the sensible world and the natural intellectual light by which we make abstract concepts from these images. In both these respects human knowledge is helped by the revelation of grace' (iii, p. 43). Moving on to a narrower use of 'revelation', a revealed knowledge contained in Scripture, 'a word of God', Aquinas continues: 'The light of grace strengthens the intellectual light and at the same time prophetic visions provide us with God-given images which are better suited to express divine things than those we receive naturally from the sensible world' (iii, pp. 43, 45). Here are Farrar's supernatural images and the transition from the 'imaginative' character of all language and the limitations which it imposes on knowledge of God, to the illumination supplied by God's grace and finally to God-given images, the revealed knowledge of God in Scripture has been made.

Maimonides remarks that God's acts are indicated in the Hebrew bible by ascribing bodily organs to him:

> God . . . has had bodily organs figuratively ascribed to him in order that his acts should be indicated by this means. And those particular acts are figuratively ascribed to him in order to indicate a certain perfection, which is not identical with the particular act mentioned. For instance an eye, an ear, a hand, a mouth, a tongue, have been figuratively ascribed to him with a view to indicating apprehension in general. (i, p. 99)

Moses and Moses only heard a voice which was created by God (Exod. 20.23), but this does not imply that God speaks. The 'voice of God' which Moses heard is a uniquely miraculous event, but it is case of 'overflow' and has to be analysed as 'the created voice from which the speech (of God) was understood' (ii, p. 365). 'The fundamental principle was given, which I have never ceased explaining, namely that to every prophet except Moses our Master prophetic revelation comes through an angel' (ii, p. 367). Moreover, as we shall discover later, such communication with all the prophets except Moses is enclosed in a visionary experience. Hence the pre-eminence of Moses and the uniquely miraculous character of the voice which he heard on Mount

Sinai. This is a mystery which cannot be penetrated and which we should not seek to pierce:

> After the prophecy and mystery of Moses have ... been set apart in your mind – seeing that the extraordinary character of his apprehension is similar to the extraordinary character of his actions – and after you have come to believe that his is a rank we are incapable of grasping in its true reality, you shall hear what I say in all the chapters about prophecy and about the degree of the prophets in respect of prophecy, all these degrees being after the degree of Moses. (ii, p. 369)

> For it is impossible to expound the gathering at Mount Sinai to a greater extent than they spoke about it, for it is one of the mysteries of the Torah. The true reality of that apprehension and its modality are quite hidden from us, for nothing like it happened before and will not happen after. (ii, p. 365)

Supernatural truth in propositional form lurks behind Farrar's images and he may not have avoided entirely what he describes an an error in the 'mediaeval scholastic mind' (1948, p. 44). His intention is to make reflective or systematic theology secondary in the scheme of biblical theology which is described as 'the analysis and criticism of the revealed images'. 'Theology tests and determines the sense of the images but it does not create it. The images themselves signify and reveal' (1948, p. 44). The troublesome question is whether Farrar's supernatural images are not a disguised kind of supernatural, propositional truth or, at any rate, a substitute for it.

Amid the uncertainties and whatever limitations there may be on my part to understand Farrar, the supernatural and anti-rational character of his account of biblical truth is unmistakeable. This can be asserted despite his defence of metaphysics and it is even confirmed by the form of that defence:

> For if our craven-heartedness surrenders the ground of metaphysics, it will have surrendered the bridgehead which the supernatural liberator might land upon. Get a man to see the mysterious depth and seriousness of the act by which he and his neighbour exist and he will have his eyes turned on the bush in which the supernatural fire appears, and presently he will be prostrating himself with Moses, before him who names himself: 'I am that I am'. (1948, p. 78)

Farrar exalts supernatural images above reason and gives them monopoly rights in the matter of access to Christian truth. Metaphysics is awarded a consolation prize – it is a propaedeutic, no more: 'We have to listen to the Spirit speaking divine things: and the way to appreciate his speech is to quicken our own mind with the life of the inspired images' (1948, p. 44). By comparison, the fruits which can be gathered in the pursuit of a rational or natural theology, which depends on the establishing of analogies between the human and divine, are meagre. These rational analogies are also images, but rational analogies and revealed images do not function in the same way: 'We can express the difference by saying that rational analogies are *natural* images: the revealed images are not in the sense intended *natural*' (1948, p. 94).

This links up with the discussion about the parabolic character of revealed images and the leap which has to be made from the parable to the truth which it images. By saying that rational analogies are natural Farrar is pointing to a more intrinsic relation, a path of reason, between the analogy and the goal which it strains to reach, for example, when we use our volition as an analogy of God's will and creative energy. The statement which stands out and makes the contrast stark is the following:

> Unless finite things put themselves upon us as symbols of Deity, we can have no natural knowledge of God. Revealed images do not do this: they are authoritatively communicated. The stars may seem to speak of a maker, the moral-sense of a law-giver, but there is no pattern of being we simply meet which speaks of the Trinity in the Godhead or the efficacy of the sacraments. (1948, p. 94)

This is as uncompromising an antithesis between reason and revelation as we could find. It leaves us with a sense of the utter mysteriousness of the body of Christian truth to which there is access only through supernatural images. But is the doctrine of the Trinity and the efficacy of the sacraments really communicated through images? We might seem to be reaching the conclusion that all of this is no more than a novel way of expressing the old doctrine that God has revealed the mystery of truth in the Bible through a process of verbal inspiration. This is denied by Farrar, though too much weight should not be attached to his disclaimer that he does not intend his account to apply to the whole of the New Testament:

> Now it will be said, and rightly said, that however vital a place great images hold in the text of the New Testament, they by no means fill it all. Thus to say that the apostolic mind was divinely inspired by the germination of the image-seeds which Christ had sown, is not to give a plain and uniform account of the text of Scripture, comparable with the old doctrine of inerrant supernatural dictation. But surely this is no blemish. For the doctrine of the

unchallengeable inspiration of the whole text is a burden which our backs will no longer bear. (1948, p. 52)

But the information that Farrar's account is to be applied only selectively does not help me very much.

A more important difference between Farrar and those attached to the doctrine of the plenary inspiration of the Bible emerges when we appreciate that his attitude to the Bible is Catholic rather than Protestant, that the New Testament is a literary deposit of what had a prior existence in the Church. Hence the New Testament, even a New Testament which contains supernatural images by means of which Christian truth is revealed, does not function as a fountainhead of revealed truth to whose judgement the Church must submit, though this is the Protestant context in which claims for the plenary inspiration of the Bible are located. On these matters Farrar remarks:

> We cannot say that the primary instrument of the Pentecostal Spirit was the Bible. No, it was the apostolic Church, of which the apostles and prophets were sensitive organs. If the biblical books had not been taken to express the apostolic mind, they would not have been canonized: and we shall rightly suppose that the dominant images of the New Testament were the common property of the teaching Church. (1948, p. 53)

It is clear that this necessarily involves some reduction in the claim that the New Testament writers were inspired: they were not inspired in the sense intended by those who make the claim in a Protestant context. According to Farrar's statement, they were not vehicles of the Holy Spirit for the disclosure of new divine truth. Farrar, however, is concerned to preserve in a modified form the claim that the New Testament writers were inspired:

> But it would be mistaken to infer that direct and immediate inspiration played a small part in the composition of the books. It may be that the decisive shaping of the images took place elsewhere. But the images are still alive and moving in the writers' minds, not fixed or diagrammatic. They continue to enter into fresh combinations. The composition of the books may be on the fringe of the great process of inspired thinking, but it is still inspired thinking, much of it as vivid and forcible as anything one could well conceive. (1948, pp. 53f).

It may be asked whether what is attributed to the biblical writers here is not better described as an exegetical skill which draws out the content of the so-called supernatural images and so a secondary process of rearrangement, reinterpretation and adaptation rather than one which makes them inspired writers.

The oddity of the conclusion which Farrar has reached is connected with his persuasion that individual human beings are the seat of theories of inspiration and revelation, combined with his inability to find these individuals in the New Testament writers. The historical Jesus, in whose teaching the supernatural images are said to originate, is such an individual; but if the images are the common property of the apostolic Church, this suggests that they emerged in a believing community, not that they arose in inspired individuals, and this seems to be a different solution or dissolution of the problems associated with revelation and inspiration. Were there or were there not inspired individuals who were illumined by supernatural images within the primitive Church prior to the New Testament writers? If not, there is a lacuna in Farrar's account of supernatural images and inspired individuals are not accommodated in it. The problems of inspiration and revelation are especially severe when the psychology of the process in relation to an individual recipient is explored. Farrar is unable to grapple effectively with the problem of inspiration on the foundation which he lays in the New Testament, but when he turns to the Hebrew prophets he faces the question more resolutely. On this topic Schökel (1967, p. 224) says:

> We should reject ... any notion of an amorphous community which is somehow creative; there is no such thing as a literary work produced by 'everybody' and there is no need to revive the romantic theory which dissolved a work of art into the masses. We reject this latter idea not because it is romantic, but because it is wrong. There were many intuitions in that school of thought which will have to be re-thought one day, but this aspect of the *Volksgeist* view of literature is certainly not one of them.

Literature for Chapter 1 is listed at pp. 41-2.

2

THE LIMITS OF OUR KNOWLEDGE OF GOD

I

Let us consider the limits which Maimonides places on our knowledge of God and the economy which he imposes in making affirmations about God. He follows a *via negativa* which emphasizes the distance between us and God and does not accumulate positive statements, pressing the analogy of our human nature to increase our understanding. Awareness of the limits of our knowledge of God is a grasp of 'the impossibility of everything which is impossible' (1963, i, p. 139) with regard to our knowledge of him. An indication that we have fallen into error is the adding of any attribute to him additional to his essence. 'Righteousness', 'Holiness' or 'Mercifulness', attributed to a human being is a mark of perfection, but if these qualities are attributed to God, they are additions to his essence and they destroy his irreducible unity:

> When you make an affirmation ascribing another thing to Him, you become more distant from Him in two respects: one of them is that everything you affirm is a perfection only with reference to us, and the other is that He does not possess a thing other than His essence, which, as we have made clear, is identical with His perfections. (i, p. 139)

When there is a reference in unphilosophical language (the language of the sages [i, p. 124]; the language of the sons of man [i, p. 140]) to the moral qualities of God, this in reality refers to God's action: 'He performs actions which resemble the actions in us that proceed from moral qualities, but the meaning is not that he possesses moral qualities' (i, p. 125). In Ps. 103.13 'pity' or 'compassion' used of God means that he acts towards us in a manner which resembles the action of a father towards a child, but 'not because of passion or change' (i, p. 125). 'Grace' in our language means showing generosity to someone who has a claim on us, but God is called 'generous' in so far as 'He brings into existence and governs beings that have no claim on Him with regard to being brought into existence and governed' (i, p. 125). When vengeance, hostility or anger is attributed to God, this does not signify that his actions are a consequence of anger, hostility or vengefulness, but only that the effects of these actions resemble those which are the product of human anger, hatred or vengeance.

Hence, when language used of human attributes is applied to God, univocality of language cannot be preserved and discourse cannot be ordered on a single scale of meaning maintained throughout differences of degree. The gulf between God and ourselves cannot be bridged by having resort to the comparative degree, by stating that 'His existence is more durable than our existence, His life more permanent than our life, His power greater than our power' (i, p. 130). Equivocation has to be acknowledged and, in that case, 'existence' or 'power' used of God will belong to a different system of meaning from 'existence' or 'power' used of us. Reliance on the meaning of 'existence' 'power', or any other attribute in a human context as a bridge to our understanding this vocabulary when used of God must be given up: 'The terms "knowledge", "power", "will", "life" as applied to Him ... and to all those others possessing knowledge, power, will and life are purely equivocal, so that their meaning when they are predicated of Him is in no way like their meaning in other applications' (i, p. 131).

It is then evident that this language, when applied to God, will suffer from lack of definition and that great restraint will have to be exercised in filling it with semantic content: 'Accordingly it behoves us to believe with regard to the attributes featuring in the revealed books [the Torah] or the books of the prophets that all of them are mentioned to direct the mind towards nothing but His perfection ... or that they are attributes referring to actions proceeding from Him, as we have made clear' (i, p. 147). Since, however, God's actions do not involve passion or change (i, p. 125), it is evident that univocality has not been achieved when God's attributes are interpreted as effects of his will or purpose. This discussion has to be conducted in the context of God's creative activity, whether as creator or sustainer of the world, but a fundamental matter in this connection is his self-containment as an Active Intellect which is always *in actu* and, unlike our intellects, has no state of potentiality which achieves actuality only from time to time:

> It follows necessarily that He and the thing apprehended are one thing, which is His essence. Moreover, the act of apprehension, owing to which He is said to be an intellectually cognizing subject, is in itself the intellect which is His essence. Accordingly He is always the intellect as well as the intellectually cognizing subject and the intellectually cognized object ... In us too the intellectually cognizing subject, the intellect, and the intellectually cognized object are one and the same thing, wherever we have an intellect *in actu*. We, however, pass intellectually from potentiality to actuality only from time to time. (i, p. 165)

Before an attempt is made to draw conclusions from this, it should be related to a passage where Maimonides sets himself the task of explaining the meaning of 'God's will'. He remarks that the ultimate cause of the created order, or any causal nexus within it, is expressed by some as 'God willed it so' and by others as 'God's wisdom decreed it so'. These are identical formulations because his will and his wisdom are not 'things extraneous to His essence' (i, p. 170). Maimonides continues:

> I mean to say that they are not something other than His essence. Consequently He . . . is the ultimate end of everything; and the end of the universe is similarly a seeking to be like to His perfection as far as is in its capacity. This . . . is the meaning of His will which is His essence. In virtue of this it is said of Him that He is the end of the ends. (i, p. 170)

Another passage with a bearing on the same subject is the following:

> Thus we are obliged to believe that all that exists was intended by Him . . . according to His volition. And we shall seek for it no cause or other final end whatever. Just as we do not seek for the end of His existence, so we do not seek for the final end of His volition, according to which all that has been and will be produced in time comes into being as it is. (1963, ii, pp. 454f)

One important conclusion which I draw from this, influenced by Maimonides' statements that God's intellect is always *in actu* and that his volition is not separable from his essence, is that the phrase 'God's will' is not univocal language and that the attribution of volition to God does not mean that he makes decisions. If this sense were attached to 'God wills', a consequence would be that his intellect passes from potentiality to actuality and this would contradict what Maimonides has said about God as always Active Intellect. Moreover, if 'God wills' were interpreted as 'God makes a decision', this would amount to the assigning of passion and change to him (cf. i, p. 125) and would also distinguish God's will from his essence which, according to Maimonides, cannot be conceived.

Hence, though it might appear that Maimonides exempts volition from the veto which he puts on assigning attributes to God, this is not so in the final analysis. 'God's will' is also equivocal language and it is not to be likened to human wills in a single scale of meaning or universe of discourse by presupposing a univocality which survives a gradation or difference of degree. The concentration of interest on 'God's will', on the creative energy and wisdom of God, transfers interest from the internal attributes, which, according to Maimonides, are wrongly assigned to God, to the effects of which he is the cause and this is the area where Maimonides concentrates the discussion. The created order, or any causal nexus within it, is accessible to investigation and God as 'the end of ends' is the Ultimate Cause. When the most stringent measures have been taken to expunge equivocation from the language used, the statement 'God willed to create the world and it is an expression of his creative energy and wisdom' has to be reduced to 'God is the Ultimate Cause of the created world'.

The general outcome of all this is that the content of affirmations about God will have an external rather than an internal character, and they will be indirect rather than direct. Even then great reserve has to be shown in making inferences from the order which God has created, or of which he is the Ultimate Cause, whether animate or inanimate, animal or human. The evidences of his power and goodness which are detected in these effects of his creative energy are not to be transformed into statements that 'God is powerful' or 'God is wise' or 'God is good'. All evaluations made by human beings about the created order of which they are part are couched in a language whose statements, when they assign attributes to God, are not univocal. The residual problem, if this is accepted, is how to relate God to his created order. The definition of the indivisibility of his essence and of his self-containment as an Active Intellect is so stringent that it is difficult to discern how his relation to his created order can be expressed. In what sense can he operate as an Ultimate Cause? If Maimonides' strict linguistic regimen is observed, we are reduced to silence on this matter.

It is in this connection that Maimonides introduces his concept of 'overflow' (Arabic, *fayḍ*). This appears in the context of a *via negativa* in the following passage:

> We say accordingly that He ... is eternal, the meaning being that He has no cause that has brought Him into existence. We apprehend further that the existence of this being, which is its essence, suffices not only for His being existent, but also for many other existents flowing from it, and that this overflow – unlike that of heat from fire and unlike the proceeding of light from the sun – is an overflow that, as we shall make clear, constantly procures for those existents duration and order by means of wisely contrived governance. Accordingly we say of Him, because of these notions that He is powerful and knowing and willing. The intention in ascribing these attributes to Him is to signify that He is neither powerless nor ignorant nor inattentive nor negligent. Now the meaning of our saying that He is not powerless is to signify that He apprehends – that is, is living, for every apprehending thing is living. And the meaning of our saying that He is not inattentive nor negligent is to signify that all the existing things in question proceed from their cause according to a certain order and govern-

ance – not in a neglected way so as to be generated as chance would have it, but rather as all the things are generated that a willing being governs by means of purpose and will. We apprehend further that no other thing is like that being. Accordingly our saying that He is one signifies the denial of multiplicity. (i, pp. 135f)

I have quoted this so as to make it the basis of a discussion and it will be convenient to cite another passage on 'overflow' at this point:

> The action of the separate intellect is always designated as an overflow, being likened to a source of water that overflows in all directions and does not have one particular direction from which it draws while giving its bounty to others. For it springs forth from all directions and constantly irrigates all the directions nearby and afar. Similarly the intellect in question may not be reached by a force coming from a certain direction and a certain distance; nor does the force of that intellect reach that which is other than itself from one particular direction, at one particular distance, or at one particular time rather than another. For its action is constant as long as something has been prepared, so that it is receptive of the permanently existing action, which has been interpreted as an overflow. Similarly with regard to the Creator . . . inasmuch as it has been demonstrated that He is not a body and that the universe is an act of His and that He is its efficient cause . . . it has been said that the world derives from an overflow of God and that He has caused to overflow to it everything that is produced in time . . . For nothing is more fitting as a simile of the action of One that is separate from matter than this expression ('overflow'). For we are not capable of finding the true reality of a term that would correspond to the true reality of the notion. For the mental representation of the action of one who is separate from matter is very difficult, in a way similar to the difficulty of the mental representation of the existence of one who is separate from matter. For just as the imagination cannot represent to itself an existent other than a body or a force in a body, the imagination cannot represent to itself an action taking place otherwise than through the immediate contact of an agent or at a certain distance and from one particular direction. (ii, pp. 279f)

The first thing to notice is that the concept of 'overflow' operates in the context of a *via negativa* and has itself the form of a *via negativa*. Overflow is described as a surplus creative energy with rational and benevolent characteristics which spills over from God's essence and constantly provides for other existents 'duration and order by means of wisely contrived governance'. But it is defined negatively: it is an overflow unlike that of heat from fire and unlike the proceeding of light from the sun. Overflow is a causation of a special kind and its employment introduces a method which reduces the account of God's relation to the created order to a more chaste philosophical language. It is a move from the internal attributes which have been wrongly assigned to him to a modification of his causal relationship to the world as Creator which has been affirmed. The reduction of God's attributes to volition and the the circumscribing of the concept of God's will have already been noticed. The problem of relating God, with his self-contained essence, to the created order is met by formulating a *via negativa* in connection with the concept of 'overflow' whose domain is the created order.

Inferences about God are made from the nature of the created order which has been brought into being and is sustained by an overflow from his essence, but these inferences are expressed by negations, not by affirmations which make him a Cause. But the foundation for the statements that 'He is neither powerless nor ignorant nor inattentive nor negligent' would not be secure if it were only affirmed that this 'overflow' from God brought the world into being. In order to validate the inference that 'He is neither powerless nor ignorant nor inattentive nor negligent' the assumption that an overflow from God is continuously and constantly operative is indispensable. This part of Maimonides' argument is illustrated by his onslaught against Muslim theologians (Mutakallimum) which takes the following form:

> Know, however, that in some people from among the Mutakallimum engaged in speculation, ignorance and presumption reached such a degree that finally they said that if the non-existence of the Creator were assumed, the non-existence of the thing that the Creator brought into existence – they mean the world – would not follow necessarily. For it does not necessarily follow that that which has been effected passes away when the maker has passed away after having effected it. Now that which they have mentioned would be correct if He were only the maker and if the thing that He effected had no need of Him for its permanence ... as in the case of the carpenter upon whose death the chest does not pass away, for he does not continually endow it with permanence. Now as God ... is also the form of the world ... and as He continually endows it with permanance and constant existence, it would be impossible that He who continually endows with permanence should disappear and that which is continually endowed by Him, and which has no permanance except in virtue of this endowment, should remain (i, pp. 170f)

'Overflow' is a constantly operative causal energy which holds the world in being, but its special characteristic as a cause derives from the circumstance that it is an overflow from God's essence and that its source is therefore an incorporeal Being or Intellect. Maimonides employs this metaphor ('overflow') in order to differentiate incorporeal causation from a cause which is physical or corporeal. There are several limitations or reservations which Maimonides has to make in order to ward off the objection that he is falling into inconsistency. The first is that this overflow from God's essence, which is a kind of causation, must not override the axiom that God is not subject to passion or change. Hence the constancy and continuity of this causal efficacy is not to be translated into a perseverance of God's will, since decision-making by God implies change. The second matter relates to Maimonides' explicit statement that the causation associated with the concept of 'overflow' is too elusive or mysterious to be captured by any terminological apparatus and so defies definition: 'For we are not capable of finding the true reality of a term that would correspond to the reality of the notion' (ii, p. 279).

The intention of the metaphorical language ('overflow') is to substitute allusiveness for definition and, in so far as it is safe to impose an interpretation, the consequence is a kind of causation which does not require the direct participation of a cause, which is multi-directional and whose effect is constant: God does not act either through immediate contact or at some particular distance, for he is not a body. His overflow is like that of a source of water which 'overflows in all directions and does not have one particular direction from which it draws while giving its bounty to others' (ii, p. 279). Similarly God's overflow does not reach 'that which is other than itself from one particular direction, at one particular distance, or at one particular time rather than another. For its action is constant as long as something has been prepared, so that it is receptive of the permanently existing action, which has been interpreted as an overflow' (ii, p. 279). The difficulty of grasping the nature of the causation indicated by the concept of 'overflow' is connected by Maimonides with the limitations of our imagination which 'cannot represent to itself an action taking place otherwise than through the immediate contact of an agent, or at a certain distance and from one particular direction' (ii, pp. 279f).

II

These matters had to be considered in order to provide an adequate context for Maimonides' account of prophecy. One feature, the denial of speech to God, has a general character, and also a special application, since the formula 'These are the words of Yahweh' or the like has to be analysed in the light of it. It has a general significance for Maimonides, because speech ascribed to God is held to be part of the created order and the distance between God in his essence and the created order, which the concept of 'overflow' safeguards, applies to any speech which is attributed to him. Even the Torah which was delivered to Moses, to whom Maimonides accords a special prophetic rank and to whom God spoke 'face to face' (Exod. 33.11), has to be reconciled with this framework of interpretation.

The difference between Moses and all the other prophets consists in the nature of the divine overflow to him: the imaginative faculty did not enter into his prophecy, 'since the intellect [God's intellect] overflowed towards him without its intermediation. For, as we have mentioned, several times, he did not prophesy like the other prophets by means of parables' (ii, p. 373). The overflow to Moses was realized in his rational faculty and was not mediated through the imaginative faculty, as is the case with the canonical prophets. The product of the overflow to Moses was the Torah and this Torah, which issued from the rational faculty, has a higher epistemological status than the 'parables' which issue from the imaginative faculty. That the prophetic overflow has to be subsumed under the general concept of 'overflow' is clear, because Maimonides mentions it in connection with the general concept (ii, p. 279).

Torah, as revelation, has an undiluted rationality which is not possessed by the revelation granted to the canonical prophets. The latter is shaped by the imaginative faculty and assumes forms of expression proper to that faculty. Nevertheless, the Torah which Moses received is no more the speech of God in a literal sense than is 'the word of Yahweh' received by the canonical prophets and no 'supernaturalism' is implied in Maimonides' use of the word 'revelation': the prophetic endowment is special but it is located within the created order and 'speech of God' has also to be contained within that order. In a passage where he discusses the delivery of the Torah to Moses and the meaning of 'speech of God' Maimonides has this to say:

> You do not require that the denial of the attribute of speech with reference to Him be explained to you. This is the case particularly in view of the general consensus of our community on the *Torah* being created. This is meant to signify that His speech that is ascribed to Him is created. It was ascribed to Him only because His words heard by Moses were created and brought into being by God, just as He has created all the things that He has created and brought into being ... The intention here is to indicate that predicating speech of Him is similar to predicating of Him all the actions resembling ours. (i, p. 158)

God's speech has to be located within the created order and should receive the same elucidation as 'God's mountains' or 'God's ocean'. On the other hand, though Maimonides' account of the prophets dispenses with supernatural apparatus, it is not a humanist view of the prophetic endowment. The exceptional effects of the overflow within those who are naturally endowed to be prophets sets them apart and confers a special authority on them as recipients of revelation:

> Thus the minds of the people are rightly guided toward the view that there is a divine science apprehended by the prophets in consequence of God's speaking to them . . . so that we should know that the notions transmitted by them from God to us are not . . . mere products of their thought and insight. (i, p. 158).

Another approach by Maimonides to this subject is his transforming of 'saying' and 'speaking', as applied to God, into 'willing':

> Now in all cases in which the words *saying* and *speaking* are applied to God, they are used in one of the two latter meanings: . . . they are used to denote either will and volition, or a notion that has been grasped by the understanding having come from God, in which case it is indifferent whether it has become known by means of a created voice or through one of the ways of prophecy (i, pp. 158f).

The prophet is overwhelmed by the certainty that he has discerned the will of God and he transforms this certainty into the representation that it is God who speaks the words which convey it.

The further analysis which 'volition', used of God, receives from Maimonides has been noticed, but the main matter is the confirmation that he denies speech to God in the continuation of the above passage:

> The terms in question never signify that He . . . spoke using the sounds of letters and a voice, nor that He . . . possesses a soul into which notions are impressed, so that there would subsist in His essence a notion superadded to that essence. For these notions are attached and related to Him in the same way as all other actions. (i, p. 159)

III

In Maimonides' view, unless it is informed by the rational faculty, the imaginative faculty is a source of error and it does not have access to truth. On the other hand, a defective imaginative faculty produces imbalance, even where the powers of the rational faculty are fully exercised. The prophetic endowment consists of a perfect integration of the imaginative and rational faculties. This is a natural endowment, intellectual, temperamental and physiological, which is realized only in a prophet, which makes him a kind of super-man and equips him to appropriate truth specially revealed by God. This revelation overflows to his rational faculty from the Active Intellect, but it is expressed in imaginative language through the medium of the imaginative faculty which itself receives an overflow from the rational faculty. Let us pause to consider this and, first of all, Maimonides' account of the dangers inherent in the imagination being disengaged from reason and of the other limitations to which it is subject.

One of the defects of the imagination on which Maimonides comments is that it does not grasp the special kind of causation which is bound up with the concept of 'overflow', so that it 'cannot represent to itself an action taking place otherwise than through the immediate contact of an agent, or at a certain distance and from one particular direction' (ii, pp. 279f). In this connection Maimonides mentions as a specific error induced by the imagination a literal understanding of the statement 'God speaks' or 'God commands' and this has importance for our enquiry: It is believed

> that He ... gives a command to a particular thing by means of speech similar to our speech – I mean through the instrumentality of letters and sounds – and that in consequence that thing is affected. All this follows imagination, which is also in true reality the *evil impulse*. For every deficiency of reason or of character is due to the action of the imagination or consequent upon its action. (ii, p. 280)

The 'evil impulse' is the Rabbinic *yeṣer hāraʿ* and Maimonides points to the imaginative faculty as a source of error in as much as a literal interpretation of 'God speaks' is induced by it. From this it can be concluded that he does not himself use 'God speaks' literally, but, on the other hand, it is not his intention to attribute 'the speech of God' heard by a prophet to the evil impulse. The problem consists in navigating the strait between this Scylla and Charybdis: 'God speaks' must not be understood literally, but the claim, in a prophetic context, that God speaks should not be reduced to an evil impulse caused by the imagination.

Among those whose imagination is not adequately informed by the rational faculty are, according to Maimonides, those who govern cities, legislators, soothsayers, augurs and dreamers of veridical dreams (ii, p. 374). This list divides easily into two: those who are active in the ordering of affairs in public life, on the one hand, and those who have prophetic affiliations, on the other. The laws made by those who govern cities are explicitly differentiated by Maimonides from 'the divine Law', that is, the Torah; they are classed as a product of opinion and as not expressive of the truth:

I shall explain this to you in order that the matter should not be obscure to you and so that you should have a criterion by means of which you will be able to distinguish between the regimens of *nomoi* which have been laid down, the regimens of the divine Law and the regimens of those who took over something from the *dicta* of the prophets, raised a claim to it, and gave it out as their own. (ii, p. 383).

Rules which are directed exclusively to the ordering of a city are the product of the imaginative faculty and have the status of opinion inadequately informed by the rational faculty:

> It you find a Law the whole end of which . . . is directed exclusively toward the ordering of the city and of its circumstances and the abolition in it of injustice and oppression; and if in that Law attention is not at all directed to speculative matters, no heed is given to the perfecting of the rational faculty, and no regard is accorded to opinions being correct or faulty – the whole purpose of that Law being, on the contrary, the arrangement, in whatever way this may be brought about, of the circumstances of people in their relations with one another and provision for their obtaining, in accordance with the opinion of that chief, a certain something deemed to be happiness – you must know that the Law is a *nomos* and that the man who laid it down belongs . . . to those who are perfect only in their imaginative faculty. (ii, pp. 383f).

Maimonides compares this kind of law (*nomos*) with Torah. The latter has legislative authority, but he uses *nomos* to signify a law promulgated by a legislator who does not have prophetic status. The perfect integration of reason and imagination, a state of affairs which is unusual but which is a feature of the prophetic endowment, does not obtain with the politician. Another kind of contrast between the prophet and the politician appears in a passage where Maimonides notices that an individual with a prophetic disposition is not hungry for the power of public office and that the absence of such ambition is the mark of a true prophet who has been set free from 'the desire of the various kinds of ignorant and evil glorification' (ii, p. 372): 'It is likewise necessary that the thought of that individual [a prophet] should be detached from spurious kinds of rulership and that his desire for them should be abolished – I mean the wish to dominate or to be held great by the common people and to obtain from them honour and obedience for its own sake' (ii, pp. 371f).

There is another class consisting of men of science engaged in speculation who enjoy an 'overflow' towards their rational faculty but none towards their imaginative faculty, 'because of some deficiency existing in the imaginative faculty in its natural disposition, a deficiency that makes it impossible for it to receive the overflow of the intellect' (ii, p. 374). The class which is made up of those who have a well-developed imaginative faculty but who are rationally defective comprises not only rulers but also 'the soothsayers, the augurs and the dreamers of veridical dreams' (ii, p. 374). Of these Maimonides says:

> All those who do extraordinary things by means of strange devices and secret arts, and withal are not men of science, belong likewise to this third class ... Some people belonging to this class have – even while they are awake – extraordinary imaginings, dreams and amazed states, which are like *the vision of prophecy*, so that they think about themselves that they are prophets. And they are very pleased with what they apprehend in these imaginings and think that they acquired sciences without instruction. They bring great confusion into speculative matters of great import, true notions being strangely mixed up in their minds with imaginary ones. All this is due to the imaginative faculty, to the weakness of the rational faculty and to its not having obtained anything – I mean thereby that it has not passed into actuality. (ii, p. 374)

Those gathered into this group may have a special imaginative power which produces positive results (passes into actuality), while, on the other hand what their imagination delivers may be purely subjective, so that they are self-deceived. 'Veridical dreams' are an achievement of men of this class, but such dreams have to be distinguished from prophetic dreams and not everyone who has seen a veridical dream is a prophet (ii, p. 397). Laban and Abimelech, who are credited with such veridical dreams (Gen. 31.24; 20.3), do not have the moral endowment of prophets:

> However in the cases where it is said 'God came to so and so in a dream of the night', there is no prophecy at all nor is the individual in question a prophet... For we do not doubt that Laban the Aramaean was a perfectly impious man, and moreover an idolator. As for Abimelech, though he was a righteous man in comparison with his people, yet Abraham our Father said of his land and kingdom, 'Surely the fear of God is not in this place'. (ii, p. 387)

The distinction between dreamers of veridical dreams and prophets is made in terms of the differing degrees of rationality attaching to each:

> You know too the actions of the imaginative faculty that are in its nature, such as retaining things perceived by the senses, combining these things and imitating them. And you know that its greatest and noblest action takes place only when the senses rest

and do not perform their actions. It is then that a certain overflow overflows to this faculty according to its disposition, and is the cause of veridical dreams. The same overflow is the cause of prophecy. There is only a difference in degree not in kind. . . The action of the imaginative faculty in a state of sleep is also its action in a state of prophecy; there is, however, a deficiency in it [the imaginative faculty in a state of sleep] and it does not reach its ultimate term. (ii, p. 370)

The imaginative faculty can yield truth only where there is an overflow to it of the rational faculty and such an overflow occurs in the case of dreamers of veridical dreams. Nevertheless, such dreams experienced in sleep are different from the dream or vision of a prophet, where a perfectly formed imaginative faculty is subject to thoroughgoing rational control. The errors generated by the imaginative faculty are attributable to a deficiency or absence of such rational control. In Maimonides' language they are to be associated with a defective overflow from the rational faculty to the imaginative faculty or with its absence. In this situation the effects of the imagination are portrayed in dark colours by Maimonides. It creates confusion and error and is an agent of the 'evil impulse'. Into this framework false prophets are to be inserted. They are the victims of an imagination which is imprisoned in subjectivity and is cut off from knowledge and truth. They spawn irrational opinions and have no awareness of a distinction between personal opinions and publicly established truth. Their dreams simply regurgitate persuasions which they have held in their waking lives prior to their dreams, but these are misapprehended as a new revelation. In a passage which follows a description of the true prophet, in which it is emphasized that the imaginative faculty is perfected by an overflow from the rational faculty, Maimonides has this to say of false prophets:

This is the true reality of the notion of prophecy, and these are the opinions that are peculiar to the prophetic teaching. In my exposition I have put in the proviso that it refers to true prophets only. This was in order to exclude from it people ... who have no rational conceptions at all and no knowledge, but only imaginings and whims. Perhaps what these people apprehend are merely opinions which they once had and of which traces have remained impressed on their imaginings together with everything else that subsists in their imaginative faculty. Accordingly when they void and null many of their imaginings, the traces of these opinions alone remain and become apparent to them; whereupon they think that these are things that have unexpectedly occurred to them and have come from outside ... Hence you will find that certain groups of people establish the truth of their opinions with the help of dreams that they have seen, thinking that what they have seen in sleep is something else than the opinion that they believe in, or that they had heard while awake. Therefore, one ought not to pay attention to one whose rational faculty has not become perfect, and who has not attained the ultimate term of speculative perfection. For only one who achieves speculative perfection is able to apprehend other objects of knowledge, when there is an overflow of the divine intellect toward him. It is he who is in true reality a prophet (ii, pp. 377f)

Concerning 'men of science', who are engaged only in speculation and in whom, for one reason or another, there is a malfunctioning of the imaginative faculty, Maimonides remarks:

> You should know that the case in which the intellectual overflow overflows only toward the rational faculty and does not overflow at all toward the imaginative faculty is characteristic of the class of men of science engaged in speculation. This happens either because of the scantiness of what overflows or because of some deficiency existing in the imaginative faculty in its natural disposition, a deficiency that makes it impossible for it to receive the overflow of the intellect. (ii, p. 374 – modified).

Hence there are those possessed of intellectual power and capable of a high level of ratiocination who nevertheless suffer from imaginative impoverishment and who, because of the defect, are incomplete and lop-sided human beings. The most fundamental difference between them and those who have the prophetic endowment is expressed thus: 'If, on the other hand, this overflow reaches both faculties, I mean both the rational and the imaginative . . . and if the imaginative faculty is in a state of ultimate perfection owing to its natural disposition, this is characteristic of the class of prophets' (ii, p. 374).

The prophet enjoys an all-round excellence of natural endowment, one of flawless comprehensiveness in the consummate interaction and balance of all the elements which contribute to it, physiological, rational and imaginative. The catalogue of prophetic qualities which Maimonides compiles shows that there are certain moral attributes and traits of character which the prophet must possess. He should be aloof from the scramble for worldly power and preferment, but, on the other hand, he must not be withdrawn or timid and should be able to act with resolution and courage (ii, pp. 376f; cf. ii, pp. 361f). Everything that goes into the making of a prophet is set out:

> After these preliminary propositions you should know that the case to be taken into consideration is that of a human individual the substance of whose brain at the origin of his natural disposition is

extremely well-proportioned because of the purity of its matter and of the particular temperament of each of its parts and because of its size and position. It is not affected by hindrances due to temperament, which derive from another part of the body. Thereupon that individual would obtain knowledge and wisdom until he passes from potentiality to actuality and acquires a perfect and accomplished human intellect and pure and well-tempered human moral habits. Then all his desires will be directed to acquiring the science of the secret of what exists and knowledge of its causes. His thought will always go toward noble matters, and he will be interested only in the knowledge of the deity and in reflection on His works and on what ought to be believed with regard to that. By then he will have detached his thought from, and abolished his desire for, bestial things – I mean the preference for the pleasures of eating and drinking and sexual intercourse ... For most of the thoughts of those who are outstanding among the men of knowledge are preoccupied with the pleasures of this sense [that is, 'touch' which is connected by Maimonides with 'copulation'] ... And they wonder how it is that they do not become prophets, if prophecy is something natural [that is, not supernatural]. (ii, p. 371).

Here then is another deficiency of 'men of science' – their inability to exert over their conduct the moral discipline which is the hallmark of a prophet. It might be supposed that Maimonides is prescribing an ascetic regime for prophets, but, in a piece of anti-Christian polemic which he inserts elsewhere, he designates moderation as an aspect of justice and warns against the imbalance of an excessive mortification of the flesh. A course should be steered between burdensome self-denial and excess, between 'monastic life and pilgrimage and similar things' and the 'being engrossed in the indulgence of appetites' (ii, p. 380). Since there is a physiological basis to the harmony of elements which constitutes a prophetic disposition, fatigue, anger or sorrow can have an injurious effect on a prophet's capacity: 'Now the imaginative faculty is indubitably a bodily faculty. Accordingly you will find that the prophecy of the prophets ceases when they are sad or angry, or in a mood similar to one of these two' (ii, p. 372). The prophetic endowment is entirely natural and is a product of the created order, but it is an exceptional all-round perfection, bestowed only on a few. It is realized when there is a perfect functioning of reason and imagination, a strength of character which cannot be undone and a high moral seriousness:

Know that the true reality and quiddity of prophecy consist in its

being an overflow overflowing from God . . . through the intermediation of the Active Intellect, toward the rational faculty in the first
place and thereafter toward the imaginative faculty. This is the
highest degree of man and the ultimate term of perfection that can
exist for his species; and this state is the ultimate term of perfection
for the imaginative faculty. This is something that cannot by any
means exist in every man and it is not something that may be
attained solely through perfection in the speculative sciences and
through improvement of moral habits, even if all of them have
become as fine and good as can be. There is still needed in addition
the highest possible degree of perfection of the imaginative faculty
in respect of its original natural disposition. (ii, p. 369)

One particular consequence of the perfect co-ordination of rational
and imaginative faculties in a prophet is the ability to leap to true
conclusions, apparently without engaging in the processes of argument
on which they depend and through the mediation of which a 'speculative thinker' would arrive at them. This insight or intuition is correctly
explained, according to Maimonides, as a kind of reasoning which is so
swift that the processes cannot be discerned, rather than as an exclusion
of the rational faculty. The 'faculty of intuition' is general, but it is
present in individuals with differing degrees of efficiency and power
and it achieves a highly specialized effectiveness in those who have the
rational and imaginative constituents which combine to make a
prophet: 'You will find a man . . . whose conjecturing and divination are
very strong and habitually hit the mark, so that he hardly imagines that
a thing comes to pass without its happening wholly or in part as he
imagined it' (ii, p. 376).

This intuition attains final expression in the imaginative faculty, but
Maimonides is concerned to establish that it is a product of the co-
operation of the rational and imaginative faculties and is not a non-
rational illumination, even if 'by means of his speculation alone a man is
unable to grasp the causes from which what a prophet has come to
know necessarily follows' (ii, p. 377). The rational component of prophetic truth is an intuition which reaches its goal immediately and the
expression of this truth in the imaginative faculty, in forms which are
apparently derived from sense experience, is, in reality, dependent on
an overflow from the rational faculty, where the truth was intuited.

The contention that the expression of prophetic truth is associated
with a condition where the senses are at rest leads on to a fuller consideration of how the mental states in which a prophet is active are to be
envisaged and a 'vision of prophecy' is said to be one such state:

In a state such as this the senses . . . cease to function, and the overflow ... comes to the rational faculty and from it to the imaginative faculty, so that the latter becomes perfect and performs its function. Prophetic revelation begins sometimes with a vision of prophecy. Thereupon the terror and strong affection, consequent on the perfection of the action of the imaginative faculty, become intensified and then prophetic revelation comes. (ii, p. 385)

Though Maimonides expunges the supernatural from his account of prophecy, it would be a mistake to suppose that his main thrust is to rehabilitate the humanity of the prophet or to establish that the prophet is always a stable and well-rounded human being. The authority which a prophet wields is not reducible to 'mere products of his thought and insight' (i, p. 158). Again his dictum 'nor can a man not be a prophet on a certain evening and be a prophet on the following morning' (ii, p. 361) might appear to be directed against a Jekyll and Hyde view of a prophet: against the view that the prophet is normally a representative human being, but that this condition is periodically and exceptionally interrupted by prophetic states which generate prophetic activity. Maimonides is not affirming that the prophet is always both a a man and a prophet; he is adhering to the opinion that prophecy is the product of exceptional mental states and that a prophet is not always a prophet. Prophecy is generated by periodic supernormal states which trigger prophetic activity and which interrupt the normal tenor of the prophet's human condition. The contention of Maimonides which establishes the particularity of his position is that a man who is not *born* a prophet, whose native endowment – whose genes – do not make him a prophet, cannot *become* a prophet. If he does not have this delicate balance of ability and disposition as an inborn endowment, he cannot subsequently acquire it. He cannot become a prophet, if he is not already a prophet in the womb. It is in this context that 'nor can a man not be a prophet on a certain evening and be a prophet on the following morning' has to be interpreted.

This is connected with Maimonides' rejection of supernaturalism and it is an affirmation that whether or not a person is a prophet depends on a natural endowment which he either has or does not have and which he cannot subsequently acquire. It is consistent with a separation of prophet and man and Maimonides enforces this in so far as he encloses all prophetic experience within the framework of states of vision or dream. The details of this representation need not be rehearsed in great detail. Prophetic symbolic action is explained exclusively as a product of visionary experience and its literary expression is described as 'parable'. These are not dramatic performances which belong to the outer world and which were done in full public view. They belong to an inner world of the prophet's imagination and arise from visionary states. The

prophetic dream is especially associated by Maimonides with the reception of the 'word of God' (ii, pp. 385–95) and it is to this part of his
exposition that I turn.

It is clear that Maimonides has rejected the idea of a God who speaks:
the literal sense 'God speaks' makes nonsense of his *via negativa* and he
has explicitly associated such a belief with the erring propensities of an
imaginative faculty which is undisciplined by the rational faculty and
serves the ends of the 'evil impulse'. But, if this is so, the other conclusion which has to be avoided is that the 'word of God', which a
prophet hears in a dream or vision, and which is generated by the
imaginative faculty, is imagination in a pejorative respect, where imagination is opposed to truth. Such a polar interpretation is clearly not
in accord with Maimonides' intention, because the truth of prophetic
experience is assured by an overflow from the rational faculty into the
imaginative faculty. Nevertheless, the circumstance that prophetic
truth is realized in the imaginative faculty, which has corporeal connections, must be regarded as a limitation, and when Maimonides says that
God speaks or that the hearing of his word takes place in the imagination he is underlining this limitation.

Hence the confining of prophetic experience to states of vision or
dream takes on a new significance. Prophetic perceptions which arise in
the imagination when the senses are at rest have a striking similarity
with sense perceptions and with the language in which these are
expressed, but they are separate from the kind of awareness which
characterizes sense perceptions and they owe the measure of truth
which they possess to the rational faculty. From this point of view
'God's speaking' which takes place in the prophet's imagination is not
to be confounded with a speaking 'through the instrumentality of
letters and sounds' (ii, p. 280) which would be heard by the hearing of
the ears. A literal sense of 'God speaks' is then excluded by two considerations: it is incompatible with Maimonides' understanding of God
in his essence and it disagrees with his separation of speech heard in the
imagination from speech heard by the ears.

It should be said, however, that, though what goes on in the imagination, in vision and dream, is limited in the respects noted, it is the
best knowledge of God available to human beings and that it is only
accessible to a prophet. A prophet is special in a sense analogous to that
in which a record-breaking athlete has been made special by happy
coincidences of physiological characteristics and biochemical functioning. The prophet has the exact ingredients, mental, moral and disposit-
ional of a prophetic endowment. So endowed he will become a prophet,
unless there are extraordinary blockages or failures of function (ii, p.
361). The thought of self-discipline is applied in connection with the
rational and moral fitness of a prophet and there are elements of asceti-

cism in the training programme which is laid down. The prophet has an access to divine truth which outruns that of other persons.

There is no doubt that Maimonides attaches a pre-eminence of religious authority and of knowledge of God to those who are prophetically endowed and that, though he excludes supernaturalism, he sets the prophet apart from our common humanity. His dictum 'nor can a man not be a prophet on a certain evening and be a prophet on the following morning' rules out the possibilty that anyone who does not have the natural endowment of a prophet from the outset can become a prophet: that the same person can be now a man and now a prophet, subject to episodic divine interventions and infusions associated with a doctrine of 'inspiration'. Maimonides' doctrine, however does not contribute to the integration of prophecy with an enrichment of the prophet's human discernment and commitment, since he maintains his special version of the Jekyll and Hyde view of prophecy with its differentiation of the prophetic and the human state. He does this by limiting prophetic experience and prophetic knowledge to visionary and dream states and thereby severing them from waking life and normal conditions of awareness and consciousness. There is a sharp cleavage of prophet and man and this is a clear indication that the enlarging and cherishing of a prophet's human dimensions are not at the centre of Maimonides' concern and that the exit of supernaturalism does not make room for a greater concentration on the prophet's human condition. We are driven to the conclusion that when he is not caught up in prophetic visions and dreams, the exceptional nature of a prophet's endowment does not obtrude and that his common humanity emerges. When he is the recipient of prophetic knowledge, his extraordinary endowment is activated and his experiences are extraordinary, and though there are no supernatural implications, he acquires the status of a super-man and his knowledge of God has the character of 'revealed truth'.

Literature for Chapters 1 and 2

Aquinas, St Thomas, *Summa Theologicae*, vol. ii and iii (London, 1964), in the edition by the Blackfriars.

Bevan, E. R., *Symbolism and Belief* (London, 1938).

Buber, M., *I and Thou*, translated by R. Gregor Smith, 2nd edition (Edinburgh, 1958).

Campbell, C. A. *On Selfhood and Godhood* (London, 1957).

Farrar, A., *The Glass of Vision* (London, 1948).

Maimonides, Moses, *The Guide of the Perplexed*, i and ii, translated by S. Pines (Chicago, 1963).

McKane, W., *Studies in the Patriarchal Narratives* (Edinburgh, 1979).

MacQuarrie, J., *God-Talk: An Examination of the Language and Logic of Theology* (London, 1967).
Mansel, H. L., *The Limits of Religious Thought*, Bampton Lectures 1858 (London, 1859³).
Schökel, L. A., *The Inspired Word: Scripture in the Light of Language and Literature*, translated by F. Martin (London, 1967).
Tillich, P., *Systematic Theology* (Chicago, 1953).
Van Buren, P., *The Edges of Language* (New York, 1972).

3

MINIMAL BIBLICAL CRITICISM AND ITS ADVANCE

I

The influence of the ideals of Renaissance humanist scholarship is well seen in the attitudes struck by William Fulke towards new English translations of the Bible in his *Defense of the sincere and true Translations of the holie Scriptures into the English Tong* published in 1583, The emphasis on the return to the sources, the *ad fontes* prescription of Renaissance scholars, is evident in Fulke's description of the Hebrew bible and the Greek New Testament as 'the first fountain and springs'. His search for biblical truth is concentrated on a new examination of these sources and a translation into English done directly from them. Fulke combines a scientific and humanist temper in relation to linguistic matters and problems of translation with a high doctrine of biblical truth and the line of demarcation is not always easily found.

In essential respects he is a Renaissance man and has a background of preoccupation with science and rational enquiry. In 1560 he had written a book against astrology in which he had opposed the light of reason to the occult and superstitious; his interest in natural philosophy is seen in a book on meteorology which he published in 1571. He asserts the autonomy of biblical science of which textual criticism, lexicography and translation are the contents. That Fulke sometimes fails in scientific rigour in these departments can be shown, but the principles which he lays down for the translation of the Bible from Hebrew and Greek into English are those of a humanist scholar who makes accuracy the primary test of the worth of the process of translation and who holds that the only way of repairing defective scholarship is better scholarship. What he expects to arrive at by an accurate translation of the Bible is nothing less than the mind of the Holy Ghost, but the means of achieving this do not transgress the limits of humanist scholarship and linguistic science.

In building up his argument against Gregory Martin, his Roman Catholic opponent, Fulke outlines his connection with pre-Tridentine Roman Catholic scholars who, like himself, were inspired by Renaissance ideals of scholarship. He identifies himself with the scholarship of Sanctes Pagninus (1470–1536), an Italian Dominican, Isidore Clarius (b. 1495; *CHB* iii, p. 92), who became Bishop of Foligno, and Arias Montanus (1527–1598), who superintended the preparation of the

Royal Polyglot Bible printed in Antwerp by Christopher Plantin and published in 1572 with the patronage of Philip II of Spain. These scholars were devoted to the study of Hebrew and Greek and made strenuous efforts to master the Hebrew bible and the Greek New Testament. They produced critical editions of the Vulgate, compiled dictionaries of Biblical Hebrew and made new translations into Latin of the Hebrew bible and the Greek New Testament. Their great works of comparative biblical scholarship, represented by the Polyglots, expressed a concern to advance the employment of the Ancient Versions by bringing them together with the originals in a synoptic format. Spanish scholars, in the period before the Inquisition, had produced the Complutensian Polyglot as early as 1522.

Fulke's book is especially concerned with translation and a more deliberate consideration of how he defines the limits of humanist scholarship or biblical science in relation to the Bible is necessary. We have already noted that with respect to translation his case is founded entirely on humanist ideals of scholarship and that it is tidy and coherent. The only authority which a translation of the Bible from Hebrew or Greek possesses consists in its agreement with the best text-critical, grammatical and lexicographical science available at the time when it is done. Bad translation may disseminate heretical tendencies but, essentially, bad translation issues from defective scholarship.

The scope of Fulke's humanism and scientific temper in relation to the Bible is not to be exaggerated. The boundary line can be drawn roughly but usefully by stating that it does not go beyond the production of an English translation of the Bible. The aim of the product is that it should be the best approximation of the mind of the Holy Ghost, given the present state of linguistic science with the acknowledgement that there are obscure passages which await further elucidation. The entrance of the Holy Ghost at this point seems to mark the exit of humanist scholarship. We are removed, for the most part, from anything akin to what later generations called 'higher criticism', from any discernment that the translation achieved brings us into the presence of human authors and their several idiosyncrasies and into the different political and social textures of the societies out of which they spoke and wrote at diverse historical periods.

The ownership claimed for the Holy Ghost wrests the translation achieved by humanist scholarship out of human hands, sets it at a great distance from the time-bound characteristics of its historical origins and makes it an approximation to eternal truth which is liberated from chance and change. This needs a little qualification, and it is important to establish that, in limited respects, Fulke continues to exercise scholarly judgement deeper into the territory of biblical interpretation. For example, there is an indication in his attitude to the authorship of the

Epistle to the Hebrews (pp. 28–33) that he recognized a diversity of literary style in biblical books which could be considered and pursued only on humanist assumptions, and another area where linguistic propriety and the refusal to fly in the face of good scholarship determine his attitude is the Christological interpretation of Old Testament texts which he thinks has gone too far (p. 313). He believes firmly that the Hebrew bible, as an embodiment of the mind of the Holy Ghost, contains Christological truth and that exegesis must draw this out, but he finds room in this area for hard, lexicographical scholarship which, allied with considerations of context, checks the extravagance of Christological interpretation.

II

In all of this Fulke, who is an Anglican leaning to Puritanism in the second half of the sixteenth century, is striking an attitude which in general agrees with that adopted by Continental reformers. Baumgartner in his book on Calvin published in 1889 (A. Baumgartner, *Calvin Hébräisant et Interprète de L'Ancien Testament*) notices that a division of labour between the Hebrew Chair and the two Chairs of Biblical Exegesis and Theology is set out in a document of the Genevan Academy (*Les Leges Academiae genevensis*), first published in 1559 (Baumgartner, p. 24). The professor of Hebrew at Geneva was required not only to teach the language, but also to read books of the Hebrew bible with a view to imparting grammatical and linguistic knowledge. Calvin was one of the two professors of theology and, though he uses his linguistic knowledge in his Old Testament commentaries, his exegesis is directed towards theology rather than philology. It would not be seriously wrong to conclude that the Professor of Hebrew operated within the limits of a biblical science which comprised grammar, lexicography and translation, though Calvin, as an Old Testament commentator, supplies his own Latin translation. Nevertheless we can discern the laying of a foundation by the acquisition of humanist scholarship and then a limit applied to its operation, at a point where a biblical theology assumes responsibility for the interpretation of the Old Testament.

So far as Calvin's lexicography is concerned we can judge it by the meanings which he attaches to Hebrew words mentioned explicitly in his commentaries and the degree of his dependence on Kimchi is noticeable. He may have had access to this through Münster's Lexicon which was a compilation of Jewish lexicography, founded principally on *Kimchi's Book of Roots*. There is a copy in the University library at St Andrews, published at Basel in 1539. In assessing the thoroughness of Calvin's lexicographical comments we have to bear in mind the kind of works in which they appear and the nature of Calvin's Chair at Geneva. He certainly knew more Hebrew than Richard Simon, the seventeenth-century French Roman Catholic scholar gave him credit for. His opinion that Calvin knew no more than the characters of the Hebrew alphabet is a considerable under-estimation (*Histoire Critique du Vieux Testament*, 1685, p. 435).

Allowance has to be made for the fact that Calvin rarely indicates his sources but that he tends to do it when he is disagreeing with an earlier authority. This has to be taken into account in any attempt to assess the degree of Jewish influence on his lexicography. A dependence on the Jewish mediaeval commentators, Rashi and Kimchi, can regularly be established, though it is unacknowledged and perhaps indirect. Whether or not Calvin could read these mediaeval commentaries cannot be determined, but the general, and sometimes hazy, way in which he refers to their exegesis when he is disagreeing with it suggests that it was mediated to him by someone else and that he did not have direct access to it. The other factor is that some of Calvin's work on the Old Testament (The Twelve Prophets, Jeremiah, Daniel, Ezekiel 1–20) originated as lectures delivered in the academy which were taken down by students, vetted by Calvin and eventually published. Given these circumstances of their origin, it would not be surprising if the final printed product had imperfections.

Though Calvin's exegesis of the Old Testament owes more to mediaeval Jewish commentators than it does to his predecessors in the Christian Church, he is aware of the earlier dominance of Jerome and refers to his exegesis, again with the tendency to mention him only when he is rebutting him. His view of Jerome as a biblical scholar is coloured by the relentless anti-Roman polemic in which he engages. Yet there is more to the attention which he gives to Jerome's scholarship than the finding of an occasion for an attack on the Roman Church. There is in it something of the awareness that whatever he may say about the abuses of Romanism, Jerome's scholarship is of such a character that it cannot be ignored. Through Jerome Calvin shows an interest in the Vulgate.

In Calvin's day Jerome's Latin translation of the Hebrew bible (the Vulgate) was no longer regarded as the inevitable point of departure for the study of the Hebrew bible, because new translations from Hebrew into Latin and vernacular languages were beginning to appear. Santi Pagnini, an Italian Dominican, had produced such a Latin translation in 1528 and Münster's Latin translation appeared at Basel in 1535, a year after Calvin's arrival. Calvin's cousin, Pierre Robert Olivetan, translated from Hebrew into French, giving birth to the Neuchâtel Bible in the same year. Calvin himself, as has been noted, supplies his own Latin translations for his Old Testament commentaries (Hall,

CHB iii, p. 89) These new translations are fundamental expressions of a revival of Hebrew scholarship. They are embodiments of Renaissance ideals and are found in both Roman Catholic and Protestant camps. They represent a dissatisfaction with any enquiry which does not originate at the beginning of the way. They are a refusal to rest on any mediate authority however celebrated and an insistence on going back to the primary sources. In order to achieve this end with the Hebrew bible Christian scholars were heavily dependent on Jewish scholarship.

A review of Calvin's Old Testament exegesis reveals the extent to which he is influenced by a Jewish model. The Old Testament, according to Calvin, is a dispensation of Law and its foundation is supplied by the first five books. In granting such a place of supremacy to the Pentateuch Calvin is in accord with the Jewish view of the structure of the Hebrew bible and in attributing the authorship of the Pentateuch to Moses he falls into line with traditional Jewish scholarship. We have to judge all this in the light of the pre-critical age of biblical learning in which Calvin was largely located, but a very broad comparison will show that the earlier flowering of critical scholarship gave precedence to the pre-exilic canonical prophets and regarded the Law as a derivative of prophecy, whereas more recent critical trends, inspired by Noth and, especially, von Rad, have had the effect of restoring the order Law and Prophets and have devised new ways of describing the dependence of prophetic literature on Law.

Calvin is untroubled by critical considerations and his account of the structure of the Old Testament is uncomplicated. The Old Testament worshipping community is described by him as a Church. It may be that 'Church' sometimes has a wider connotation and that the term embraces 'nation', but this does not seem to be the case for the most part. The discernment that the Old Testament Church is rightly ordered when its sole criterion is the Law is linked by Calvin with his conviction that the order of the Christian Church must be determined solely by the Scriptures of the New Testament. This analogy furnished him with a contemporary homiletic of a polemical kind. The priest and prophets of the Old Testament who did not know the Law and led the people astray have their counterparts in the clergy of the Roman Church and the apostasies and idolatries which are writ large in the pages of the Old Testament are being re-enacted in the Roman Church. He also uses this scheme of interpretation to blast those who boast of their emancipation from Romanism and have adopted the licence of antinomianism.

There is consequently a strong ecclesiastical interest in Calvin's exegesis, and though it would have pained him to hear it said there are resemblances between Jerome and Calvin in this focusing of interpretation on an ecclesiastical centre. Jerome also discerned correspondences between the history of apostasy recorded in the Old Testament and abuses in the Church of his own time and he developed his exegesis of the Old Testament in order to excoriate heretics, bogus ascetics and Princes of the Church living in the lap of luxury. Exegesis of this kind enabled Calvin to move from the past to the present and to give a contemporary point to his exposition, without straining too much to achieve the transition. It rests on no more than the intuiting of analogies and does not involve any 'Christianizing' of the Old Testament. It is because Calvin regularly operates in this area that he devotes a great deal of attention to the plain sense of Old Testament texts in their historical settings. He discusses them faithfully and then uses them to generate contemporary, homiletical comments. Much of Calvin's commentary on the book of Jeremiah has this character and it is understandable why an inveterate allegorizer, like the Lutheran Hunnius (*Calvinus Judaizans*, 1595), who searched widely for Christ in the Old Testament, should have regarded Calvin as a Judaizer.

Calvin's interpretation of the prophetic literature depends on his understanding of the prophetic office and one aspect of it is that he appears to exhaust the content of that office with the description 'teacher': the prophets are no more than teachers of the Law. This derivative character of the prophetic office is so emphatically marked that Calvin's interest in the revelatory nature of the prophetic word, indicated by such a formula as 'These are the words of Yahweh', is not considerable. The thought of prophetic oracles is not a major preoccupation and there is no agonizing over the theological problems of inspiration and revelation. The matter is different when he identifies a prophetic utterance as Messianic and so Christological (see below), but, apart from this special category, he underestimates the difference between an Old Testament prophet who is claiming to speak the word of God, and so create Scripture, and a Christian minister whose teaching activity has the form of the interpretation of Scripture. The analogy which he employs in order to move from the past to the present involves a reduction of the prophetic office. Calvin makes large use of this correspondence between the Old Testament prophet and the teacher or minister of the Christian Church: the teaching of the prophet rests on the authority of the Law and the teaching of the minister on the authority of the Gospel.

Calvin's tendency is to give a Christological interpretation to prophetic oracles of salvation and this will always happen if there are Davidic and so Messianic elements in these oracles. Calvin has a general principle of interpretation that the content of weal in these oracles can never be satisfied by referring them to historical kings of David's line or to any this-worldly polity and that they require a point of fulfilment in Jesus Christ. Hence Calvin's Christological exegesis of the Old Testament is mostly concentrated on texts which he supposes to refer to a Messianic figure of David's line.

Here the question may be asked where Calvin stands in relation to the different senses of Old Testament Scripture which were recognized in mediaeval exegesis. The mediaeval view was that certain passages did not have a 'literal' meaning and that they had only a Christological sense. This has a critical bearing on the concept of fulfilment which is applicable to these passages. Calvin translates Isa. 7.14 as 'A virgin will conceive and bear a son and call him Immanuel' (Hebrew, 'A young woman will conceive and bear a son and call him Immanuel'). He holds that this text has no 'literal' sense, that is, Jewish sense; it is Christological and nothing else. In that case it cannot be interpreted in connection with the historical circumstances out of which it arises and it has no meaning in its Old Testament context. This is what is intended by the mediaeval assertion that it has no literal sense and this is Calvin's position in respect of Isa. 7.14. In that case it is no longer possible to say that the original writer wrote better than he knew, that the clarity of the hope which he cast into the future was veiled from him, that he had another form of fulfilment in mind and that only when the fulness of time brought forth the One who would fulfil the hope was the final reference of the text manifest.

There are other places where Calvin's attitude is similar and where he appears to recognize only a Christological sense. Commenting on Isa. 11.1 ('Then a shoot shall grow from the rod of Jesse, and a branch shall spring from its roots') he comments: 'Hence we infer that this prediction applies solely to the person of Christ, for till he came no such Branch arose'. On Ps. 2.8 ('I shall give you the nations as your inheritance, the ends of the earth as your possession') he remarks: 'That David prophesied concerning Christ is clearly manifest from this that he knew his own kingdom to be merely a shadow.' On Isa. 52.13 ('Behold my servant will succeed, he will be raised and exalted high') his comment is 'The servant is Christ' and on Ps. 110.1 ('The Lord said to my Lord, sit at my right hand, until I make your enemies a stool for my feet'), 'In this psalm David sets forth the perpetuity of Christ's reign and the eternity of his priesthood'. Here Calvin is influenced by the circumstance that Jesus applies the text to himself (Mt. 22.42–45) and that there are references to Melchizedek in the Epistle to the Hebrews. The type of Old Testament priest on whom he seizes in order to define the priesthood of Christ is this mysterious figure, an unworldly king and a priest without a successor. The crux of Christ's eternal priesthood is his office as Mediator, so that, along with the assertion that the sense intended by David was Christological, there are elements of typological exegesis in this psalm.

There are other passages which Calvin regards as ultimately Christological, but where he allows a worldly as well as a spiritual interpretation. Here there is a tendency to reproduce the antithesis of carnal and spiritual after the pattern of mediaeval exegesis. Such passages are Isa. 9.5 ('A child has been born to us, a son given to us and the responsibility will rest on his shoulders'); Jer. 30.10 ('You Jacob, my servant, have no fear, do not be terror-stricken, O Israel, says the Lord. I shall bring you back safe from afar and your offspring from the land where they are captives; and Jacob shall be at rest once more, prosperous and unafraid'); Ps. 45.10 ('Listen, my daughter, hear my words and consider them. Forget your own people and your father's house'). An attempt is made to preserve two levels of interpretation: the first refers to the return of the Jews from Babylon to their own land and the second to Christ. It is argued that the Christological interpretation is indispensable, because at no time did the Jews in any worldly polity satisfy the content of these passages and, in this respect, the spirituality and otherworldliness of the final Christological fulfilment is contrasted with the political or carnal character of the lower order of interpretation.

Where Calvin maintains two senses of Scripture in passages which he regards as ultimately Christological, he is sometimes driven towards allegorical interpretation and those who suppose that allegory is foreign to him should give close attention to Ps. 45. He acknowledges that this psalm deals with Solomon and his Egyptian bride, but he is, in the manner of Origen, persuaded that unless it had possessed a fuller and more edifying sense it would never have attained to the rank of Scripture. So too much attention should not be devoted to an exegesis which yields no more than 'obscene or unchaste amours' and v. 10 is to be interpreted as a reference to Christ and his chaste bride, the Church. The bride who leaves her father's house and her people signifies 'all the corruptions which we carry with us from our mother's womb or derive from evil custom'. Verses 13–15 contain a description of the Church richly clad, not designed to attract the notice of men but only for the pleasure of Christ, the King.

So far as I can see Calvin does not say of any passage which he deems Christological that David or a prophet did not discern the ultimate meaning. They are always, on Calvin's view, aware of the Christological content of what they say and the 'literal' or 'carnal' meaning is then accounted for by a doctrine of accommodation. The prophets provide a carnal envelope for the inner, spiritual content, because they wanted their audiences, who were incapable of grasping the inner mystery to take something from their words.

III

That accurate translation of the Hebrew bible and the Greek New Testament was thought to exhaust the contribution of specialist, humanist scholarship to biblical interpretation is clear in the context of Zwingli's first disputation at Zurich in January 1523. Zwingli had been reappointed as preacher in the Minster by the Council at Zurich on 10th October 1522 and he was offered the opportunity of defending and expounding his teaching at a public disputation to be held in January, 1523, where he would advance propositions which were to be defended against any who would oppose them. The primary purpose of this event was to establish Zwingli's position in Zurich and to give him the opportunity of vindicating his stance of *sola scriptura*, and it should be noticed that it was the Council of Zurich who issued the invitations to the debate which was to be held on 29th January 1523. They went to the clergy of their own state, to the bishop of Constance and then to every state of the confederation. They received a dusty answer. Of the other Swiss states only Schaffhausen and Berne were represented and the Bishop of Constance sent four observers to maintain a watching brief. They were not to take part in the discussions, though in a preliminary contribution they protested that the assembly had no standing. Latin, the language of the Church and of specialists in biblical and theological matters, was not to be used. Proceedings would be public and were to be conducted in German. This is another indication of the hand which the Zurich councillors played in organizing the disputation and of the influence which they exercised on its transactions. They had no Latin, they had a stake in the outcome of the debate and it must not be a mumbo-jumbo with which they were completely out of touch. They would draw their own conclusions, but, if they were to be a jury, they must hear the arguments.

This is a reminder that Zwingli worked in tandem with the civil power and rendered to Caesar the things which were Caesar's, but its connections with his *sola scriptura* emphasis are perhaps the more important. His assumption is that laymen are as competent as specialists (clergy) to decide what the Bible teaches and that it is only what the Bible contains which counts. The councillors are a body of Christian men, a jury good and true, and provided they have been supplied with accurate translations of the Hebrew bible and the Greek New Testament, they can follow the debate and decide whether Zwingli's propositions are valid. It is striking that Zwingli is so completely assured that humanist scholarship, lexicographical learning, linguistic ability – the equipment of specialists – has exhausted its usefulness once a reliable translation of the Bible is available. At this point reliance can be put on the democratic intellect of Christian men as opposed to linguists, critics or theologians. A hierarchy of priests or a meritocracy of scholars is not needed to weigh the evidence once the Hebrew and Greek has been translated. It is an untimely and almost violent death which is decreed for critical biblical scholarship which has suddenly become

redundant and has given place to the mind of the Holy Spirit declared
in a vernacular which laymen can understand and interpret. It is an
unreal foreclosing of biblical criticism, a gratuititous assumption that
the mind of the Holy Spirit has been revealed with such clarity in the
Bible that when Christian laymen of goodwill and sturdy judgement
have access to it they will achieve unanimity in its exegesis.

Bainton sketches well the gulf between Zwingli's position and that of
the representatives of the Church of Rome who were present at the
disputation in 1523. It was wide and deep and was unbridgeable. They
were at cross-purposes in so fundamental a way that a meeting of minds
was precluded from the outset. Whatever might be the outcome it could
not be a concerted decision. The gathering was grounded before it had
taken off; it was deemed unconstitutional and was declared null and
void. The thought that a debate called by the counsellors of Zurich
could rule on matters which concerned the whole Church would have
been laughable if it were not so deplorable. Thus spoke the delegates of
the Bishop of Constance. A debate in Zurich arranged by its Council in
order to give Zwingli an opportunity to air his opinions was entirely
unacceptable to them. The conflict was one of incompatible premises
and irreconcilable presuppositions. Bainton writes:

> The delegates of the Bishop of Constance protested that such an
> assembly could not judge of doctrine and change ancient custom.
> This only a general council could do. A village like Zurich could
> not legislate for Christendom. What would Spain, Italy and France
> and the northern lands have to say on the subject. The universities
> must be consulted, Paris, Cologne, Louvain. Zwingli facetiously
> interjected 'Erfurt and Wittenberg'. Then, when the laughter sub-
> sided, he turned to a serious refutation. The present assembly, he
> said, was perfectly competent to judge of doctrine and usage,
> because an infallible judge lay on the table in Hebrew, Greek and
> Latin, namely Holy Writ, and there were those present quite as
> conversant with these languages as any at the universities named.
> Here the humanist Zwingli assumed that the understanding of
> Scripture required philological competence. Yet, he went on, after
> the manner of Luther, to say that the assembly contained also
> Christian hearts who through the Spirit of God could tell which
> side rightly and which side wrongly interpreted Scripture. (*CHB*
> iii, p. 4; Potter, 1977, pp. 20–22)

This is the same attitude to humanist biblical scholarship as was
noticed in Fulke and a similar function and scope are assigned to it. It
aims at providing as perfect an access as possible to the fundamental
sense of the Bible and this is achieved characteristically by translating
the Hebrew bible and the Greek New Testament. What is thus pro-

vided is nothing less than the infallible word of God whose further interpretation can be entrusted to Christian hearts, that is, to those who are illumined by the Holy Spirit and discern the mind of the Spirit as it is declared in the Bible.

IV

A related conflict but in a different setting and proceeding from different premises was sparked off by the seventeenth-century French Roman Catholic scholar Richard Simon, whose *Histoire Critique du Vieux Testament* was published in Paris in 1678 only to be suppressed and burned by Louis XIV abetted by J. B. Bossuet, Bishop of Meaux. An edition in French appeared in Rotterdam in 1685. It was not at all a *sola scriptura* tendency which awakened opposition to Simon in France and far from affirming that a translation of the Hebrew bible would make its sense transparent and that the mind of the Holy Spirit could be read from it, he focused on the obscurity of the Hebrew bible, even when it had been translated. It was not that he showed no interest in the translation of the Hebrew bible and the Greek New Testament, but he did not attach the theological or doctrinal significance to it which appears in Fulke, Calvin and Zwingli. His concern is both to achieve critical freedom and to demonstrate that this is compatible with his remaining a Roman Catholic priest. He was an accomplished text-critical and lexicographical scholar and employed the resources of the Ancient Versions to further the study of the Hebrew bible. He was involved with Protestants in projects to produce a French translation of the Bible, though he finally came to the conclusion that if it was to have liturgical impact, the translation into French would have to be made from the Vulgate and his Trevoux version of the New Testament (1702), which was condemned by Bossuet, still pursuing him, as 'Socinian', was done from the Vulgate (*CHB* iii, p. 350; *Dict. de la Bible*, ii, 1899, 2369). Why he encountered such unbending resistance in France is a matter which will receive further consideration.

The ripples from *Histoire Critique du Vieux Testament* reached the other side of the Channel and John Dryden's response to Simon's book can be inspected in his *Religio Laici* (1682). Dryden was an Anglican at the time and the circumstance that he converted to Roman Catholicism in 1685 has no bearing on the nature of the riposte which he made to Simon in *Religio Laici*. He writes as an Anglican layman and he resents what he regards as a denial by Simon that the Scriptures are reliable, though he does not claim that they are inerrant and he is not an out-and-out biblicist in the mould of Calvin and Zwingli. He acknowledges that Scripture and Tradition are complementary, as also did Fulke, another Anglican, who, however, was nearer to the stance of Calvin and

Zwingli than Dryden. The primacy of Scripture, is, nevertheless, a main premiss of Dryden's argument in *Religio Laici*. The nature of the relationship between Scripture and Tradition outlined by Simon was entirely unacceptable to him and he was deeply offended, because he supposed that Simon had flaunted his critical expertise to debunk the Old Testament.

Let us deal with Dryden first. In the parts of *Religio Laici* which may be regarded as the dutiful contributions of a Poet Laureate, Dryden attacks the Roman Catholic Church. In the Preface he targets especially the Jesuits and, among the Dissenters, especially the Calvinists (Kinsley, 1958, pp. 306–11). They are potential regicides (Kinsley, 1958, p. 310). The Roman Catholics, because they placed the authority of the Pope above that of the king, and the sectarians, because they had already murdered one king and were republicans at heart. The Roman Catholics held that the Pope had a right to depose kings and the dissenters founded their right to topple monarchs on their tendentious biblical exegesis.

More important, and nearer the centre of our interest, are the evidences in *Religio Laici* that Dryden had a serious concern with revealed religion and was alive to matters of biblical criticism. He writes as a well-informed Anglican layman who had shown his manuscript to 'a judicious and learned Friend, a Man indefatigably zealous in the service of the Church and State' (Kinsley, 1958, p. 303), thought by some to have been John Tillotson who became Dean of St Paul's Cathedral. He steers a moderate Church of England course: the establishment of the Church and the union of Church and Throne are corner-stones; Roman Catholicism and Calvinism are equally intolerable forms of dissent and both are politically noxious.

It is in the light of his concern for biblical religion that the long passage on deism (42–60, 168–83) in *Religio Laici* has to be judged and his criticism of Simon's *Histoire* springs from it. Winn is to be followed in dismissing as 'preposterous' the opinion that Dryden was a closet deist when he wrote *Religio Laici* in 1682 (J. A. Winn, 1987, p. 604 n. 93). Dryden's statement that he was 'naturally inclin'd to Scepticism in Philosophy' (Kinsley, 1958, p. 302) and the passage in the poem pressed into service to support the claim is seen, when taken in its context, to show almost the opposite. When Dryden writes in the preface to *Religio Laici* that the way of reason will not reach God (Kinsley, 1958, p. 304), he is not indicating that he has been attracted to deism. On the contrary, he is signifying that a rational religion cannot be constructed and that the foundations of religion are biblical revelation. The theme is a recurring one and the conclusion is unmistakeable. The flickering, guttering candle of reason throws shadows; it is the Bible that lights up the path to God. The light of reason is contrasted with the supernatural light shed by the Bible. 'Reason grows pale at religion's sight and *dissolves in Supernatural Light*' (10–11).

These conclusions explain Dryden's concern for the authority of the Bible which, he supposes, has been damaged by Richard Simon's book. It was probably through the publisher Tonson that he became aware of it. Tonson had undertaken to publish an English translation, but when the French original (1678) was burned shortly after its publication he had second thoughts and withdrew from the undertaking. The English translation of Simon's *Histoire* was done by Henry Dickinson and was published by Walter Davis in January 1682 (Winn, 1987, pp. 372, 603 n. 82). That Dryden is searching for a concert of biblical authority and Tradition is clear. He rejects Roman Catholic imperialism and dissenting enthusiasm is equally unacceptable to him. Exegesis of the Bible should be a public activity and should be under the aegis of the Church. Dryden cannot endure private, unregulated, undisciplined exegesis such as he finds among some sectarians and his quarrel with Simon is not that he assigns a role to Tradition but that he does it in such a way as to create a monopoly of theological significance for it at the expense of the Bible:

> Not that Traditions parts are useless here:
> When general, old disinteress'd and clear. (334–5)

> Nor can we be deceiv'd, unless we see
> The *Scripture*, and the *Fathers disagree*. (439–40)

He is alive to the danger of biblical exegesis done by 'Christian hearts':

> The Book thus put in every vulgar hand,
> Which each presum'd he best cou'd understand,
> The *Common Rule* was made the *common Prey*;
> And at the mercy of the *Rabble* lay.
> The tender Page with horny Fist was gaul'd;
> And he was gifted most that loudest baul'd. (400–5; cf. *The Medall*, 156–61, 165–6)

Dryden has a much lower view than Zwingli of the capacity of laymen to interpret Scripture. Nor is he urging that the Bible is inerrant, that the mind of the Holy Spirit can be discerned in it and that it is the sole arbiter of Divine Truth (*sola scriptura*). There is a couplet in *Religio Laici* which, though it is a polemic against the Roman Catholic Church in the context of the poem, is, nevertheless, an admission that biblical interpretation is not self-authenticating and that there is a problem in finding a seat of authority for it:

> Such an *Omniscient* Church we wish indeed;

'Twere worth *both Testaments* and cast in the *Creed*. (282-3)

On the reliability of the Scriptures Dryden remarks:

> More Safe and much more modest 'tis to say
> *God wou'd not leave Mankind without a way*:
> And that the *Scriptures*, though not *every where*
> free from Corruption, or intire, or clear,
> are uncorrupt, sufficient, clear, intire,
> In *all* things which our needfull *Faith* require. (295-300)

Simon has exaggerated the degree of corruption in the Hebrew bible
and his contention that '*Scripture*, though deriv'd from *heav'nly birth*,
has been but carelesly preserv'd on *Earth*' (258-9) is a *reductio ad
absurdum*. Dryden has grasped the outlines of Simon's *Histoire* and his
criticism is trenchant so far as it goes. His knowledge of its contents is
not profound, and that the Scripture is derived from heavenly birth is
Dryden's premiss not that of Simon.

It is clear that Dryden objects to the divorce between Christian belief
and biblical criticism which Simon argues for. Simon's position is the
reverse of *sola scriptura*. Far from being the sole arbiter of Christian
truth the Scriptures have a very small part in it, according to Simon's
scheme. It is an inerrant Roman Catholic Tradition which formulates
Christian doctrine and biblical critics can be allowed an unfettered,
intellectual freedom without putting it at any risk. Dryden, on the
other hand, holds that the Scriptures are a fountain of Christian truth,
that their authority is primary, but that they need the reinforcement of
ecclesiastical Tradition. Certainly biblical exegesis ought not to be the
province of lay enthusiasts with sectarian leanings and Dryden antici-
pates a possible objection that he, a layman, has entered a theological
debate (Kinsley, 1958, p. 302). It is possible that Dryden smelled the
same rat as Simon's opponents in France and was convinced that
Simon's principal concern was to achieve intellectual freedom as a
biblical critic from the restraints imposed by the Church and that his
professed reverence for *les véritables traditions* was a smokescreen.

Simon's attitude is connected in important respects with a concept of
'obscurity' which he attaches to the Hebrew bible. It will be enough to
say at the moment that this special obscurity with which Simon is
exercised would not be overcome even if all the technical difficulties
attaching to the Hebrew bible, of which Simon has a lively appreciation
and with which he grapples, were solved. If textual criticism could
provide a pure Hebrew text, a perfect recovery of the original, if the
philologists and lexicographers unravelled the grammatical perplexities
of the Hebrew bible and discerned the meaning of the many rare words,
and if the translators rose to great heights of accuracy, sensitivity and

luminosity, this theological obscurity would not be relieved. It arises from the fundamental circumstance that the Bible as a whole is not theologically self-explanatory and that its theological interpretation must be supplied from without by the dogma and Tradition of the Roman Catholic Church. This account will do for the time being, but the matter has such importance for Simon's account of the relation between biblical criticism and biblical theology that we shall return to it.

It would be easy to gather a wrong impression of Simon's *Histoire* from the statements that are regularly made about him. He is said to be the 'Father of Biblical Criticism' and there is a tendency to interpret this in terms of higher or source criticism. It is sometimes coupled with the statement that he limited the Mosaic authorship of the Pentateuch to the laws which are contained in it. Scholars who do not know very much about Simon tend to know this and to give the impression that his critical boldness was of this kind and that he led the charge of the higher critics into the territory of the Old Testament. It is generally true to say that one is not well prepared for an encounter with the *Histoire* by summary references to it in books. Simon's denial of the Mosaic authorship of the entire Pentateuch is a minor item, occupying only a small part of the book, and it is not a clue to the principal tendencies and concerns of his biblical criticism. An undue concentration on this higher-critical foray at the beginning of the book distracts attention away from the scale and plan of his work, and he focuses, for the most part, in a different area of biblical criticism. In important regards his practice of a humanist, biblical scholarship has similarities with that of William Fulke, but his aims diverge entirely from those of Fulke: he is not concerned to make Bible translation the foundation of Christian truth, but to establish that biblical criticism does not infringe on the boundaries of theology and that there is no reason why it should raise the hackles of dogmatic theologians. His work consists of text-critical expertise and appraisals of translations of the Hebrew bible, and, in the field of textual criticism, he ranges widely and enters into great detail. He explains the relation between the Hebrew bible and the Ancient Versions; he has views on Massoretic scholarship and lexicography. He gathers up all his scholarship into a critique of translations of the Hebrew bible and its exegesis. The gist of his contention is that throughout this complex of scholarly activity the biblical critic may be granted complete intellectual freedom without inflicting any damage on Roman Catholic theology.

Simon is well versed in Patristic theology, though it is his intention to escape from its chains. He accepts the irreversibility of Jerome's Vulgate, but he criticizes its textual and linguistic scholarship. Simon has a view of the Vulgate which goes along with the pronouncements of the

Council of Trent and which reveals a conservative streak in him. His translation of the New Testament into French (Trevoux, 1702) was one of the last things which he did and it was made from the Vulgate. It was a declaration by him that only a translation from the Vulgate could make an impact on the liturgy of the French Church. Scholarly translations from the original languages of Hebrew and Greek, embodying new and better scholarship, should be produced, but this activity should not be an attempt to replace the Vulgate.

It was not that Simon made the extravagant claims that Jerome's translation was inspired and inerrant. On the contrary, he was convinced that there were deficiencies in Jerome as a textual-critic and translator. His perception may have been that the Vulgate was so inextricably bound up with the dogmas of the Roman Catholic Church that it was irreplaceable. Jerome succeeded in imposing a new translation on the Church, but the shock of discontinuity and the tremors of instability which would be induced by another such departure in a later age was something which could not be contemplated. One interpretation would be that Simon, the critic, was bowing to ecclesiastical authority, though this would be an over-simplification and would not take full account of the complex of considerations which influenced him.

Certainly the gap opening up between the respective stances of Fulke and Simon can be perceived, for what did Fulke want new translations of the Bible for if not to instal them in a place of supremacy and make Christian truth and ecclesiastical structures answerable to them? On the other hand, by not requiring the Roman Catholic Church to make a translation of the Bible from Hebrew and Greek which were products of better biblical scholarship than that possessed by Jerome, Simon may have been aiming at giving consistency to his claim that the Church could have an easy mind in the face of Simon's exercise of unbridled freedom as a biblical critic. The liberty claimed by Simon was larger than and different from that exercised or desired by Fulke.

One particular criticism of Jerome which Simon makes is that his concept of *Hebraica veritas*, 'the Hebrew truth', is defective. Jerome assumes that the Hebrew text from which he translates is the original Hebrew text, but we know that the Hebrew text did not enjoy such a massive stability nor achieve such a perfection of transmission. Hence (so Simon) Jerome does not do justice to the Septuagint, because he does not appreciate that the Seventy Alexandrian translators had before them a Hebrew text which was different from the one which was established in his time. The concept of the 'Hebrew truth' which Jerome used in connection with his translation into Latin from Hebrew and not from Greek is not so transparently true as he supposed. Why should it be supposed that the Hebrew text which Jerome had rather than the one which was available to the Seventy contained the 'Hebrew truth'? The simplicity and force of Jerome's appeal to 'Hebrew truth' is seen on closer examination to disintegrate.

Moreover, the Seventy had a Hebrew text which was unvocalized and an examination shows that differences of interpretation between them and Jerome arise not from a divergence of the consonantal text but from a different vocalization of the same text. It can be shown that there are cases where the Greek translation of the Seventy reflects a correct vocalization of the Hebrew and where Jerome's departure from the Seventy in his Latin translation is a consequence of the incorrect vocalization of the Hebrew (so Simon).

Thus the recovery of the Hebrew original requires the vocalization of the Hebrew consonantal text and this is a process of interpretation which precedes translation. It is a further indication that Jerome's *Hebraica veritas* is an over-simplified slogan. All of this can be aimed against the Protestant *sola scriptura*, the view that the translation of the Old Testament from the original Hebrew is a sure way of recovering the mind of the Holy Spirit. According to Simon, Jerome undervalued the Septuagint, but Protestants have made the additional assumption that the interpretation of the Hebrew consonantal text made by Jewish scholars, the Massoretic vocalization, is entirely correct. It may be mostly correct, but it should be regarded as no more than one interpretation which should, for example, be compared with the one made by the Seventy. The intention of this argument which is developed by Simon is to torpedo Jerome's *Hebraica veritas* and to demonstrate that the Protestant claim is misconceived and is invalid. The translation of the Hebrew text in the form in which it has been interpreted by the Massoretic vocalization is not a return to the 'first fountain and springs'. Simon makes his point well, but he protests too much and exaggerates the extent of the ambiguity and obscurity which are created by the circumstance that the consonants of the Hebrew text are primary and the vowels secondary.

Simon's intention is to empty the Hebrew bible of a transparent, theological content and to assign to the Church the task of supplying a theological interpretation in conjunction with its formulation of dogma. It would follow naturally from this that the 'inspiration' of the Old Testament writers should not have exercised Simon unduly and this, to some extent, is the case, though not altogether. He works with a rough and ready idea of *genre*, according to which all the material in the Old Testament is historiographical. No more need be shown than that it has been safely stored in archives and conserved and edited by competent archivists. These editors are preserved from error by a special divine oversight and they sometimes indicate the archives from which they are selecting (1 Kgs 11.41; 14.19; 2 Kgs 24.5). Their task of judicious editing seems to be a human, intellectual activity and is disengaged from direct divine endowment or 'inspiration'. It is, nevertheless, thought to involve a divine enabling, so that their editorial judgements are free from error. Editorial judgement, exercised on archives, and a theological doctrine of 'inspiration' is a marriage of incompatible partners.

Auvray (1974, p. 175 n. 2) describes Simon's view of inspiration as 'Molinist' and describes Molinism as an anti-docetic tendency, an attempt to do more justice to the human dimension of the Bible. The trouble with Simon's account is that he does not succeed in combining the divine and human aspects of the Bible in a credible way. Those who are exercising editorial judgement in their selection of the archives are unaware of any divine reinforcement as they undertake their tasks. 'Inspiration' does not influence or enter into their intellectual method. The so-called 'inspiration' is not part of their mundane competence – it is a kind of over-ruling Providence which operates independently of it and mysteriously keeps it from error. No explanation is given of how this coherence between intellectual judgement and divine inspiration is effected and they have the appearance of mutually exclusive alternatives rather than that of partners who could co-operate with each other. The state of affairs which is described is 'either-or' not 'both and'.

Simon's interest in the Hebrew bible is mostly a critical one and he claims unfettered freedom in pursuing it on the ground that such scholarship does not impinge on the authoritative teaching of the Roman Catholic Church on doctrine and morals. An indication that he intends his scholarship to stop short of theology is the circumstance that he confines himself to what mediaeval scholars called the 'literal' sense of Old Testament texts and he abstains almost entirely from any element of Christian interpretation of the Old Testament. He thinks this is beyond the limits of Old Testament exegesis as a biblical science and he finds fault with scholars who have confused this kind of interpretation with the critical study of the Old Testament. It will be perceived that there is a great gulf in this respect between Simon and Fulke for whom the Christological content of the Old Testament was an assumption of his scholarship, though he issued a warning against the extravagances of Christological exegesis. If we ask, with respect to Simon, what are the limits which are to be fixed for the critical study of the Old Testament, the answer seems to be that there are no limits and that, at this level of investigation, the whole of it is the province of humanist scholarship.

There are some features of Simon's work which appear to contradict this conclusion, but his principal contention is that it is the theological interpretation superimposed on the Old Testament by the Church which must support the truth of Christianity. Simon conjures up 'inspiration' and smuggles it into the Hebrew bible, but he makes little use of it and his kind of critical scholarship does not need it. A defect from the point of view of Roman Catholic orthodoxy is that he does not display convincingly the interpenetration of Scripture and Tradition, because he is, for the most part, absorbed in a critical, humanist investigation of the Hebrew bible. It has been noticed that Dryden disliked Simon's cavalier treatment of the Bible, but Simon's concept of 'obscurity' goes deeper than the alleged 'corruption' which Dryden parodied, though this is a consideration which Simon raises: 'The Church has always kept the truths contained in Scripture, but to achieve this she has not given the spirit of sincerity to copyists who wrote down the exemplars of the Bible and has not prevented them from introducing corruptions into their copies' (*Histoire*, p. 492).

However, it is the theological obscurity or inadequacy of the Bible which is the more important of Simon's contentions. There are two passages in which the theological priority and self-sufficiency of Roman Catholic tradition over against the obscurity of Scripture are clearly expressed by Simon:

> It is necessary to have recourse to another principle, a deposit of Religion [meaning Christianity] which has always been in the Church independent of Scripture, in terms of which one resolves the difficulties which are found in the Bible. This is what is meant by Tradition, which Tradition was present in the Church before there was any Scripture, and she never neglected to conserve it at a time when there was no Scripture. (*Histoire*, p. 405)

The second passage occurs on the same page in a context where Simon is appraising Patristic exegesis of the Old Testament and where he seems to say that the Christian, theological content of this exegesis is derived from Tradition and that Scripture is used by the Fathers as a homiletically apt and effective way of communicating these doctrines.

Simon is asserting that all the armoury of biblical science is to be employed in the investigation of the Hebrew bible, but that this science of criticism, which is a humanist activity, has no part to play in determining how the Bible relates to Catholic Tradition. Scholars must provide the Church with a translation, but, having given authority to a translation, the Church will interpret it so that it agrees with true Religion, a system of belief and morals prior to and independent of the translation. Simon separates the critical study of the Hebrew bible, which has no Catholic theological constituent, from its theological elucidation which is supplied by the Church.

What were Simon's motives? He is rejecting Protestant claims that the Bible when translated from Hebrew and Greek into a vernacular language, is the fountain of Christian truth and that Christian laymen

are competent to determine the content of that truth. There was
nothing in that affirmation which would have been objectionable to the
Roman Catholic Church. It could not have been other than sweet music
in the ears of those who heard it. But, in separating the critical study of
the Hebrew bible from Roman Catholic dogma, Simon was also fighting his own corner. He was not solely engaged in exalting *les véritables
traditions* above the Protestant Bible. Other interests were at work and
he was endeavouring to peg out a wide area of biblical scholarship
which was not subject to dogmatic *diktats* and where critical autonomy
would prevail. In view of the suppression of the *Histoire* in 1678 we
must suppose that the Roman Catholic Church was unconvinced by his
statement of the relation between Scripture and Tradition. There may
have been a deep suspicion that he was more exercised to achieve
unrestricted liberty and the widest sphere of operation for a humanist
biblical science than he was to give a satisfactory account of the complementarity of Scripture and Tradition.

V

Let us finally look briefly at the historical context in which the publication of Simon's book is set and at the two men, Louis XIV and
Bossuet, who were responsible for its suppression and subsequent
burning. Which of them played the principal part? This is not a simple
question to answer. To suppose that the part of the king in the affair
was a minor one and that Bossuet was the prime mover may not correspond with the facts. Certainly Bossuet was the Dauphin's tutor from
1670 to 1680 and while he fell out with Louis between 1662 and 1665
and in 1676, he had the confidence of the king for the most part (*Dict.
de Biographies Françaises*, vi, 1954, 1152–1156). He was in an influen-
tial position at court and, as the Dauphin's tutor, he would have had the
ear of the king. But it would be a mistake to suppose that Bossuet took
advantage of his position to convey his *animus* against Simon to the
king, that this is simple case of *odium theologicum* and that the king's
part in it was no more than that of a royal executioner doing the bidding
of a favourite. It is evident that Bossuet was regularly involved in
controversy throughout his life, that he was combative and was something of a war-horse, but he does not seem to be a Prince of the Church
who had become conformed to the world. He was not a cleric who had
become a courtier and statesman rather than a bishop. Ingold urges
(*Dict. de la Bible*, v, 1908, 1743–1746) that he had a deep and sincere
concern for the integrity of the Faith which he perceived Simon's book
to have endangered. His response was not nakedly reactionary; it was
not brute obstinacy or intransigence. Bossuet was serious in his pursuit
of sacred learning and his scholarly output bore this out. He had been

prominent in ecclesiastical contexts and had played an active role in seeking a rapprochment with French Protestants.

The other side of the coin is that there was a close relationship between Crown and Church and that a Churchman at court was not out of his element. By virtue of his coronation oath Louis XIV was the protector of the French Roman Catholic Church. He strenuously upheld the liberties of the Gallican Church and defended it against the claims of the Pope, and Bossuet was associated with him in this. Louis' clash with Pope Innocent XI over Church revenues led to the threat of excommunication and to the Declaration of Four Articles (1682) by an Assembly of the Clergy of France which Louis had summoned. The Four Articles of 1682 were a revision by Bossuet of a more abrasive first draft:

> There is no power except from God... Therefore anyone who resists authority resists the command of God... It follows that kings and princes cannot be subordinated by God's command to any ecclesiastical power, nor deposed directly or indirectly by authority of the heads of the Church, nor their subjects dispensed from fealty or obedience or released from their oath of allegiance ('a riposte to the threat of excommunication'; Mousnier, *Louis XIV*, 1973, p. 13)

Hence while the theological niceties of Simon's book were, in all likelihood, beyond the interest and comprehension of the king, its publication in the historical context just sketched raised an important matter of state. Simon's writings had been condemned as heretical by the Pope and it would have been awkward if the *Histoire* had opened up another line of attack on the Gallican Church and was cited as a confirmation of its heretical tendencies. Louis had enough on his hands and did not want his differences with Rome to be aggravated by doctrinal complications.

Yet the circumstance that Simon did not gather any support in France is surprising. It was not that he was born before the time was ripe; currents of criticism were flowing in his favour and it might be thought that he had sailed on the tide, discerned the *Zeitgeist*. Ingold (op. cit., 1744) draws up a formidable list of moral scars and temperamental defects by which Simon was disfigured, warts which made him unprepossessing. His character was bad, his satires were cruel, he was a practised liar and he had an objectionable streak of vanity. Even so, he concludes, this is not a sufficient explanation of the unanimous rejection which he suffered. So far as Bossuet's motives are concerned, we should suppose that they were genuinely theological in kind and that the bargain which Simon tried to strike was seen by him as a Satanic temptation. He demanded a complementarity of inspired Scripture and *les véritables traditions* and he rejected the division of labour which Simon had proposed and the antithesis which he had created. The price which Simon asked for bestowing a monopoly of dogmatic authority on Tradition was too high.

Literature

Auvray, P., *Richard Simon 1638–1712. Étude bio-bibliographique avec des textes inédits* (Paris, 1974).

Bernus, A., *Richard Simon et son Histoire Critique du Vieux Testament: La Critique Biblique au siècle de Louis XIV* (Lausanne, 1869).

Bainton, R. H., 'The Bible in the Reformation', *Cambridge History of the Bible* (*CHB*), iii (Cambridge, 1963), pp. 1–37.

Baumgartner, A. J., *Calvin Hébräisant et Interprète de L'Ancien Testament* (Paris, 1889).

Calvin, J., *Biblical Commentaries*. Calvin Translation Society (Old Testament Commentaries: Edinburgh, 1845–1854).

Fulke, W. *A Defense of the sincere and true Translations of the holie Scriptures into the English Tong* (London, 1583).

Hall, B., 'Biblical Scholarship: Editions and Commentaries', *CHB* iii, pp. 38–93.

Ingold, A., 'Richard Simon', *Dictionnaire de la Bible*, v (1908), 1743–1746.

Kinsley, J., *The Poems of John Dryden*, vol. 1 (Oxford, 1958).

Limouzin-Lamothe, R., 'J. B. Bossuet', *Dictionnaire de Biographies Françaises*, vi (1954), 1152–1156.

Mousnier, R., *Louis XIV* (1973).

Potter, G., *Ulrich Zwingli* (1977).

Simon, R., *Histoire Critique du Vieux Testament* (Rotterdam, 1685). *Critical Enquiries into Various Editions of the Bible* (London, 1684).

Simon, R., *Le Nouveau Testament de notre Seigneur Jésus-Christ* (Trevoux, 1702).

Vigouroux, F., 'J. B. Bossuet', *Dictionnaire de la Bible*, i (1895), 1864–1866.

Winn, J. A., *John Dryden and his World* (Yale, 1987).

4

OLD TESTAMENT CRITICISM AND THE CANONICAL PROPHETS (I)

I

The original Dutch edition of Kuenen's book on Old Testament prophecy was published in 1875 and the English translation (*The Prophets and Prophecy in Israel*) appeared in 1877. A broader treatment of Old Testament religion is offered by Kuenen in his Hibbert Lectures for 1882 (*National Religions and Universal Religions*) and this theme will serve as a point of departure. It is an approach which coincides, in important respects, with that of Wellhausen and Robertson Smith. Nor does such a starting-point dilute the concentration on the canonical prophets which is advertised as the subject of this chapter, because these prophets are placed by all three scholars at the centre of a process by which the nationalistic limitations of Yahwism were overcome and its advance to the stature of an ethical monotheism, capable of universalization, was achieved.

A consequence of this framework of interpretation is the theological devaluation of the public expressions of Yahwism, the religious institutions in which they were embodied and by whose transactions they were expressed. All the institutional projections of Yahwism are thought to belong to an ethnic religion, corresponding with religions of restricted vision, cramped by nationalistic boundaries, religions which are characteristic of the nations surrounding Israel. They are on the same level as as the institutional expressions of the religions of Moab, Edom and Ammon and, hence, a great gulf is fixed between the canonical prophets, who are spiritual aristocrats (cf. Mulder, 1993, p. 78; in Dirksen and van der Kooij, *Abraham Kuenen*) and the popular, public Yahwism which is the religion of the multitude. The prophets are not disengaged from their community; they are not unconcerned about it and they are not distant theorizers. The differences between them and institutional Yahwism are generated in the heat of conflict with it. They take their stand where the current of popular Yahwism is flowing strongly against them. They have a vision which they cannot communicate effectively, because they have horizons which are wider than those of their community.

Kuenen, Wellhausen and Robertson Smith all describe the prophets from the eighth century BC to the exile in these *élitist* connections, the heroic stature of the prophets as giants among the pygmies being a special feature of Wellhausen's portrayal (1894, p. 81; cf. Kuenen, 1882, p. 148). The Yahweh of these prophets, so it is argued, is not the Yahweh of institutional Yahwism. He is not limited to a special area of territorial responsibility within which he identifies himself with the interests of a particular community and is their shield and defence. He cannot be understood or grasped apart from ethical values which transcend ethnic or national boundaries and are universally human in their application. This is Kuenen's Universal Religion or Ethical Monotheism. That Yahweh is a God of justice and that justice is as wide as humanity is a leap to universalism which is achieved by means of a costly and sorrowful solidarity with a community from which the prophets are alienated, because it has no access to their vision. It is what they see there, inhuman infringements of justice between individuals in society and the triumphs of greed and hardness of heart over the claims of generosity of spirit and brotherhood, that awaken their understanding and shape their convictions. As they enter into the sorrow of fundamental betrayals in their own community they are enabled to discern the contours of a Yahwism which is universal in scope.

II

It is not the intention of this diversion to outline how more recent Old Testament scholarship has reacted against the claim that the canonical prophets are to be severed from institutional Yahwism and that the forms of prophetic literature have no cultic connections. I have gone into these particular matters elsewhere (1979, pp. 163–88; 1982, pp. 251–66). The diversion is limited to the more general contention of Eichrodt that Old Testament theology, in fundamental respects, has an institutional character and to the 'Patternist' or 'Myth and Ritual' scheme of interpretation which attaches far-flung institutional features to its ideology, but which, otherwise, parts company with Eichrodt's theology.

Eichrodt has a serious concern to establish the distinctiveness and superiority of Yahwism, and the community and culture which it created, over against the nations which comprised the environment of Ancient Israel. What may be regarded as a new departure in Eichrodt is the extent to which this has been undertaken not only in terms of religious ideas but especially with reference to institutional coherence, since 'covenant', on which he depends so largely in his demonstration of the stability and mutual compatibility of the theological structure of Yahwism, is an idea which is shown to have created the institutions, officers and offices of Yahwism, to have penetrated them deeply, to have influenced decisively the forms they assumed and the spirit in which they functioned. Such an extension of the base of Old Testament theology is cited as a constructive feature of Eichrodt's work, a liberation from a narrow concentration on religious ideas. This, it is maintained, is a too theoretical approach to the theology of the Old Testament. A drawing into the theological enquiry of institutional embodiments of religion is better able than religious ideas, defective because they are too cerebral, to grasp how a community participates in its religious beliefs and how they are incorporated in observances which were for the many rather than the few.

On 'Patternism' I shall not dwell on fine distinctions between different schools. The names called to mind are those of S. H. Hooke who edited *Myth and Ritual* (1933), *The Labyrinth* (1935), and *Myth, Ritual and Kingship* (1958); A. R. Johnson who contributed to the second and third of these volumes and who wrote *Sacral Kingship in Ancient Israel* (1967^2); I. Engnell whose contributions include *Studies in Divine Kingship in the Ancient Near East* (1967^2) and *Critical Essays on the Old Testament* (1970). The second of these is an English translation of thirteen essays from *Svenskt Bibliskt Uppslagsverk* (1962). Engnell is concerned to establish that his 'pattern' (Divine Kingship) is restricted to 'a distinct cultural area' (the Ancient Near East) and to a historical period (Antiquity) and that it does not 'cross all boundaries of time and space' (1970, p. 25). He is not a scientist of religion and his method is not phenomenological like that of G. Widengren (*Religionens varld* [1953^2]). This is translated into German as *Religionsphänomenologie* (1969).

These are distinctions which do not affect the comments I propose to make on Patternism as a method of Old Testament interpretation. The institutional emphasis in Eichrodt's theology of the Old Testament was designed to focus on distinctive institutions of Yahwism and so to emphasize the special character of the Israelite community; the function of the institutionalism of Patternism is to subsume Yahwism and Yahweh's community under the cultural area of the Ancient Near East by using the institution of Divine Kingship as a master key which unlocks every door. For the interpretation of the Old Testament this becomes the ultimate, single hypothesis which clears away the lumber of a plethora of hypotheses. If we think of this in terms of 'myth and ritual', the religious institution in whose ritual the community is involved is that of the New Year Festival and the myth which interprets the ritual is that Yahweh is incarnate in or is represented by or is identical with the reigning king in the cultic drama of the festival. The king *qua* God is exposed to suffering and humiliation, is held captive in the land of the dead, rises victorious to new life, is anointed and enthroned, repeats the victory of creation over chaos in the primaeval conflict and brings to the community the guarantee of a stable and ordered world, of fertility and well-being (Widengren, 1969, pp. 360–93; Engnell, 1967, pp. 97–173).

Engnell asserts categorically that in the Jerusalem New Year Festival the theme of Yahweh's kingship or enthronement is not separable from that of the sacral (that is, the Davidic or Messianic) king (1970, pp. 105f). Consequentially he holds that the Suffering Servant of Deutero-Isaiah is a Messianic not a prophetic figure and that he emerges as a metamorphosis of the suffering and humiliation of the king in the ritual of the New Year Festival (1948, pp. 54–93). A perplexing aspect of the account of the king's part in the Jerusalem New Year Festival, as it is postulated by Widengren and Engnell, is that they assign to him what appear to be two irreconcilable roles. On the one hand, he acts *qua* Yahweh and, on the other, he is the representative or embodiment of the community. If the king acts *qua* Yahweh, he cannot also be the 'Servant of Yahweh' and he cannot have a 'covenant' relationship with Yahweh in the context of the ritual. It is to be hoped that this will not receive the dusty answer that the fault lies in our 'western logic' (Engnell, 1970, p. 20; Widengren, 1969, pp. 360f, 392f).

Engnell holds that the two themes, 'Kingship of Yahweh' or 'Enthronement of Yahweh' and 'Messianic King' are inseparable (1970, p. 106). The enthronement of Yahweh as a part of the ritual of the postulated New Year Festival involves the participation of the Davidic king as one whose identity with Yahweh holds within this specific cultic field. Engnell holds that the 'Kingship of Yahweh' theme (Pss. 97, 99) and the 'Messianic king' theme (Pss. 2, 110) are not antithetic in the book of Psalms. This may be so, but it is not obvious that they combine with each other in the ritual of a New Year festival. Psalms like 2 and 110, which are about the accession and enthronement of a Davidic king and his adoption as a 'son of Yahweh', do not obviously refer to an enthronement ritual in the context of a festival in which the Davidic king plays the part of Yahweh. A once-for-all coronation ritual is a different matter from a regularly repeated enthronement festival in which the king takes the part of Yahweh and is identified with him in a cultic drama. Psalms which are royal and Messianic are not obviously connected with the kingship or enthronement of Yahweh and psalms which are about the kingship of Yahweh are not obviously Messianic.

The main matter to which attention should be drawn, in the context of this chapter, is that Patternism is a scheme of Old Testament interpretation which contradicts the view (Kuenen, Robertson Smith, Wellhausen) that prophets, who were spiritual aristocrats, created a new and distinctive Yahwism and that their religion transcended the limits of institutional Yahwism. Opposed to this is the contention of the Patternists that the foundation of the structure of the Old Testament is a cultic festival, a ritual and ideology of Divine Kingship, which was common to the Ancient Near East. This is the seed which produces the manifold growth of the Old Testament, and the Messianic king is more centrally located in the Old Testament than the canonical prophets. Joel and Habbakuk are cultic poetry, Nahum is probably an imitation of cultic poetry and the book of Deutero-Isaiah, who was a Messianic not a prophetic figure, certainly is. The Suffering Servant's mission corresponds to a scheme of suffering, death and resurrection, the source of which is the Jerusalem New Year Festival, where the Davidic king, as the incarnation of Yahweh, participated in a ritual drama with such a pattern (Engnell, 1948, pp. 54–93; 1970, p. 167). The alternation of oracles of doom and salvation in the canonical prophets has its roots in the ritual and ideology of the New Year festival (1970, p. 169). Messianism is an important criterion for determining genuine 'prophetism' and 'it is an element which holds a dominant and critical place in the main ideological line of Israel's religion and history' (1970, p. 162).

III

Account should be taken of a theological divergence beween Kuenen and Robertson Smith, an opposition of natural and supernatural, which is focused on an evaluation of Old Testament prophecy. It will subsequently appear that the divergence is not so clear as might appear from this bald statement. The complications are on the side of Robertson Smith and will be considered in the next chapter. It will be enough to say now that Robertson Smith is dissenting from Kuenen's view that no appeal to the supernatural should be made in connection with the utterances of the canonical prophets and that their theological contribution to the Old Testament should be elucidated without recourse to the concepts of inspiration and revelation. What is more difficult to express, and will require further consideration, is how Robertson Smith escapes from this conclusion, given that, up to this point of disagreement, there is such impressive unanimity between him and Kuenen on the prophets and the prophetic literature.

There is a relation between Kuenen's theological (or 'non-theological') conclusion that the 'ethical monotheism' of the prophets is a religion which is a human product and his account of the history of Israelite religion which he regards *in toto* as a human product (*The Religion of Israel*, i (London and Edinburgh, 1874; the Dutch edition was published in 1869). 'Revelation' by God or the 'inspiration' of prophets by God plays no part, according to Kuenen, in the history of Israelite religion. One should be aware of this link between 'the ethical monotheism' attributed by Kuenen to the canonical prophets and his comprehensive account of the history of Israelite religion. But if the interest and concern of the enquiry is whether the canonical prophets derived their religion from their own enlightment or from a supernatural source – if it is this which is being investigated – one should not become too involved in the problems of constructing a detailed history of Israel's religion (cf. Emerton, 1993, pp. 8–28).

Nevertheless, as Emerton has noticed (1993, p. 20, *Abraham Kuenen*), the assumption of Kuenen's history of the religion of Israel, that it derives entirely from the evolutionary thrust of men who attained progressively higher levels of religious refinement, hangs together with the conclusion about the nature of the destination which is reached – the ethical monotheism of the canonical prophets. Moreover, where the emphasis lies on 'high moral seriousness' (Matthew Arnold's phrase), a bridge has been constructed between morality and theism: the elevated prophetic morality and the ethical demands made by the prophets reflect a universal moral order which Yahweh upholds and he is best grasped by moral perceptiveness and commitment at a human level (cf. Mulder, 1993, pp. 65–90, *Abraham Kuenen*). However, although the fading away of ecstasy and abnormal psychological states (trance) and the onset of a condition of rational coolness is part of Kuenen's portrayal of the canonical prophets, the excellence which he ascribes to them is primarily religious not intellectual. He does not make them into great thinkers or moral philosophers; it is 'the peculiar excellence of their religion' (Kuenen, 1877, p. 356) on which he fastens (cf. Mulder, 1993, p. 6, *Abraham Kuenen*). What makes them extraordinary is religious excellence, a penetrating insight which is exceptional and separates them from their community, but which is to be explained as native endowment not as divine inspiration.

The response of some Dutch scholars (especially Wildeboer; Houtman, 1993, pp. 43–6, *Abraham Kuenen*) was to accept Kuenen's critical framework, and the evolutionary character of the history of Israelite religion which it implied, but to reject Kuenen's exclusion of 'revelation' from the account. Instead, the evolutionary aspect of the process was described as a progressive revelation by God who cast as much light on the human scene as could be borne. The establishment of a correlation between service of God and obedience to ethical demands had already been made by Moses and the ethical monotheism of the canonical prophets was the *apogée* of a gradual and progressive revelation.

Kuenen's book, *The Prophets and Prophecy in Israel* (1877; Dutch edition 1875), has been thought by many to be excessively tedious – an example of over-kill. There is an element of unfairness in this and it is not free from anachronistic tendencies to which we are prone. It is forgotten that what may now appear to us to be a mouse of a problem near the end of the twentieth century was a burning question in the second half of the nineteenth century, when Kuenen was writing his book. It is largely dull reading for us, because it expends so much intellectual energy in destroying beliefs which many do not hold. Kuenen was not shadow-boxing; he was waging a serious contest. He was attempting to demolish the belief that the canonical prophets were recipients of supernatural truth and the chief proof of this, at the time, was thought to be the accuracy of the detailed predictions which the prophets had projected into the future. To win the argument Kuenen had to destroy these alleged proofs and he went into great detail to do so. That this was his plan of action can be discovered in his own statements:

> In order to obtain certainty with regard to the truth of the traditional view, we accompanied the supernaturalist on his way, and subjected the prophecies, one by one, to the test of the requirements which, according to him, they should necessarily have corresponded. This enquiry led us to a negative result, namely the absence of the supernatural divine inspiration which the knowledge of the hidden things of the future would presuppose. But at the same time it opened our eyes for that in which the power and significance of the prophets lie, for their religion and their religiousness. (1877, pp. 586f, cf. pp. 94f)

The concern which engaged Kuenen was not only a negative one. He viewed the work of demolition as a clearing of the ground preparatory to the emergence of an understanding of the prophets which would capture the significance of their intervention and the scale of their achievement.

The value of Kuenen's undertaking can be discerned and its worthwhileness asserted without the expression of complete agreement with him. He is, for example, almost certainly mistaken in supposing that the question whether or not the prophets were recipients of divine truth – whether all supernatural elements should be excised from their interpretation – is to be focused on an enquiry into the degree of accuracy which attaches to their predictions about the shape of the future. There are more interesting and significant areas where these questions can be pursued. He is, however, not mistaken that the intense preoccupation with the predictive power of the prophets was unhealthy and that, while it prevailed, both prophetic religion and the God of the prophets would be cheapened. It cheapened prophetic religion by a too great concentration on proving their supernatural endowment in terms of the accuracy of their predictions, rather than in relation to the truth which they spoke in the present. This would be a valid criticism, even if Kuenen's further claim that the words which they addressed to their contemporaries should be evaluated without any recourse to a supernatural explanation, were not allowed. It cheapened God by laying too much weight on displays of his prescience and by presenting these as proofs which commanded belief in him, whereas the crucial area of belief and unbelief for the prophets was the present and not the future. That they were rejected as witnesses to the truth in the situations in which they addressed their contemporaries is the centre of the study of the canonical prophets and their literature.

A further investigation of Kuenen's attitude to prophetic predictions is facilitated by dividing the subject into predictions of doom and predictions of blessing in which the future is filled with hope. On predictions of doom he holds that these are always conditional and that the primary purpose which they serve is to induce repentance in those who are addressed. The question whether the canonical prophets are principally proclaimers of doom or preachers of repentance was discussed in my article on 'Prophecy and the Prophetic Literature' (McKane, 1979, pp. 176f), but the context was more modern and different from the one in which Kuenen's opinions were formed. There I was dealing with a premiss of form criticism that, if prophetic oracles have an unconditional character, and there is nothing in their textual form which permits us to regard them as conditional, they must be interpreted as unconditional oracles of doom.

The scholars whose dissent from this assertion was particularly noted were Buber (1957, pp. 192–207; 1963, pp. 13–27, 173–82) and Fohrer (1967, pp. 28ff, 279ff) Both, like Kuenen, held that the prophets were, first and foremost, preachers of repentance and maintained that, even if there were no explicit conditions inserted into an oracle of doom, such an intention had to be presupposed in order to establish the credibility of the stance of the prophet. The perception was that a prophet who simply announces ineluctable doom is incredible. The idea was particularly offensive to Buber, because it had the whiff of an ideological rigidity which contradicted a fundamental postulate of his philosophy: the assumption of an institutional rot so deep that it left individuals at the mercy of an impending dissolution was a surrender of personal freedom to impersonal structures. From this point of view a discourse situation in which a prophet is doing no more than issuing threats is an unacceptable assumption. Whatever the literary form of his utterance may have been, however absolutely formulated as a threat of doom, it was not merely an intimation of coming disaster, but was presented as a powerful consideration, a means of persuading hearers that there must be a change of heart in the community and that the need to make it was urgent. This is a different argument from that of Kuenen, but the point of departure is common, namely, that the prophets are principally preachers of repentance.

Kuenen explains prophetic predictions of doom as concrete embodiments, provisional in character, of certain general ideas about theodicy which are held by the prophets. The conviction that God effectively enforces a moral order on a turbulent historical scene is projected by constructing future historical situations where his moral judgements on the nations will become effective. These should not be taken as anything more than possible future *scenarios* for the enforcement of Yahweh's theodicy and we should not suppose that they they were regarded in a more serious light than this by the prophets. What they hold as an unshakeable conviction is that Yahweh effectively maintains a theodicy, but the details which they provide about future historical applications of this theodicy are embodiments of the general idea which have illustrative value but which may not be realized in the future. Hence the prophets do not consider that the truth of their fundamental affirmation stands or falls with the fulfilment or non-fulfilment of their detailed predictions and they are not dismayed when their illustrative models of the operation of the theodicy fail to come to pass.

A further turn of the screw (Kuenen, 1877, pp. 332–64) is that, in any case, the general belief in theodicy which the prophets hold is mistaken and this leads on to a demonstration of the falsehood of prophetic predictions of a more thoroughgoing nature than the one which has just been rehearsed. The first part of the argument accepted the general affirmation of a theodicy for the purpose of establishing the merely illustrative character of predictions of doom. The second part declares the premiss to be false and proceeds to the conclusion that if the primary assumption is false, all the detailed prophetic predictions generated by it must also be false. This brings Kuenen to a consideration of the relation between prophetic confidence in the operation of a theodicy and political wisdom of a similar kind to the one which I undertook in *Prophets and Wise Men* (1965), especially in the final chapter (pp. 113–30). 'It cannot', Kuenen says, 'be asserted that the action of the prophets, in general, advanced the welfare of the Israelitish nation' (1877, p. 517). He discerns that, from a political point of view, the prophets were agents of political instability and hastened the disintegration of the society to which they preached; that their loyalty to what they were convinced was prophetic truth made them, in the eyes of the statesmen who were resolved not to exchange political wisdom for a belief in a theodicy, the enemies of the state.

When we turn to prophecies which encourage hope in a better future, issues of a different kind are raised. The first is the extent to which Kuenen's attitudes are influenced by his concept of 'scientific exegesis'. There is a hint of this in his statement that the Israelite prophet 'is a unique phenomenon in history' (1877, p. 591). There is here something of the point of view considered in chapter 8, in connection with the *Religionsgeschichte* school, that the emergence of the pre-exilic canonical prophets signalled an exceptional historical period chosen by God for the disclosure of religious and moral truth and that this truth is entirely contained in the elucidation of these utterances in the historical contexts in which they were uttered. 'Scientific exegesis' is the rigorous application of a historical-grammatical-critical method and its task is completed when it recaptures the meaning which the prophet intended at the time and in the circumstances in which he spoke. Kuenen's discussion of the use of Old Testament texts by New Testament writers (1877, pp. 447–548) has to be related to these considerations. Referring to the degree of freedom which was used by New Testament writers in interpreting Old Testament texts he remarks: '*At the present day*, when the laws of grammatico-historical interpretation of Scripture are universally known, and are accepted by all as valid, such a procedure would be very difficult for many, for some even altogether impossible. *But at that time*, long before the science of exegesis was born, it would be practised very easily' (1877, p. 540). Within the same frame of reference he says: 'But they [the New Testament writers] found, moreover, in Scripture [that is, in the Old Testament] what it did not contain, or what at most existed there in germ (*implicite*). It is the task of *scientific exegesis* accurately to determine where the one case is presented and where the other' (1877, p. 544).

If the use made by New Testament writers of the Old Testament fails the scientific test and must be regarded as invalid exegesis, 'it can still preserve its significance': 'This does not depend on the exegetical correctness or incorrectness of the interpretation. In what these authors borrow from the Old Testament their own conviction is mirrored. It is not their agreement with the words of the prophets and psalmists, it is *that conviction itself* which is always the chief object' (1877, p. 544). There is a further confirmation of the line which Kuenen is taking in the following:

> For in this way the Scriptures of the Old Testament were brought closer to the Christian community and became for it the source of abundant edification, which probably might not have been enjoyed, or enjoyed in a less degree, if the historical interpretation had from the beginning exercised unlimited sway. Now, only after we have learned to keep separate scientific judgement and the religious appreciation – only now can the heart receive a beneficial impression without the understanding being surrendered as a captive. For us the value, for example, of the description of Jahweh's suffering servant in Isa. lii.13–liii.12 is independent of its application to Jesus; we can explain it historically, and still admire it. But for former generations that was different; the impression which they received became immediately transmuted into a less

correct exegesis and could not be dissociated from that without being wholly lost. In so far, we can rest satisfied with the slow progress of science, while at the same time we rejoice that its full light now shines on us. (1877, p. 545)

By attending to all this a number of things can be discovered about Kuenen's attitude. In the first place his attack is directed against the claim that the sense of Old Testament texts, related to hopeful fulfilment, which was intended by Old Testament prophets when they uttered them, is precisely the sense which they have in the New Testament contexts where they appear. It is this which he is primarily concerned to demolish, because it brings out what he regards as one of the worst features of supernaturalism. It is destructive of historical-critical exegesis and so it is unscientific, since for him historical-critical exegesis is biblical science. It dehumanizes the prophet in a most objectionable way: his utterance is loosed from its historical moorings; he is disengaged from the historical setting of the despair which he is trying to relieve and the kind of hopeful future which he descries is obliterated. His voice becomes that of a ghost, with no anchorage in a human setting of time and place, which intimates in a vacuum a distant Christian fulfilment. Thus the main target of Kuenen's attack is the contention that the intention of hopeful prophetic utterances is precisely that which is present when they are applied to new situations centuries later than the period of the utterance.

The second matter is that Kuenen's consideration of the scope for the reinterpretation of hopeful prophetic predictions is limited by his firm adherence to the view that only historical-critical exegesis constitutes biblical science. He is not, however, so rigid in his application of this principle as to rule out a degree of openness to the future in prophetic predictions which makes it legitimate to reinterpret and reapply them. He remarks that on scientific examination this might prove to be a drawing out of a significance already implicit in the original utterance and that every case has to be judged on its merits. It is clear, nevertheless, from his statements that many cases of the reapplication of Old Testament texts in the New Testament would have to be deemed, on his criteria, as unscientific exegesis and that their value would consist solely in the religious conviction of which they had become homiletical vehicles. Emphasis on the normative character of historical-critical exegesis, while it does not blind Kuenen to the possibility that prophetic predictions may acquire enhanced significance, when appropriated in a new situation as elucidations of fulfilment, does hamper him from taking a positive view of the proverbial openness and indeterminate allusiveness of Hebrew poetry. We should be willing to view some of the predictions as cast into the future and available for reinterpretation.

We should do this rather than be disposed to conclude that once they have failed in respect of the fulfilment which the original prophet intended, their life has come to an end and the only purpose which they serve is as examples of predictions which were falsified by events. They should be regarded as living on and as capable of enriched meaning when the time is ripe for them.

IV

Kuenen faces up to the problem that the prophets ascribe what they say to Yahweh and not to themselves and that they cast their utterances into the form of words spoken by Yahweh. They represent that they are messengers of Yahweh sent to speak his word. He asks how this can be reconciled with the view that prophetic oracles are to be elucidated without recourse to supernatural explanations and he is occupied with this throughout chapter iv whose title is 'The Conviction of the Israelitish Prophets with regard to their Divine Commission' (1877, pp. 68–97). It ends inconclusively and he takes up the matter again in a later chapter (ix) entitled 'The Prediction of the Future and the Religious Belief of the Prophets of Jahweh' (1877, pp. 332–64) and supplies an answer which is in accord with his thinking as we have so far followed it.

He accepts that an unusual state of mind is indicated where, in the context of visionary experience, a prophet claims that he has heard Yahweh speak to him and represents that the words spoken are Yahweh's words. The major prophets (Isa. 6 and Jer. 1) had visions and heard Yahweh speak in connection with their calls to the prophetic office and we should assume a state of trance or ecstasy:

> The prophets could use this form when they themselves and their hearers were satisfied that Jahweh had made known his will, or revealed the secrets of the future, in visions. But we can advance a step farther. The character of those visions also admits of being determined with certainty. They are beheld by the prophet when he is in a state of trance or ecstasy. All the representations coincide in fact with each other, and therefore with the reality, in this, that the prophets *behold* and *hear* things which cannot be discerned with the bodily eye and ear: it is the supersensuous forms, images and voices which they mention in their descriptions. (1877, p. 82)

On the other hand, it should not be too readily assumed that literary accounts which are given of prophetic visions are always uncomplicated transcripts of such extraordinary psychological experience. A freedom demanded by literary artistry and a bowing to conventions may effect a metamorphosis and the furthest reach of this would be literary accounts of prophetic visions which have no foundation in the psychological experience of a prophet (1877, pp. 78–82).

Kuenen is not affirming here that 'God speaks Hebrew' or resiling from his insistence that the content of prophetic utterance does not have a supernatural source. He is elucidating an extraordinary psychological state (ecstasy or trance) as the expression of the absolute conviction of the prophet that he knows Yahweh's will. It is not in his view something more than a mysterious psychological state. It is not a revelatory experience and if, when he was caught up in it, the prophet heard a voice, it was not produced by the organs associated with speaking (it was 'supersensuous') and it was not the voice of God. None of this can be transmuted into theology, into a doctrine of 'revelation' and 'inspiration'.

Another factor which might seem well suited to a supernatural explanation is noticed by Kuenen, with special reference to the prophet Jeremiah. This is the degree of compulsion to which a prophet is subjected and the distinction which he draws between the word of Yahweh which he must proclaim and his own desires and inclinations. Jeremiah confesses that his message of doom is so uncongenial to him that he would rather not utter it, but it burns within him like fire and will not be denied release (McKane, 1986, on Jer. 20.9). Kuenen, however, sets his face against the claim that 'trance' and 'ecstasy' are revelatory states, that all prophetic utterances are associated with these extraordinary psychological conditions and that they are indispensable accompaniments of the delivery of oracles – only a prophet who is so psychologically prepared will speak the words of Yahweh:

> The difference between the prophetical literature and the revelation to the prophets would certainly have been very great, if the revelation was granted to them while they were in state of trance. Where we discover clear marks of reflection, deliberation and study may we not confidently infer the absence of ecstasy? Let it be considered besides, that the prophets are not in the habit of appealing to the visions as the only or usual means by which the word of Jahweh came to them. (1877, p. 84)

The strong interest which Kuenen has in maintaining the rationality of the canonical prophets comes to the forefront here. His conclusions about how the 'word of God' should be analysed are not further revealed in chapter iv, but he does sum up the relation between ecstasy or trance and the manner in which the prophets produce their oracles. What he says in essence is that there is a gulf between abnormal psychological states and prophetic truth which cannot be bridged and that to describe trance as a revelatory state blurs this distinction. In opposing a theory that the prophet is always so pyschologically conditioned when he prophesies, Kuenen remarks:

> The certainty which the ecstasy could have given to a prophet was first of all purely subjective; he alone knew that he had witnessed a vision and that he proclaimed the revelation which had been made to him in that manner. We can have no control over the one or the other, but must accept both on his testimony. In the second place, a specific, supernatural character can in no wise be ascribed to the trance; its divine origin is not at all self-evident. Phenomena of that nature were far from uncommon in ancient times and in the middle ages, and occur even at this present day. It is true that for a long time people had no hesitation in ascribing them to supernatural influence. They seemed so singular and extraordinary that this explanation forced itself quite naturally on men's minds. What could not be derived from God was therefore regarded as a display of the power of evil. But we now no longer occupy this standpoint. Ecstasy is now accurately studied, compared with other affections allied to it, and is explained from the human organism itself, specifically from the nervous system. It may be – on that point I determine nothing at present – that the trances of the Israelitish prophets were of a nature altogether different: but that must be proved separately; for ecstasy in itself is no supernatural phenomenon. It does not therefore advance us a step in determining the origin of Old Testament prophecy. (1877, pp. 85f)

Kuenen's argument is that unusual psychological phenomena cannot transcend the limits of the psychological domain and should not be confused with supernatural truth. When the individual experiences them they are real elements of his experience, but they are enclosed in the private world of the subject and cannot acquire the objective and public characteristics of truth. Whether a prophet is true or false depends on the content of his utterance which is available to public scrutiny, whether as heard or read, and not on the interior psychological state associated with his utterance. The correctness of this analysis should not be doubted and it has important applications in teasing out confusions which have arisen in discussions on 'revelation' and 'inspiration'. Much clarification results from grasping it. For the time being it will be enough to say that Kuenen connects it with the disposal of the entire baggage of revelation and not with an alternative way of analysing and expressing the concept. His main point is that there is nothing supernatural about prophetic truth and he is refuting a claim that abnormal psychological states are supernatural evidences.

V

It remains to pick up Kuenen's final resolution of the problem created for him by the circumstance that the prophets represent that the words which they speak are the words of Yahweh. He solves what he describes as a principal difficulty 'as with one stroke' (1877, p. 362):

> The great self-confidence with which the prophets published their threatenings and promises as the 'word of Jahveh' is now no longer an enigma to us. If their predictions had had no foundation in their religious belief, then in order to utter them in Jahveh's name, they would have required a definite warrant, and one, so to say, renewed on every occasion... But the matter assumes a different aspect now that the prediction of the future also may, on good grounds, be regarded as the result of the religious conviction of the prophets. It could now be an object of no doubt for themselves. It must have been as certain to them as the religious life itself, which had grown along with their own inner life and had become inseparable from it. The 'Thus saith Jahveh' must have flowed from their mouth quite involuntarily and naturally, for did they not know that Jahveh, the God of Israel, was the Holy and the Righteous? Even the disappointments of the expectations thus expressed could not perplex them or make them doubt of being in the right; because, as we recently remarked, they limited that disappointment, at once and of course, to the form of their anticipations, and remained as firmly convinced as before of the truth of the matter itself. (1877, pp. 362f)

Kuenen is partly going over the ground which we have already covered. Prophetic predictions have their ground in religious and moral values of whose truth the prophets are seized with unshakeable conviction. The predictions themselves are hypothetical particularizations which may be proved wrong, without damage being done to the confidence which the prophets have that their grasp of the truth is in principle unflawed. The circumstance that the prophets preface their word with 'Thus saith Yahweh' is explained as a consequence of their irrefragable confidence that their principles and convictions, which on Kuenen's view have no supernatural support, embody a content of religious and moral truth. This is the claim which is made by the preface and by the oracular style of their utterance.

According to this analysis the conflict which Jeremiah describes between his prophetic responsibility and other courses of action which recommend themselves to him as less sorrowful and desolating are not to be explained by setting up an antithesis between natural and supernatural. It has to be seen as arising from a granite-like determination not to forsake the path of duty however forbidding its aspect. He must speak hard words if he is to pursue it, but, in any case the force and intensity of the prophetic message will not be denied expression. His resistance arises from the awareness of the human cost to himself, as a member of a community, in making such a stand: it is colossal and he is tempted to turn away from it. This is not a cool consideration about the respective merits of truth and falsehood, duty and expediency. It is the deep questioning of a sensitive and suffering human being whether he can endure against such a wall of hostility, such impenetrable mis-understanding, personal debilitation and rejection, as speaking the truth will entail. '*The earnestness and warmth of his religious conviction –* that is the chief matter. It is that which makes the true prophet, because it accounts for the confidence with which he comes forward as an interpreter of Jahveh' (1877, pp. 363f).

It is clear that Kuenen has excluded the supernatural, but we should attend at greater length to a matter which was touched on earlier. Kuenen does not make the canonical prophet into a cool natural theo-logian or a moral philosopher. The possession of religious insights which reach to the heart of the mystery and grasp the truth or of a piercing moral sensitivity which discerns wrongs in society, cries out against them and suffers anguish in the knowledge that they exist, all of this comes out of an identification with others which is urgent, intense and touched with suffering, the more so since it is maintained in the face of loss of esteem and rejection. The native endowment of the prophet is stressed by Kuenen, but he is not the kind of person who argues his way to the existence of God by a process of ratiocination. I sum up this discussion with a final quotation from Kuenen:

> It will indeed be quite superfluous to remind the reader that by these words [that is, 'ethical monotheism'] in the present connec-tion is not meant the intellectual conviction of God's unity and moral attributes. Our whole preceding examination teaches that the prophets were not conspicious as philosophers, but as religious men. By the formula 'ethical monotheism', therefore, as succinct a description as possible is given of the peculiar excellence of *their religion*. Just on account of that they have, apart from the result, even for the very nature alone of their struggles, a claim upon our respectful admiration. Heartful trust in God and moral earnest-ness: these two things, connected with each other in the closest manner, inspired them from the beginning and sustained them to the end. (1877, p. 589)

VI

It may be helpful at this point to introduce a comparison between Kuenen's account of the canonical prophets and that of the Hebrew prophets which appears in Maimonides. There are differences between the two, but the fundamental similarity is that both dispense with supernatural explanations of prophetic activity and describe the prophetic endowment as native. Maimonides reproduces an opinion of the 'philosophers' which perhaps is to be identified with his own opinion. He notices that it coincides with the opinion of the Torah, except in one regard: according to the Torah one who is fit to be a prophet and prepared for it may be debarred by the divine will. Maimonides reproduces the opinion of the 'philosophers':

> According to this opinion it is not possible that an *ignoramus* should turn into a prophet; nor can a man not be a prophet on a certain evening and be a prophet on the following morning, as though he had made some find. Things are rather as follows. When, in the case of a superior individual who is perfect with regard to his rational and moral qualities, his imaginative faculty is in its most perfect state, and when he has been prepared in the way that you will hear, he will necessarily become a prophet, inasmuch as this is a perfection that belongs to us by nature. According to this opinion, it is not possible that an individual should be fit for prophecy and prepared for it and not become a prophet, except to the extent to which it is possible that an individual, having a healthy temperament, should be nourished with excellent food without sound blood and similar things being generated by that food... For it is a natural thing that everyone who according to his natural disposition is fit for prophecy, and who has been trained in his education and study should become a prophet. (1963, ii, p. 361)

Again:

> With regard to one of the most ignorant among the common people, it is not possible, according to us, that God should turn one of them into a prophet – except as it is possible that he should turn an ass or a frog into a prophet [that is, a mere possibility not deserving consideration]. It is our fundamental principle that there must be training and perfection, whereupon the possibility arises to which the power of the deity becomes attached... For this is the state of every prophet: he must have a natural preparedness in his original, natural disposition. (1963, ii, p. 362)

The following quotations have a special bearing on the moral qualifications required by the prophet – 'his thought will always go towards noble matters' (1963, ii, p. 371). Maimonides is describing the attachment of 'men of knowledge' to sensual pleasures, among which he regards the sense of touch, whose ultimate satisfaction is copulation, as the most degrading:

> For most of the thoughts of those who are outstanding among the men of knowledge are preoccupied with the pleasures of this sense and are desirous of them. And then they wonder how it is that they do not become prophets, if prophecy is something natural. It is likewise necessary that the thoughts of a prophetic individual should be detached from spurious kinds of rulership and that his desire for them should be abolished – I mean the wish to dominate or to be held great by the common people and to obtain from them honour and obedience for its own sake. (1963, ii, pp. 371f)

And finally:

> It is known that with regard to these three aims set forth by us – namely the perfection of the rational faculty through study, the perfection of the imaginative faculty through natural disposition, and the perfection of the moral habit through the turning away of thought from all bodily pleasures and the putting an end to the desire for the various kinds of ignorant and evil glorification – there are among those who are perfect very many differences in rank; and on the differences in rank with regard to these aims there depend the differences in rank that subsist between the degrees of all the prophets. (1963, ii, p. 372)

The distinctive aspect of Maimonides' account derives from a feature which Kuenen does not share with him, that prophetic activity is to be located in the context of visionary or dream experience and to be dissociated from the state of consciousness or awareness which obtains in waking life (1963, ii, pp. 385–95). One has to think in terms of a prophetic temperament and constitution, a combination of natural characteristics which fit a person to be a prophet. A prime necessity is the ability to rearrange the images given by sense data in states other than those of waking life, whether the intense concentration of a visionary state which is all-absorbing or the involuntary imaginative activity which arises in dreams when sleep has prevailed. These states may be described as 'revelatory' and the resulting prophetic content as 'revelation', provided it is understood that no special supernatural intervention by God is implied. It is simply that individuals are so constituted in respect of their natural endowment that personal qualities combine to give them a prophetic capacity.

The prophet is special in the way that a record-breaking athlete has been born special by happy coincidences of physiological characteristics and bio-chemical functioning. So endowed temperamentally an individual will become a prophet, unless there are extraordinary blockages or malfunctioning (cf. 1963, ii, p. 361). But the thought of training and self-discipline is also applied in connection with moral fitness and here Maimonides comes nearer to Kuenen. There is more asceticism in the regimen which he prescribes, but he, like Kuenen, introduces elements of moral seriousness and a preference for truth over political advantage in his description of the prophetic figure.

An important coincidence between their views follows from their common rejection of supernaturalism. Maimonides differs most significantly from Kuenen in distinguishing between a normal human state and special prophetic states (visionary experience). For Kuenen a prophet is always a man and always a prophet. He does not wear two hats, doffing one when he puts on the other. His prophetic discernment and commitment are permanent conditions of awareness and consciousness and he is not raised to special and temporary visionary states in order to acquire prophetic powers. The man/prophet dichotomy, which is associated with a supernatural view of prophecy, is not overcome by Maimonides.

VII

In a review of Kuenen's *De propheten en de prophetie onder Israel* Wellhausen (1876, 203–8) affirms the excellence of Kuenen's scholarship: 'The chief characteristics of Kuenen as in his other books are a fundamental mastery of the material and the literature, the putting of the right questions, calm appraisal, precise judgement, the avoidance of all heat and nastiness' (208). It is evident from the correspondence between Wellhausen and Kuenen from 1874 on (Smend, 1993, pp. 113–27, *Abraham Kuenen*) that he did not only admire Kuenen as a big brain, but that there was human warmth in their relationship and, after he had visited Kuenen in Leiden (1878), he wrote a letter to Robertson Smith (Smend, 1993, p. 119): 'I have made a short visit to Kuenen in Leiden, the man is even more remarkable than his books' (12.10.1878). In a letter to Kuenen (23.10.1878) Wellhausen remarks that he has hitherto known Kuenen's *Geist* through his books but that now he has encountered him as a kindred spirit, has been received into his home and has been delighted by his hospitality. Hence Wellhausen's reservations about Kuenen's book on the prophets expressed in his review of 1876 are not to be connected with any incompatibilty on the level of personal relationships between the two men. Wellhausen concluded that Kuenen was not at home with the canonical prophets and that they were not a congenial subject for him (1876, 208). This has nothing to do with a perception that Kuenen was not a well-rounded human being, but it does point to differences between the two as scholars and in temperament.

In a letter to A. Jülicher (8.11.1880; Smend, 1993, p. 118) Wellhausen observes that Kuenen is unsurpassed as an analyst and as a man, but that he is not so good at synthesis and this is in line with his opinion about *De propheten en de prophetie onder Israel*. The book is more effective in clearing away the debris than it is in reconstruction. It has not offered a positive elucidation of the phenomenon of prophecy and it was not in Kuenen's mind to achieve this end. The book has a negative orientation and constructiveness is not a strong side of the work. In spite of all his warmth for the subject he does not find it congenial in the way Ewald did (1876, 203–8). Wellhausen is not enamoured of the polemical tone of the book and he connects this with the Dutch context out of which it came. It is understandable that he finds Kuenen's long contests with his scholarly opponents wearisome and he judges the book so wide-ranging that it loses its shape. Wellhausen's method was not that of Kuenen. He did not expend his energy with frontal assaults on opinions which differed from his own and did not obtain satisfaction in leaving his adversaries for dead. Such prolonged refutation was tedious and negative and Wellhausen's concern was rather to find the *mot juste* and let the positive conclusion, memorably expressed, which was the child of his extraordinary perceptiveness and literary skill, stand out (cf. Smend, 1993, p. 116).

Writing to Robertson Smith about the new edition of *Historisch-critisch onderzoek* (1885) Wellhausen remarks that he finds the shape of the book unhappy, although the logic is sound. He has skimmed through it and confesses: 'I find the whole thing, by degrees, becomes so wearisome that I cannot resolve on a proper study of it' (21.1.1885; Smend, 1993, p. 117). Yet it may be asked whether Kuenen's book on the prophets, despite all its warts, is correctly summed up as 'negative'. A consideration of what Wellhausen himself has to say about the canonical prophets will show how his attitudes compare with those of Kuenen and to this we now turn.

The Torah, which consists of priestly decisions on legal matters and, more generally, of guidance which is given in accord with a traditional 'knowledge of Yahweh' was part of the Yawhist institution. Hence Yahwism is more than 'cultus', which refers to worship and, particularly, to the sacrificial system, since, in connection with the priestly office, there is an institutionalizing of Torah. This inserts a special Yahwistic presence into the institution which differentiates it from the cults of other national gods. The position then is that in respect of cultus there is no distinction between Yahwism and other national religions, but that in respect of Torah there is:

> The Torah of the priests was like a spring which runs always, that of the prophets like a spring which is intermittent, but when it

does break forth, flows with all the greater force. . . . After the spirit of the oldest men of God, Moses at the head of them, had been in a fashion laid to sleep in institutions, it sought and found in the prophets a new opening; the old fire burst out like a volcano through the strata which once, too, rose fluid from the deep, but now were fixed and dead. The element in which the prophets live is the storm of the world's history, which sweeps away human institutions; in which the rubbish of past generations with the houses built on it begins to shake, and the foundation alone remains which needs no support but itself. When the earth trembles and seems to pass away, then they triumph because Jehovah alone is exalted. (1885, pp. 397f; German edition, 1883)

The reference to 'the rubbish of past generations' should be noticed in view of Wellhausen's criticism that Kuenen has dwelt too much on the canonical prophets as clearers of debris and has neglected their positive achievements. Wellhausen like Kuenen refers to the prophets as a spiritual aristocracy and remarks that a tension between them and the remainder of the people has always existed. It is, according to Wellhausen, a battle of the giants against the pygmies and it is the giants who clear away the rubble (cf. Kuenen) which the pygmies have accumulated. Innumerable, anonymous pygmies create the culture and it is the giants who remove the rubbish which is inevitably accumulated. Religious progress usually consists in the removal of the rubble – hence there is an enmity between popular culture and prophetic religion (1905, p. 81). But Wellhausen is not referring in the quotation given above to the canonical prophets in particular, but to 'true' or 'real' prophets in general, and he is not asserting that the Torah inserted into the Yahwistic institution the association of Yahwism with moral demand. He traces the origins of the Torah to Moses, but he does not suppose that it was Moses who received the Decalogue (1891, p. 112; 1905, p. 93). In this regard Moses was not a pioneer of the religion of the canonical prophets: 'One should not suppose that Moses made justice and morality supreme in the cultus. The old Israelite religion was, as every other national religion, predominantly cultus. It did not become something different until the prophets made it so' (1905, p. 77).

The prophets are essentially individual figures and 'notoriously they have no father' (1885, p. 397). They are not amenable to institutionalization; their Yahwism is inward and has its centre in the perceptiveness and the commitment of extraordinary individuals: 'What they were unconsciously labouring towards was that ethical individualism which has its historic source in the national downfall and manifested itself not exclusively within the prophetical sphere' (1891, pp. 88, 122f). This emphasis is a clue to what Wellhausen had in mind when he refers to the mystery of the prophets' individuality and its relation to the springs of all truth as one which was hidden from Kuenen (1876, 208). The essence of his criticism of Kuenen's book on the canonical prophets is not associated with its radical theological conclusions, the denial that the source of their utterances is supernatural. Wellhausen found this debate tedious and thought that an inordinate amount of intellectual energy had been misspent, but it is unlikely that his hackles were raised by it or that he felt his own theological position threatened. He had no theological position to defend. It was rather that he was convinced that there were more important things to consider about the canonical prophets than this, but in so far as he describes them as exceptional individuals, as giants and heroes, Kuenen's conclusion that we are dealing with cases of extraordinary native endowment and not with those who have received a revelation from God was not one which Wellhausen would have found inhospitable.

Wellhausen holds up the canonical prophets as exemplary individuals and supposes that the spread of true religion involves the liberation of individuals from the shackles of corporate religion. This individualization is a necessary prerequisite of religious maturity, and the self-sufficiency of the individual, whose relation with God is independent of external circumstances and institutional supports, is the fullest realization of religious trust. Rejected by men, Jeremiah took refuge in God who had chosen him as his messenger. His despised prophecy was a bridge to an inward intercourse with the Godhead and out of his mediation which was fruitless there originated a private religion, a relationship between him and Yahweh. In suffering he acquired the certainty of a personal communion with God, and a new, deep piety was set free in him. He experienced victory in defeat and his piety was inherited by later generations (1894, pp. 105f; similarly 1905, pp. 96f). But it could be inherited only by exceptional individuals and prophetic religion could not be communicated to the multitude and become corporate religion. The religion of giants and heroes cannot be grasped or appropriated by ordinary individuals. Hence 'ethical monotheism' may be accepted as a description of prophetic religion, the religion of exceptional individuals, but it cannot be organized into a system of corporate religion, a legacy left to the world by the canonical prophets, as Kuenen supposed: 'What was thus revealed to the eye of their spirit was no less than the august idea of the moral government of the world' (1882, p. 124). It should be noticed that Kuenen also makes statements which resemble those of Wellhausen: 'The prophets had not succeeded in making their conception of Yahweh the possession of the people. This is not meant as a reproach. Neither the wish to reform the nation in its entirety, nor zeal and perseverance in the attempt, had been wanting. But the demands of the prophets were too lofty to be at once allowed by and complied with by the masses' (1882, p. 148). Nevertheless, the portrayal of the canonical prophets as tragic heroes, suffering for a vision of God which was incomprehensible to their community is to be associated with Wellhausen rather than Kuenen.

This view that the canonical prophet is a heroic (cf. Smend, 1991, pp. 183f) and tragic figure is the deepest understanding of prophecy which Wellhausen achieves: 'In brief, history in its effect on individuals is tragedy, and no tragedy has a happy ending' (1894, p. 77). 'The prophets are tragic figures, because the effect of their work is the destruction of the nation' (1891, pp. 88, 122f). The faith which can endure when the world is hostile, when society crumbles and the terror of disintegration appears, is the faith which is fully grown. A prophet like Jeremiah is born to suffer, because he sees too clearly and feels too deeply. He has left behind the world of surface impressions and illusory expectations, which is all that his contemporaries have, so that even their religion is nourished by them. The religious confidence of the people and the institution in which it is embodied appear strong and enduring, but it is all illusory. It is a shell which is wafer-thin and when the truth comes in the form of Yahweh's judgement, the wreckage will be terrible and the ruin complete. Jeremiah is consumed with a concern for his community, but he is helpless and cannot reach them, for there is a barrier to communication which is insurmountable. The relation between Yahweh and Israel has been fractured and he is not present in the life of his people, despite the confidence which is exuded by public religion and the expectations which are cherished that that he will always be present to sustain and defend them. These are the ingredients of the tragedy which engulfs Jeremiah: the feel of the prophet for the world and for God, the impressions which he receives from the human existence in which he is immersed, lead him to a valley of tears and a tragic appropriation of the truth.

VIII

Duhm's book *Die Theologie der Propheten als Grundlage für die innere Entwicklungsgeschichte der israelitischen Religion* was published in the same year (1875) as Kuenen's *De propheten en de prophetie onder Israel*, but, as the title suggests, his interests in the canonical prophets, a locating of them in the 'inner history of the development of Israelite religion', takes a different shape from that of Kuenen. For Duhm 'theology of the prophets' is, more or less, synonymous with a survey of prophetic books (Amos, Hosea, Isaiah, Micah, Isaiah and his successors, Jeremiah) with whom he associates the zenith of a process of *Religionsgeschichte*. He gives the same impression as Wellhausen that he is unwilling to spend time on a consideration of the use made of the doctrines of 'inspiration' and 'revelation' in connection with the endowment of the prophets but, like Wellhausen, he turns up his nose at the prospect of engaging in a polemic directed against such supernaturalism. It is not at all the case that either Wellhausen or Duhm were fighting a defensive action, only that they were not convinced of the value of undertaking what they regarded as a protracted and wearisome process of demolition after the manner of Kuenen. The task was superfluous, because the walls had already crumbled. The fate of the old doctrines did not trouble them; they felt that the subject was *passé*, that the focus of the investigation had changed and that they had a historical and human context within which they could develop a new and positive estimate of the canonical prophets. Duhm affirms (1875, p. 85) that his objective is to diminish the emphasis on the doctrine of 'inspiration', to strike out on fresh paths and to give a more secure historical basis to the question: In what way were the prophets equipped for their task?

Two questions should be held apart in considering Duhm's position: 1. His own analysis of 'These are the words of Yahweh' with which the canonical prophets prefaced their oracles. 2. The sense which this formula had for the prophets themselves. On the second matter Duhm (1875, p. 88) maintains that these prophets asserted the objectivity of their standing and the reality of their direct relation with God and observes that it is not his intention to align himself either with 'the supernaturalism which ignores psychology' or with 'the naturalism which denies it'. He is impressed by the depth of conviction shown by the canonical prophets and by the circumstance that this rested on their certainty that it arose from their relation with God. Duhm is unhappy about the normal way in which the distinction is made between subjectivity and objectivity and about the superiority which is granted to external attestation over inner conviction, but he admits that the convictions of the prophets can give rise to no more than a conviction on our part and cannot supply proof that this conviction is true, that is, that the prophets were in communication with God and uttered his word.

Duhm (1875, p. 89) turns to the first question and claims that objectivity is achieved when regard is had to the public domain of history in which the canonical prophets operated and the advance of religious truth which was a feature of it. This is the only basis on which the matter of objectivity can be raised, but to achieve results we have to assume that the advances in the refinement and truth of religion, which prophetic utterances embodied, were a providential guidance. Duhm argues that if it is conceded that the personality of the individual can be epoch-making, it is then unreasonable to push God, who has a personal interest in the world, into the background and to deny him that force of personality which would give impetus to historical advances. The *necessity* of postulating such a God who supplies providential guidance and implements his wisdom cannot be demonstrated (1875, p. 90), but it is the foundation on which theology in general rests. For theology it is a compelling and absolute assumption and it must suffice for us.

Duhm describes this as a teleological principle (*Grundgedanke*) which is confirmed by further enquiries. These, in the first place, will establish that the utterances of the prophets contained a quality of discernment amounting to religious progress which verifies the rightness of their claim to have an objective relationship with God. The main point which Duhm is making is that the objective nature of the relation of the canonical prophets to God cannot be investigated directly by asking such questions as, Were they supernaturally inspired? Did they hear God speaking to them? The proof that they had an objective relation with God is mediated through their contribution to the advancement of religion and to measure this we must rely on the historical evidence. The proof is the 'progressive revelation' of religious truth which they initiated, since this should be equated with God's providential guidance and personal intervention. If so, this confirms that the prophets did not deceive themselves when they affirmed that they had an objective relation with God. In this sense they were proclaiming the Word of God.

Reverting to the second question, we should notice (1875, pp. 203f) the distinction which Duhm makes between the prophets in the Chaldaean period and those of the preceding age, especially between Amos / Isaiah (1875, p. 86) and Jeremiah. This is connected with his perception that Amos and Isaiah experienced ecstatic visionary states, whereas Jeremiah's prophethood was completely integrated with his normal human condition. It was a cry of anguish, a product of costly commitment to his vocation, but it was a profound human discernment and was not the outcome of temporary visionary states. Because of this, 'These are the words of Yahweh' when used by Amos and Isaiah should be taken literally. These prophets believed that the words which they heard in their special psychological states were indeed the words of Yahweh, that he was speaking to them, but we should resist such a conclusion in the case of Jeremiah. He parts company with the men of the preceding period in that the immediacy of God's address to him recedes as compared with the prophets who preceded him.

With Jeremiah (1875, p. 204) the advent of moral seriousness is noticeable and with this emphasis the traits of human individuality are brought to the fore. In this sense prophecy becomes more subjective. There is a new awareness in Jeremiah that when he prophesies the divine and human elements are inextricably bound up together. The formula 'These are the words of Yahweh' does not have a literal sense and the divine objectivity of his utterances is assured for him in quite another way. He challenges his adversaries to submit their predictions to the test of whether or not they eventuate: their eventuation is the demonstration of their divine origin. Otherwise Jeremiah only has a subjective assurance that his message is divine, namely, his unswerving faith in his God-given task. The objective element resides in the content of what he utters (1875, p. 206).

When one has to judge earlier stages of religious development against the highest point reached – the culmination – that prophet is the greatest whose awareness of his unity with God needs the fewest external props, the relationship being characterized by a constant and unshakeable inward persuasion. We hear the challenge of Jeremiah only if first of all we are convinced of the divine origin of his utterances from their content (1875, p. 207).

Duhm is giving his answer to some of the questions which have been asked earlier in this book. He does not waste time on the enquiry whether God communicated his word supernaturally to the canonical prophets. He shifts the investigation to the 'progressive revelation' which he perceives in the public domain of history, to the evidences of religious truth and moral seriousness which are marks of these advances and to the prophetic oracles which give expression to them. The content of these oracles, when correlated with the providential guidance and the interventions of a personal God, is the only proof of the objectivity of the prophetic word which we can have.

It was when Amos and Isaiah were overtaken with ecstatic states that they saw visions and heard an inner voice and they believed that they were being addressed by God and were listening to his words. They were prophets in virtue of this excited psychological state and they were no longer prophets when they reverted to a normal human condition. But the dictum 'A prophet is always a man and the man is always a prophet' applies to Jeremiah who used the old formula to preface his utterances ('These are the words of Yahweh'), but who did not suppose that he was being addressed by God. He was utterly convinced of the reality of his relation to God, and of the objectivity of what he uttered on the strength of its content. In him there is an integration of human and divine so intrinsic in its inwardness that his grasp of religious truth and his penetrating moral sensivitivity are not to be alienated from a reasoned human discernment and commitment.

IX

A different approach to the formulae which preface prophetic oracles appears in Auld who proposes to resolve the problem by assuming that these formulae are the product of a secondary editorial activity which is controlled by a canonical concern to establish that the Old Testament

Scriptures are the 'word of God' (1988, pp. 237–51). His observation that the 'word of Yahweh' occurs only twice in Hosea (1.4; 4.4) does not have any point for our enquiry, since 'Yahweh said to Hosea' and 'Yahweh said to me' occur in the book (1988, p. 246). But Auld continues: 'I doubt if Isaiah or Hosea or even Jeremiah actually said "Hear the word of the Lord" or "The word of the Lord came to me"' (1988, p. 247) and it becomes clear that he would apply his literary criticism to all forms of the prefatory formula in the prophetic books. This is confirmed by his definition of his theological position and his conclusion that God does not speak Hebrew and that the prophets did not converse with God: 'Essentially this Old Testament "word of God" language notes the imparting of divine decrees, the unveiling of his will; it does not describe mutual divine–human verbal communion' (1990, p. 732).

Auld will have to make deeper incisions and to practise more drastic surgery, if he is to make out a credible case for his literary criticism. It is true that textual criticism discloses differences between the Massoretic text and the Septuagint in regard to these formulae, especially in the book of Jeremiah, and also that grammatical unevenness in the body of prophetic oracles which purport to be speech of God are not absent. There are occasions where their content or part of it is not compatible with the assumption that God is the speaker. On the whole, however, they have the correct form of oracles spoken by God and received by a prophet and this circumstance requires that Auld should go on and show not only that the formulae are secondary, but also that the oracular form of the content of the oracles is secondary and that a more original text of them did not contain the portrayal of a speaking God. Such an extension and complication of his literary criticism is a formidable undertaking. It is one thing to analyse the proposition 'God speaks', to insist that all language is human language and that the limits of our knowledge of God preclude us from affirming that God spoke to Israelite prophets in Hebrew and that they spoke to him. It is another thing to rewrite the text of the Hebrew bible and to have such a confidence in our knowledge of the psychology and the beliefs of the canonical prophets as to assert that it was later men predisposed to a 'word of God' theology who made them into conversationalists with God.

Literature for Chapter 4 is listed at pp. 112–14.

5

OLD TESTAMENT CRITICISM AND THE CANONICAL PROPHETS (II)

I

Similarities between Kuenen and Robertson Smith are easily perceived and may be summed up as a concern to establish the rationality of the canonical prophets and to set them at a distance from 'heathen diviners' with features 'akin to insanity' (Robertson Smith, 1892², p. 293). This is allied with a view shared by both scholars that cultic Yahwism is a 'natural religion', not different in character and content from other ethnic religions and sharply different from the 'spiritual religion' of the canonical prophets. There are, however, particular expressions of these positions in Robertson Smith to which we should attend.

He is aware that the prophets whose religion he sets on a pinnacle are exceptional in the context of the Old Testament and that they are to be contrasted with the 'official prophets' who are installed in institutional Yahwism. He notices that the Arabic cognate of the Hebrew word for priest kōhēn) means 'soothsayer' (kāhin) and that 'in this, as in other points, the popular religion of Israel was modelled on the forms of Semitic heathenism' (1892, p. 292):

> The official prophets of Judah appear to have been connected with the priesthood until the close of the kingdom... They were, in fact, part of the establishment of the Temple, and subject to priestly discipline... They played into the priests' hands (Jer. 5.31), had a special interest in the affairs of worship ... and appear in all their conflicts with Jeremiah as the partisans of the theory that Jehovah's help is absolutely secured by the Temple and its services. (1892, pp. 292f)

Robertson Smith distinguishes prophecy of this kind from 'spiritual prophecy':

> But the prophecy which thus co-operates with the priests is not spiritual prophecy. It is a kind of prophecy which the Old Testament calls divination, which traffics in dreams in place of Jehovah's word (Jer. 23.28), and which, like heathen divination, presents features akin to insanity that require to be suppressed by physical constraint (Jer. 29.26). Spiritual prophecy, in the hands of Amos,

Isaiah and their successors, has no such alliance with the sanctuary and its ritual. It develops and enforces its own doctrine of the intercourse of Jehovah with Israel, and the conditions of His grace, without assigning the slightest value to priests and sacrifices. (1892, p. 293)

In describing the cultic or institutional Yahwism, from which the spiritual religion of the prophets is to be distinguished, Robertson Smith mentions particularly sacrifice and ritual. He has to be selective in his condemnation of institutional Yahwism, since he claims the Torah of Moses, which was part of the Yahwistic institution, for 'spiritual prophecy'. He comments on, 'Thou has forgotten the Torah of thy God' (Hos. 4.6): 'It cannot fairly be doubted that the Torah which the priests have forgotten is Mosaic Torah' (1892, p. 303). The canonical prophets deny that the priests are organs of revelation. The knowledge of the priests is traditional and is founded on old-established law. There is no doubt that the priests themselves referred their wisdom to Moses:

What is quite certain is that, according to the prophets, the Torah of Moses did not embrace a law of ritual. Worship by sacrifice, and all that belongs to it, is no part of the divine Torah to Israel. It forms, if you will, part of natural religion which other nations share with Israel and which is no feature of the distinctive features given at the Exodus. (1892, p. 303)

The 'true distinction' of Israel's religion is said to lie 'in the character of the Deity who has made himself personally known to his people and demands of them a life conformed to his spiritual character as a righteous and forgiving God' (1892, p. 303). This content of religious truth was already contained in the Torah revealed to Moses and is summed up in the Decalogue. It is not confined to the prophetic books; it is 'the standpoint of the Ten Commandments' (1892, p. 304). According to Robertson Smith, the Mosaic Torah has been corrupted by the priests through the importation of ideas and rituals from natural or ethnic religions. Moses was a prophet as well as a judge and 'he founded in Israel the great principles of the moral religion of the righteous Jehovah' (1892, p. 305). When Robertson Smith remarks that Moses was associated with the highest method of revelation (1895[2], p. 220) his concern to drive Old Testament prophecy towards moral reason finds expression: 'Moses, who received his revelation in plain words not involved in symbolic imagery, is placed above those prophets to whom Yahweh speaks in vision or in a dream [cf. Maimonides]. This view is entirely conformed to the conclusions of scientific psychology' (1895, p. 220).

In making Moses the great originator of the canonical prophets, by supposing that the union of Yahwism with moral demand was effected by a Mosaic Decalogue, Robertson Smith is parting company with Kuenen and Wellhausen who did not ascribe such high significance to the Torah of Moses or associate him with a seminal 'ethical monotheism'. Nor did they conclude that the Decalogue was Mosaic in origin. A more general impression gathered from the theological language which Robertson Smith uses is that he assumes the Scriptures of the Old Testament to be 'revealed', that Moses and the canonical prophets received a refined kind of revealed truth. Thus, though he was a controversial figure in the Free Church of Scotland and had been 'withdrawn' from the work of his Chair in Aberdeen (1880), he was a son of the manse and was concerned to defend his scholarship and exert his influence in the context of the Free Church. The twelve lectures delivered at the invitation 'of some six hundred prominent Free Churchmen in Edinburgh and Glasgow' were published as *The Old Testament in the Jewish Church* in 1881. They are an *apologia* and Robertson Smith is arguing that his scholarship establishes his position inside the Church and is not a reason for putting him out it. His case is entirely different from that of either Kuenen or Wellhausen. With Kuenen's 'ethical monotheism' he had a fundamental theological disagreement, since his account of the canonical prophets retained the 'supernaturalism' which Kuenen had thrown overboard and he clung to the doctrine that they were the recipients of 'revealed truth'. Wellhausen did not have the liking for Occam's razor which was strong in Kuenen, nor the theological *Angst* of Robertson Smith. His mind was not of an ideological stamp and he found Kuenen's logic tedious, but it did not arouse his concern and opposition. There were more important things to say about the canonical prophets and logomachy was not the appropriate medium. But Robertson Smith felt threatened by Kuenen's analysis of the canonical prophets. It provided ammunition for his ecclesiastical adversaries and it negated a doctrine of Scripture to which he was firmly attached.

The conclusion of the present discussion is that the covenant with Moses, and the Torah which issued from it, is the foundation of true Yahwism. All else was, 'but a development of the fundamental revelation' (1892, p. 305). All true Torah moves along the lines of the original covenant and this moral law is preserved by the canonical prophets who, prior to Ezekiel, have no concern with ritual (1892, p. 305). Hence Robertson Smith supposes that Israel's covenant, instituted by Moses, was a cornerstone of early Yahwism, a foundation of moral law on which the canonical prophets built, and this was an interpretation of the Mosaic Torah and of the covenant concept which was negated by Wellhausen who located 'covenant' at a later stage in the history of Yahwism: it was a post-prophetic development rather than a pillar of the 'ethical monotheism' of the canonical prophets.

Into this pattern fits Robertson Smith's view that the canonical prophets were principally preachers of repentance. This is what modern scholars would recognize as a view of prophecy represented in the Old Testament by the Deuteronomist or Deuteronomistic school of thought, but we have noticed (see chapter 4, p. 72) that it is strongly held by Buber and Fohrer. The prophets, in Robertson Smith's words, 'set forth the true doctrine of forgiveness':

> Jehovah's anger is not caprice but just indignation, a necessary side of his moral kingship in Israel. He chastises to work penitence, and it is only to the penitent that he can extend forgiveness. By returning to obedience the people regain the marks of Jehovah's love and again experience his goodness in deliverance from calamity and happy possession of a fruitful land. (1892, p. 307)

The connection which he establishes between this emphasis and the predictions made by the canonical prophets aligns him noticeably with Kuenen: predictions are to be understood as concrete projections of general ideas: 'All prophetic prediction is but the development in many forms, and in answer to the needs of Israel in various times, of this supreme certainty that God's love works triumphantly in all his judgements' (1892, p. 307).

II

Robertson Smith's distaste for prophecy which is wildly irrational has been touched on, but more attention should be given to this disposition of his mind. He asserts that 'the method of true revelation has nothing in common with the art of the diviner' (1892, p. 288) and continues: 'He [Jehovah] speaks to his prophets, not in magical processes or through the visions of poor phrenetics, but by a clear intelligible word addressed to the intellect and the heart. The characteristic of the true prophet is that he retains his consciousness and self-control under revelation' (1892, p. 289). Smith describes unusual states of consciousness and abnormal psychological experiences associated with prophetic activity. Micah is empowered by the spirit of Yahweh (3.8); Isaiah is grasped by a powerful hand (8.11); Jeremiah feels Yahweh's word as a fire burning within him and demanding release (20.9). He returns to his insistence on intelligibility: 'But it is an intelligible word which speaks to the prophet's own heart and conscience, forbidding Isaiah to walk in the way of the corrupt nation, filling Micah with power to declare unto Jacob his transgression, supporting the heart of Jeremiah with an inward joy amidst all his trials (15.16)' (1892, p. 289). This accent on reasonableness is used to distinguish the canonical prophets not only from the prophets of Baal, but also from the excited states of Israelite $n^e b\hat{i}'\hat{i}m$: 'There is nothing rhapsodical or unintelligible in the prophetic discourses; they address themselves to the understanding and the heart of every man who feels the truth of the fundamental religious conceptions on which they rest' (1895, p. 221). The canonical prophets are 'not like modern fanatics of the East'; they did not pass into 'a sort of temporary madness' to which a supernatural character was ascribed. 'Canaanite prophetism' was a kind of divination 'on the notion that the irrational part of man's nature is that which connects him with the deity' and there were men in Israel, 'calling themselves seers or prophets of Jehovah, who occupied no higher standpoint' (1892, p. 287).

Despite the measure of agreement between Robertson Smith and Kuenen, the interest which both have in promoting the rationality of the canonical prophets, the former speaks the language of 'revealed truth', while the latter jettisons every trace of 'supernaturalism'. Moreover, Robertson Smith appears to tolerate the idea that special states of prophetic consciousness can be correlated with the reception of 'revelation'. This could be interpreted as a theological correlation of 'inspiration' and 'revelation'. It will be enough at present to observe that Robertson Smith is concerned to separate such inspiration as he would allow the canonical prophets from 'the crasser forms of religion':

> This is not the place for a theory of revelation. But it is well to observe, as a matter of plain fact, that the inspiration of the prophets presents phenomena quite distinct from those of any other religion. In the crasser forms of religion the supernatural character of an oracle is held to be proved by the absence of self-conscious thought. The dream, the estatic vision, the frenzy of the Pythoness, seem divine because they are not intelligent. But these things are divination and not prophecy. Jeremiah draws an express contrast between dreams and word of Yahweh (23.25–28). And the visions of the prophets, which were certainly rare, and by no means the standard form of revelation, are distinguished by the fact that the seer retains his consciousness, his moral judgement, his power of thinking. (1892, p. 297)

The same kind of balance as is found in Kuenen is discernible here, and the resemblances are extended in so far as Robertson Smith raises the question whether the literary expression of prophetic visions are to be regarded as transcripts of prophetic experience or whether, in whole or in part, they have the appearance of a secondary craftsmanship. At their furthest reach he judges them to be shaped by a concern for homiletical aptness rather than for the preservation of a revelatory content and at this point, vision is transformed into parable. This is reminiscent of Kuenen's treatment of prophetic visions and of the problematic relation between literary form and prophetic vision which he entertains. In any case, Robertson Smith clearly does not regard the imagery of prophetic visions as a primary revelatory content and this is connected with his attitude towards the products of imagination:

> But the origin of the scenery is immaterial for the ideal meaning of Isaiah's vision [the call vision in chapter 6]; temple and seraphim are nothing more than the necessary pictorial clothing of the supreme truth that in this vision the soul met the Infinite and Eternal face to face and heard the secrets of Yahweh's counsel direct from his own mouth. Nor can it be important to us how far the description is conscious poetry and how far the pictures pass without any effort of thought or volition before the inward eye. Even in the highest imaginings of poetical genius this question would be hard to answer; much less can we expect to be able to analyse the workings of the prophet's soul in a supreme moment of converse with God. (1895, pp. 218f)

It is almost certainly Robertson Smith's intention to preserve the impenetrable mystery of the prophet's encounter with God rather than to offer an analysis of it. He is not undertaking to describe 'sensual' (to use Kuenen's vocabulary) seeing, hearing and speaking. The prophet sees with his 'soul' not with his eyes; he does not hear the voice of God with his ears and God does not speak the sounds of human language with his mouth. 'Word of God' used of 'revelation' is not literal language (cf. Maimonides). It may be that Robertson Smith would not have agreed with this kind of explicitness or that he would have doubted the wisdom of attempting to unravel the mystery. At any rate his concern is to deepen the mystery not to explain it:

> Whether a prophet merely set forth in symbolic form truths which he had reached in another way, or whether he consciously devised a symbol, in order to have the aid of an analogy to bridge over gaps in his view of divine things, or whether the symbol rose up before his mind without a conscious effort of the intellect, does not affect its value as a vehicle of spiritual truth. The value of the symbol or vision depends simply on the fact that in one or other way he was guided by the use of imagery fitted to give larger and deeper views of spiritual realities (1895, pp. 223f)

He is attracted, however, to the former view of 'symbolic form' rather than the latter: its explanation as a secondary metamorphosis of prophetic experience into a literary medium. He likens prophetic visions to parables:

> So far, therefore, as the structure is concerned, there is no essential difference between a vision and a parable or other creation of poetic fancy; and this is as strictly true for the visions of the prophets as for

those of other men, so that it is often difficult to say whether any
particular allegory set forth by the prophet is visionary or not – that
is to say, we often cannot tell whether the prophet is devising an
instructive figure by a deliberate act of thought, or whether the
figure rose, as it were, of itself before his mind in a moment of deep
abstraction, when his thoughts seemed to take their own course
without a conscious effort of will. (1895, p. 221)

From this account of Robertson Smith's attitude to the imagery which
appears in prophetic utterances the problems which arise in any attempt
to identify the content of the 'revelation' assigned to the prophet by him
can be foreseen. The prophet's encounter with God and the revelation
associated with it are obscured by the literary phenomena which are
available for inspection and have taken on the character of a mystery
which must remain unelucidated. This will receive further investigation,
but a simpler task, that of contrasting the revelation which Robertson
Smith affirms with Kuenen's rejection of 'supernaturalism', will first be
undertaken.

III

Robertson Smith rejects the assertion that 'the prophets identify the
word of Jehovah with their own highest thoughts' and remarks that they
drew a sharp distinction between their own word and God's word. 'Nor is
spiritual prophecy, as other scholars hold, a natural product of Semitic
religion... According to the prophets, all true knowledge of God is
reached, not by human reflection, but by the instruction of Jehovah
himself' (1892, pp. 297f). The prophetic awareness of a difference
between their own thoughts and attitudes and Yahweh's is here advanced
as a reason why Kuenen's account of prophetic experience is inadequate.
Robertson Smith is resting his case on the oracular form of prophetic
utterance, the kind of formulae with which they preface it, which is a
claim that they speak Yahweh's word ('These are the words of Yahweh'
or the like), but Kuenen had undertaken to accommodate this usage
without recourse to a supernatural explanation. It is not clear that the
account which Kuenen gives deals principally or satisfactorily with the
oracular form of prophetic utterance – the claim that they speak Yahweh's word. The distinction which he draws between abnormal psychological states and the content of prophetic truth does not do this, because
it is argued that a calm rationality rather than an excited state of vision or
trance is a characteristic of the canonical prophets. In view of the wide
distribution of 'These are the words of Yahweh' or the like in the
prophetic literature it cannot be his intention to hold that, wherever they
occur, they are indicative of an unusual psychological state. The distinc-

tion which he draws between prophetic experience and its transformation into literature (which Robertson Smith also makes) could be used to reduce 'These are the words of Yahweh' to a secondary embellishment associated with this process, but he does not make much of this (Auld, above, p. 91). His most direct engagement with the problem is his statement that the prophets preface their utterances with 'These are the words of Yahweh' as a claim – an expression of utter confidence – that they have discerned the truth. But this complete conviction that they have grasped a content of religious and moral truth and that they speak for Yahweh is not to be made into a claim that the words which they speak have been revealed to them and that they derive from a supernatural transaction.

In a longer passage Robertson Smith criticizes the non-supernatural elucidation of 'ethical monotheism', but its content does not suggest that he had Kuenen precisely in mind:

> It is a widespread opinion that the prophets are the advocates of natural religion, and that this is the reason of their indifference to a religion of ordinances and ritual. On the naturalistic theory of religion, *ethical monotheism* is the natural belief of mankind, not, indeed, attained at once in all races, but worked out for themselves by the great thinkers of humanity, continually reflecting on the ordinary phenomena of life and history... From this point of view the prophets are regarded as advanced thinkers, who had not yet thrown aside all superstition, who were hampered by a belief in miracle and special revelation, but whose teaching has abiding value only in proportion as it reduced these elements to a subordinate place and struck out new ideas essentially independent of them. The prophets, we are told, believed themselves to be inspired. But their true inspiration was only profound thinking. They were inspired as all great poetic and religious minds are inspired; and when they say that God has told them certain things as to His nature and attributes, this only means that they have reached a profound conviction of spiritual truths concealed from their less intelligent contemporaries.

What follows is not a transition to Robertson Smith's own opinion, but a continued exposition of the view he is criticizing:

> The permanent truths of religion are those which spring up in the breast without external revelation or traditional teaching. The prophets had grasped these truths with great force and so they were indifferent to the positive forms which make up the religion of the mass of the nation. This theory has had an influence extending far beyond the circle of those who deliberately accept it in its whole compass. (1892, pp. 295f)

Some of this is recognizable as a criticism of Kuenen, though he portrayed the canonical prophets somewhat differently: they were a spiritual aristocracy and they had a rare 'religious excellence' rather than excelling as advanced thinkers. They were not an intellectual *élite* and their exceptional grasp of God and his ways was not awakened in an ivory tower but in intense involvement and conflict with their community. Kuenen had gone out of his way to insist that the prophets were not religious theorists or moral philosophers, but had a profound vision of the truth because they combined an extraordinary religious impressionability with a fineness of moral fibre. It was this which enabled them to penetrate to the implications of belief in and commitment to a holy, righteous and merciful God for their own society and for the world.

Robertson Smith introduced the concepts of 'revelation' and 'inspiration', but in a guarded way. He had no appetite for a supernaturalism which was too overt, for an elucidation which made everything as plain as a pikestaff, for description which attempted to dot every *i* and cross every *t*. He had no ambition to convert the mystery into a dogmatic parody. So far as inspiration goes, he would not allow a prophet to be dehumanized and to become a mouthpiece of Yahweh. The entire weight of his historical-critical exegesis of the prophetic literature cried out against such a procedure. He would not permit a canonical prophet to have his rationality and self-possession overthrown by any cocktail of abnormal psychological states. With regard to revelation, he observes great caution and restraint in offering any indication of how and where the juncture of the human and the divine is realized. We have to eke these out as best as we can. His appraisal of imagery in prophetic visions shows how far removed he is from Farrar's 'supernatural images' (*The Glass of Vision*, 1948, pp. 35–56; see chapter 1, pp. 14–22). That he does not regard such imagery as the primal form of revealed truth is shown by the circumstance that he leans towards an interpretation which associates it with a secondary literary process rather than with primary revelatory experience, though he does not exclude the latter possibility.

Another reason why the imagery of prophetic visions should be allocated a subordinate role in connection with Robertson Smith's account of revelation is the theory of knowledge to which he relates it. According to this, the source of all the images which appear in visions or dreams is sense experience and nothing new, over and above what was given as sense data, can be created. The stock of images which appear in visions or dreams is, therefore, fixed by empirical constraints and the only scope for novelty is in arrangements or combinations of these images, when the volitional control characteristic of waking life is relaxed. Even then, one will not find in Robertson Smith any urge to assert that revealed truth consists in a special arrangement of images superimposed by God, and the tendency of his theory of knowledge is rather to devalue the imagination in favour of what he regards as more rational and superior expressions of truth (1895, pp. 218–24).

He has rejected Kuenen's analysis of 'These are the words of Yahweh' and has put in its place something which does not amount to a total rejection of supernaturalism, but it is difficult to find out what this is. One argument which he uses is that tradition is not enough and that, when it is traced back to its origins, it must reach a point where divine truth was communicated. This is associated with a positive view of tradition, in so far as Robertson Smith holds that Torah or instruction is an essential element of true religion and rejects the idea of a process of self-education issuing from the voice of nature and conscience:

> To say that the voice of God speaks to all men alike, and gives the same communication directly to all without the use of a revealing agency reduces religion to mysticism. In point of fact, it is not true in the case of any man that what he believes and knows of God has come to him directly through the voice of nature and conscience. All true knowledge of God is verified by personal experience, but it is not exclusively derived from such experience. There is a positive element in all religion, an element which we have learned from those who went before us. If what is so learned is true, we must ultimately come back to a point in history when it was new truth, acquired as all new truth is by some particular man or circle of men, who, as they did not learn it from their predecessors, must have got it by personal revelation from God himself. (1895, pp. 11f)

These considerations are too general to support the argument that the canonical prophets received supernatural truth by an extraordinary channel directly from God. The contention that new truth of whatever kind is 'revealed' truth in the special sense which Robertson Smith intends is much too wide and it is insupportable.

If the point about the process by which supernatural truth was revealed to the canonical prophets is pressed, the following is perhaps the best that can be done to supply an answer:

> The characteristics of the prophet is that he retains his consciousness and control under revelation. . . Thus the essence of true prophecy lies in moral converse with Jehovah. It is in this moral converse that the prophet learns the divine will, enters into the secrets of Jehovah's purpose and so, by declaring God's word to Israel, keeps alive a constant spiritual intercourse between Him and His people. According to the prophets this spiritual intercourse is the essence of religion, and the 'word of Jehovah', in the sense now explained, is the characteristic and distinguishing mark of His grace to Israel. (1892, pp. 289f)

A passage which appears in another connection describes the encounter between the prophet and God at the moment of revelation: his soul 'meets the Infinite and Eternal face to face' and hears 'the secrets of Jehovah's counsel directly from His own mouth' (1895, pp. 218f). The mixture of metaphors in this passage is striking; there is a tension in Robertson Smith's thinking and the balance which he strives to maintain is not altogether happily achieved. He is concerned to assert that God communicates supernaturally with the prophet, but the 'seeing' and 'hearing' is that of the 'soul', not of the eye and ear. He is constrained to combine 'soul' with 'face to face' and with 'hearing'; he equates 'moral converse' with God as the issuing of speech 'directly from his own mouth'.

The first of the quotations offers an analysis of 'word of Yahweh' as 'moral converse' which is more reserved and less explicit. The prophet is apprised of Yahweh's purposes and will, but the nature of the intercourse is not elucidated. It is not clear what degree of literalness Robertson Smith would have us attach to 'moral converse' but this particular point of interpretation is thrust into the foreground by the anthropomorphic language used in the second quotation. It may be that this is a kind of poetic licence on the part of Robertson Smith and not an indication that he intends 'word of Yahweh' to be taken literally, but it is off-putting and it might be thought that he is installing a God who speaks to a prophet in Hebrew at the centre of his theology of prophecy. There are reasons for not drawing this conclusion about his intentions. Any interpretation of revelation and inspiration which would debilitate the humanity of the prophet is unacceptable to him. He dismisses any tendency to analyse 'These are the words of Yahweh' as a claim that Yahweh is using the vocal chords of a prophet to make his voice heard. To establish the rational, deliberate, and so human, character of the canonical prophets ranks high in his list of priorities. Moreover, he is completely committed to the historical-critical exegesis of the prophetic literature and the content of truth which it possesses is grasped by this way of studying it. The assumption of such an approach is that the prophet is located in a particular society, at a historical moment and that the discovery of prophetic truth cannot be disengaged from the contours of the community in which it is grasped, from the human and historical context in which it appears.

Robertson Smith's caution in relation to the phenomena of inspiration and revelation and the kind of exegetical method which he employs counsel us against supposing that he is taking 'word of Yahweh' literally in the context of the moral converse which the prophets have with Yahweh. He is far removed from a dehumanizing and irrational view of revelation which reduces the prophet to a reedy voice made use of by Yahweh to divulge truth – which then exists in a vacuum, without credible historical and human support. His reticence in this regard appears in the following: 'As a rule, the supreme religious thought which fills the prophet's soul, and which comes to him not as the result of an argument but as a direct intuition of divine truth, an immediate revelation of Jehovah, is developed by the ordinary processes of the intellect' (1895, p. 221).

The truth which the prophet seizes is intuitive and is not the product of ratiocination. It has a quality of immediacy, but the content of truth which is disclosed by Yahweh to the prophet remains obscure. This passage occurs in the context of a discussion of the imagery of prophetic visions and Robertson Smith is not disposed, for the most part, to identify such visions with the content of the moment of revelation. The elusive content of the truth which is revealed in the divine-human encounter does not consist of 'supernatural images'. Robertson Smith's words 'is developed by the ordinary processes of intellect' satisfy me that the formulation of prophetic oracles, the grammatically organized series of words which constitutes them, the language in which they are expressed, are entirely a human product. What Robertson Smith says here about the relation between the disclosure of divine truth and the human language in which it is expressed is incompatible with the supposition that he intends 'word of God' literally and is committed to belief in a God who speaks Hebrew into the heart of a prophet at the moment of a divine-human encounter.

At the point where this argument has come to rest it appears that Robertson Smith's position resembles that of Fohrer who also has differentiated the mysterious divine-human transaction, which is touched with ineffability and to which we have hardly any access, from the overt linguistic forms of prophetic oracles (1967, pp. 8f, 27f; McKane, 1979, pp. 167f). Fohrer is reacting against a different, and more modern, context of scholarship, the tyranny of a form-critical method which confuses literary forms with psychological and theological categories. If it is established that the prophetic utterance is oracular, that it has the form of 'word of Yahweh', this is a correct observation, so far as it goes, but a literary description should not be transposed into a doctrine of revelation and be thought to supply transparent theological conclusions. This is a disastrous confusion of categories. Fohrer, for his part, holds that the mysterious transcendence of the prophetic message does not find expression in public utterance. It is metamorphosed into human language by the prophet.

IV

Robertson Smith also conducts a historical argument, connected with a theory of 'progressive revelation' to which he adheres, but also having

the character of an independent, empirical argument, founded on historical evidence, in general, and on the results which are obtained from
the scientific exegesis of the Old Testament, in particular. With respect
to 'progressive revelation', we find that Robertson Smith is putting this
to work in different ways. It is a method by which he answers objections
that religious truth could never, at any time, have been confined to one
nation (Israel) and to the narrow tract of its historical experience:

> But the whole conception of progressive revelation worked out in
> special dealings of God with the people of Israel is often represented
> by modern thinkers as involving something inconsistent with the
> universality of the divine purpose. There is a large and thoughtful
> school of modern theologians, fully possessed with the idea of a
> divine education of mankind, and ready to do sincere homage to the
> teaching of Christ, which yet refuses to believe that God's dealings
> with Israel in the times before Christ can be distinguished under the
> name of revelation from his prudential guidance of other nations.
> ... The prophets, who were the organs of God's teaching in Israel,
> appear to them to stand on the same line with the other great
> teachers of mankind who were also searchers after truth and
> received it as a gift from God. (1895, pp. 8f)

It appears from another passage (1895, p. 10) that the 'modern
theologians' to whom Robertson Smith refers are natural theologians
who will have nothing to do with 'special revelation' and who, dispensing
with the 'supernatural', replace it with 'providential guidance' (cf.
Duhm, above, pp. 89f) He answers the objection that the truth
'revealed' in the Old Testament suffers from historical limitations by
pointing to its New Testament fulfilment and by urging that the drawing
out of its implications had to be gradual, the intensity of its light being
graduated to what men, in the historical situations in which they received
it, were able to bear:

> There is nothing unreasonable, therefore, in the idea that the true
> religion was originally developed in the national form within the
> people of Israel; nay, this limitation corresponds to the historical
> conditions of the problem. But at length a time came when the
> message of revelation was fully set forth in Christ. The coming of
> Christ coincided under divine providence with the breaking down
> of national barriers and the establishment of a cosmopolitan system
> of culture and politics under the first Roman emperors, and so
> Christianity was able to leave the narrow field of Old Testament
> development and become a religion not for one nation but for all
> mankind. (1895, p. 13)

For the antithesis of 'natural' and 'supernatural' which the natural theologians formulate in the process of rejecting the latter, Robertson Smith creates a synthesis of 'special revelation' and 'providential guidance':

> The difference is generally expressed by saying that the modern theologians deny the supernatural, but I do not think that this phrase expresses the real gist of the point at issue. The practical point in all controversy as to the distinctive character of the revelation of God to Israel regards the place of Scripture as the permanent rule of faith and the sufficient and unfailing guide in all our religious life. (1895, p. 10)

This confirms the view already expressed that Robertson Smith is reserved in his explication of the 'supernaturalism' of the canonical prophets and that he is unwilling to explicate the mystery beyond the limits already indicated. Instead of attacking the problem at its centre and indicating how 'revealed truth' is inserted into prophetic experience so that their utterance becomes 'word of God', he transforms this particular issue into an affirmation of the adequacy and sufficiency of the Bible, about its authority 'as the permanent rule of faith and the sufficient and unfailing guide in all our religious life'. This is a general Protestant biblicism rather than a theology of the prophetic literature.

More than this, 'progressive revelation' is a different subject from 'inspiration and revelation', as I have hitherto been pursuing it in connection with the canonical prophets, and it is attuned to a historical-critical exegesis of prophetic literature rather than to these recondite theological ideas. 'Progressive revelation' is a historical-critical rather than a theological concept, as the following quotation will show: 'Thus the analogies which the Bible itself presents as our guides in understanding the work of the divine grace lead us to expect that revelation must have a history, conformed to the laws of human nature, and limited by the universal rule that every spiritual and moral relation must grow up by small degrees, and obey a principle of internal development' (1895, p. 4). An important reason why Robertson Smith objects to the equation of 'progressive revelation' with 'supernaturalism' is that he identifies the former as a truth elicited by biblical science and not a truth dependent on a theological assumption or a credal affirmation. He throws the question open to candid scholarship and is confident that an answer will emerge from a historical-critical study of the Old Testament which is untrammelled by antecedent premises or prejudices:

> Occupying this vantage-ground, the defenders of revelation need no longer be afraid to allow free discussion of the details of its history. They are not bound to start, as modern apologists too often do, with preconceived notions as to the kind of acts by which God made his

presence and teaching known in the Bible ages – they can afford to
meet every candid inquirer on the fair field of history, and to form
their judgement on the actual course of revelation by the ordinary
method of historical investigation. (1895, pp. 16f)

With this confidence that a scholarly historical method will lead to the
perception of a 'progressive revelation' Robertson Smith sets out to
examine the documents of Old Testament religion to see 'whether they
actually possess the evidence of consistent, progressive and indestruct-
ible truth which entitles them to be received as embodying a scheme of
divine teaching' (1895, p. 17).

V

The final stage of this discussion is concerned with the extension of
Robertson Smith's argument. It becomes a general affirmation that the
truth of the Bible has been vindicated by the course of history. This he
describes as 'external evidence of the truth of the Biblical revelation'
(1895, p. 16). The argument is an empirical one 'which lies behind the
question of the supernatural as it is usually stated, an evidence which lies
not in the miraculous circumstances of this or that particular act of
revelation, but in the intrinsic character of the scheme of revelation as a
whole'. He continues:

> It is a general law of human history that truth is consistent, progress-
> ive and imperishable, while every falsehood is self-contradictory,
> and ultimately falls to pieces. A religion which has endured every
> possible trial, which has outlived every vicissitude of human for-
> tunes, and has never failed to reassert its power, unbroken in the
> collapse of its old environments, which has pursued a consistent and
> victorious course through the lapse of eventful centuries, declares
> itself by irresistible evidence to be a thing of reality and power.
> (1895, p. 16)

Here he seems almost to indulge in a bombastic triumphalism and to
be strangely out of touch with the mood of our age. Not many, not even
those who are Christians, would now be so superbly confident.

He should not be judged harshly. He reflects the vigour of Scottish
Presbyterianism in the second half of the last century, its soaring morale
and robust confidence that the Gospel would be preached to the ends of
the earth and the Kingdom of God would be realized. He speaks for the
Free Church of Scotland which, in the wake of the Disruption, had
acquired a rare combination of talents and resources: evangelical earnestness, critical biblical scholars, out-going theologians and high-calibre
preachers. Add to this a well-informed and theologically articulate laity,

some of whom had combined their resilient Christian faith with business acumen and were a power in the land, and one has a context for the fuller understanding of Robertson Smith's preface to the first edition of *The Old Testament in the Jewish Church*. He was invited by 'some six hundred prominent Free Churchmen in Edinburgh and Glasgow' to deliver the twelve lectures which became that book (1881). They 'deemed it better that the Scottish public should have an opportunity of understanding the position of the newer criticism than that they should condemn it unheard. The Lectures were delivered in Edinburgh and Glasgow in the first three months of the present year, and the average attendance on the course in the two cities was not less than eighteen hundred' (1881, p. v). That lectures so intellectually severe and doctrinally challenging could have commanded such lay audiences is remarkable. Robertson Smith believed that his biblical criticism was part of the witness of the Free Church of Scotland that it harmonized with its theological stance and its wide-ranging missionary vision. His desire that he should speak for the Church, be firmly installed within it and not become a reject outside its gates, was earnest.

According to Robert Laws' biographer (pp. 44f), Robertson Smith was present at a public meeting in Aberdeen held in connection with the imminent departure of the Livingstonia expedition in 1875. This was a Free Church of Scotland enterprise, conceived as a memorial to David Livingstone, and the plan was to establish a mission station on Lake Nyasa. Robert Laws, a minister of the United Presbyterian Church and a medical practitioner, who was an Aberdonian, was a focus of interest at that meeting. He was subsequently to become the dominant figure in connection with the execution of the project. He had joined the Livingstonia party which was otherwise comprised of four Free Church churchmen, one who belonged to the Church of Scotland, one Anglican and one Baptist: 'Robertson Smith came up to Laws at the end of the meeting and said, "Have you any use for a Professor of Hebrew in Livingstonia"'. This is not to be taken too seriously, but it is not simply a jocular remark. That Robertson Smith had taken the trouble of attending such a meeting and that he had made personal contact with Robert Laws (who had not been his student) are indications of the extent of the involvement which he felt with the missionary enterprise of the Free Church of Scotland.

I had been arguing that 'progressive revelation' is a concept which falls within the area of historical-critical biblical scholarship and that it does not deal with the problems of 'inspiration' and 'revelation' as these are encountered in a direct consideration of the theology of prophecy. In another respect, the substituting of an affirmation about the authority of the Bible for a more precise investigation of the prophetic endowment, Robertson Smith grasps at a formula which indicates his unwillingness to be trapped in the antithesis of natural and supernatural. There is no doubt that he draws the boundaries of historical-critical scholarship very widely, even if he dissented from the method by which Kuenen dispensed entirely with supernaturalism. How wide the boundaries are the following quotation will show clearly: 'The first condition of a sound understanding of Scripture is to give full recognition to the human side, to master the whole situation and character and feelings of each human interlocutor who has a part in the drama of Revelation. *Nay, the whole business of scholarly exegesis lies with this human side*' (1892, p. 13). The closing words of this quotation are puzzling: 'All that earthly study and research can do for the reader of Scripture is to put him in the position of the men to whom God spoke'. With 'the men to whom God spoke' he seems to affirm 'revelation' in the old language of orthodoxy. He is referring to the authors of the Scriptures and he expresses the authority of the Scriptures by saying that they are 'the word of God'. This statement requires further consideration, but for the present it will be enough to say that it is unlikely that 'God spoke' is to be taken literally and that he is affirming that God spoke Hebrew and Greek.

The puzzle of the above quotation is that Robertson Smith's emphasis on 'the human side' of historical-critical exegesis, that it is wholly a linguistic, literary and historical study, does not sit easily with the reference to 'the drama of revelation' and 'God speaking' at its close, because his original assumption is the reasonable one that the languages (Hebrew and Greek) are human languages and only human languages. 'Revelation', however, may be equated with 'progressive revelation' in which case his emphasis is on the progress from lower to higher disclosed by historical-critical exegesis rather than on a God who reveals, and can be reconciled with his concentration on the 'human side'. His statement then has principally to do with the objectives of exegesis: to recover the sense which the Old Testament writers intended at the time and in the context in which they spoke. If this is done, a 'progressive revelation' is disclosed and he has the confidence, characteristic of his time, that these critical objectives can be accomplished. No supernatural 'pneumatic' assistance is required to achieve this end, yet what is unfolded by the exegesis, though it lies entirely on the 'human side', is 'revelation'. This is an indication of the antipathy of Robertson Smith to the equation of 'revelation' with 'supernaturalism'. He asserts the contrary, that the content of revelation is recovered and displayed by a kind of humanist scholarship, namely, historical-critical exegesis. On this analysis the concept of 'revelation' is compatible with biblical science and does not imply an appeal to the supernatural.

The Bible is to be studied in the same way as any other ancient document; the thoughts and convictions of the Old Testament writers are expressed in human language, set in a community, and a particular cultural envelope, at more or less ascertainable dates. Its mastery depends on the exercise of the appropriate scholarly skills and what counts is rigour and a discerning use of the tools of scholarship. This intimate fellowship of intelligibility is to be achieved by intellectual integrity, nice judgement and penetrating empathy. The entire enterprise of historical-critical exegesis is a humanist activity, lexicographical, philological and syntactical. It is the establishing of an accurate translation and the fixing of the historical context to which the text or passage belongs.

But this explanation of Robertson Smith's reference to 'the drama of revelation' in terms of 'progressive revelation' requires the New Testament to make it complete. He acknowledges this in the answers which he gives to the objections lodged against the concept. It is specifically a Christian idea, for it is only in the New Testament that the 'progress' evident in the Old Testament reaches a culmination. 'Progressive revelation' must mean more than progress which has been arrested before the goal was reached, a process which did not reach a climax, and it cannot be formulated satisfactorily without the New Testament fulfilment. In any case there is Robertson Smith's reference in the quotation above to a speaking God and this suggests that the tension between natural and supernatural lies still deeper.

Robertson Smith is facing a dilemma not dissimilar to that which confronted William Fulke (see chapter 3, pp. 43–5) who also endeavoured to combine Renaissance linguistic scholarship with biblical theology. In the sixteenth century he did not have to reckon with historical-critical exegesis and his procedure was much less refined and more perfunctory than that of Robertson Smith. He assumed that once an accurate translation of the Bible had been made all was plain-sailing and that the entire continuing task could be handed over to the theologians. In the seventeenth century Richard Simon (see chapter 3, pp. 53–64) was a much more complex scholar, with a sharp critical awareness and a concern to explore the Old Testament freely. He foresaw that that there was a conflict between the exercise of this freedom and regard for the dogma of his Church. He recognized this incompatibility between critical scholarhip and theology and he sought to remove it by urging that the former should be pursued with complete freedom, but that critical scholars should not aspire to be theologians. The two disciplines should be held apart and the latter should be formulated, as a separate activity, by ecclesiastical theologians. Robertson Smith is running up against what is essentially the same difficulty. If weight is thrown on historical-critical exegesis and on the baggage of scholarship which accompanies it, the point at which 'revelation' or 'word of God' is to be introduced cannot be found. Robertson Smith perseveres with this task and does not take Simon's way out, but the passage cited exhibits the extreme tension

between the language of criticism and the theological language of orthodoxy.

Robertson Smith does have a final theological move which is unsatis-
factory, because the solution which is offered is an appeal to a pneumatic
theology and is not sufficiently founded on his historical-critical scholarship. Is it evidence of the strength of his attachment to the formula of his
Church that the Scriptures of the Old and New Testament are the word
of God, a mark of the indestructibility of his early nurture? Perhaps, but
too much speculation would be unprofitable. It is noticeable that in his
fine prose there are some echoes of the language of piety and the ring of
familiar words would not have been missed by the Free Churchmen who
first listened to his lectures. But he may have been implying that the
language of 'the reformed symbols' could be analysed and reconciled
with his historical-critical exegesis. He says:

> It is only the Spirit of God that can make the Word a living word to
> our hearts, as it was a living word to him who first received it. This is
> the truth which the Westminster Confession expresses when it
> teaches, in harmony with all the Reformed Symbols, that our full
> persuasion and assurance of the infallible truth and divine authority
> of Scripture is from the inward work of the Holy Spirit, bearing
> witness by and with the Word in our hearts. (1892, pp. 13f)

Robertson Smith is here at a distance from a treatment of the topics of
'revelation' and 'word of God' as they arise in the Bible, especially in the
prophetic literature. He has moved from biblical criticism to pneumatic
theology, to 'the full assurance of faith' which the Holy Spirit bestows on
the Christian believer, who reads or hears the Bible, that it is the word of
God. He is no longer dealing with prophetic experience and prophetic
literature directly, but is affirming that the assurance of the truth of
prophetic words conveyed to the heart by the Holy Spirit is identical with
the assurance which the prophets had when they uttered them. He is no
longer wrestling with a theology of prophecy directly. He is offering a
theology of *belief* in revelation not a theology of revelation itself. It is a
conviction of the truth of the prophetic word which is imposed by the
Holy Spirit. The contents of the product of historical-critical exegesis are
not by themselves self-evidently 'word of God' in this theological sense; it
is the Holy Spirit which makes 'the Word a living word to our hearts' and
creates the unassailable conviction that it is the word of God.

A criticism of this individualistic doctrine is that it will create a legion
of Holy Spirits instead of reinforcing the unity of one Holy Spirit and in
this respect it is like von Rad's plea for exegesis done in the freedom of
the Holy Spirit, though this has a different context (see chapter 8). It is
important to be aware that Robertson Smith's pneumatic theology is not
accompanied by another layer of exegesis which overlays the historical-

critical exegesis. The objective of this exegesis is to recover the original sense of the words at the times, and in the places and historical contexts where they were uttered or written. There is no trace of Christological exegesis in this scheme. The Christian fulfilment is not adumbrated or intimated in Old Testament texts. They contain a 'progressive revelation', an ascent from a lower to a higher understanding and grasp of Yahweh, but they are significant only in connection with the time span, the historical periods, in which they originated. Old Testament exegesis is historical-critical through and through and this is why the scheme of 'progressive revelation' is an unfinished structure until its culmination is reached in the New Testament. There is no room for Old Testament texts which have shadowy or not so shadowy descriptions of Christ and which predict his coming. The crowning affirmation of 'progressive revelation' is that the New Testament is the witness of the climax which was reached and unfolds its significance.

If so, the temptation to set up Robertson Smith as a Protestant version of Richard Simon should be resisted, because *les véritables traditions* of the Roman Catholic Church in Simon's scheme are associated with an interpretation of the Old Testament which goes far beyond his own critical exegesis and which furnishes a new theological content distinct from it. There is nothing akin to this in Robertson Smith and the only content of truth which he acknowledges for the Old Testament is that produced by historical-critical exegesis. His theological goal is attained by means of an illumination granted to individuals by the Holy Spirit which produces 'a full persuasion of the infallible truth and divine authority of Scripture' (1892, pp. 13f). Notice that, so far as the Old Testament is concerned, this action of the Holy Spirit does not reveal an inner content of Christian truth. It confirms 'the infallible truth and divine authority' of the content of truth contained in the historical-critical exegesis of a text.

There is then no bridge from biblical criticism to biblical (Christian) theology in the Old Testament. There are those who are inwardly persuaded by the Holy Spirit that Old Testament Scripture has the authority of word of God, but, even they are bound to affirm that the content of their exegesis lies entirely 'on the human side'. Christian theology is hardly at all, according to Robertson Smith, a part of Old Testament scholarship; there is a dichotomy between such scholarship and Christian theology. Moreover, the kind of direct exploration of the prophetic literature whose aim is to investigate how a prophet's words can be both 'word of man' and 'word of God' is not undertaken. The gulf between Robertson Smith's scholarship and his subscription to a formula of his Church that the Scriptures of the Old and New Testament have the authority of the Word of God is notable, all the more so because of the unusualness of its form. He is not recommending that a Christian

hermeneutical method should be applied to the Old Testament and that
this should be done 'in the freedom of the Holy Spirit', after the manner
of von Rad. The assurance given by the Holy Spirit adds nothing to the
content of historical-critical exegesis and does no more than generate the
certainty that what has been explained as human and historical is unassailable truth.

His final comment on the encounter of a prophet with God is that it is
inaccessible to scholarship and 'lies beyond our wisdom'. The contention
that it is mysterious is not to be quarrelled with, but he leaves us
suspended at one remove from the mystery and does not attack the
problem of the relation of 'word of man' to 'word of God' in immediate
connection with the prophetic literature. This he cannot do, because, in
all important respects, he locates the assurance that word of man is also
word of God in an area which lies 'beyond our wisdom', beyond the
boundaries of linguistic analysis and discourse. He ends up with a
general affirmation that the Scriptures of the Old and New Testaments
are the word of God and that this certainty is communicated to believing
individuals by the Holy Spirit. He adds that when, with the help of the
Holy Spirit, we are persuaded that the prophets spoke the word of God,
we shall understand why they themselves made this claim and prefaced
their utterances with 'These are the words of Yahweh': 'It is only the
Spirit of God that can make a word a living word in our hearts, as it was a
living word to him who first received it' (1892, p. 13).

Literature for Chapters 4 and 5

Auld, A. G., 'Word of God and Word of Man'. Supplements to *JSOT* 67
    (Sheffield, 1988), pp. 237–51.
Auld, A. G., 'Word of God', *A Dictionary of Biblical Interpretation* (London,
    1990), pp. 731f.
Buber, M., *Pointing the Way* (New York, 1957).
Buber, M., *Israel and the World: Essays in a Time of Crisis* (New York, 1963²)
Dirksen, P. B., and van der Kooij, A. (eds.), *Abraham Kuenen (1828–1891): His
    Major Contributions to the Study of the Old Testament* (Leiden, 1993).
Duhm, B., *Die Theologie der Propheten als Grundlage für die innere Entwicklungs-
    geschichte der israelitischen Religion* (Bonn, 1875).
Eichrodt, W., *Theology of the Old Testament*, i and ii (London, 1961 and 1967).
    Translated by J. Baker from *Theologie des Alten Testaments*, Teil i (1959⁶) and
    Teil ii–iii (1964⁵).
Engnell, I., *Studies in Divine Kingship in the Ancient Near East* (Oxford, 1967²).
Engnell, I., *Critical Essays on the Old Testament* (London, 1970). An English
    translation by J. T. Willis of thirteen essays from *Svenskt Bibliskt Uppslagsverk*
    (Stockholm, 1962).
Engnell, I., 'The Ebed Yahweh Songs and the Suffering Messiah in "Deutero-
    Isaiah"', *BJRL* 31 (1948), pp. 54–93.

Fohrer, G., *Studien zur alttestamentlichen Prophetie (1949–1965)*, BZAW 99 (1967). Especially 'Bemerkungen zum neueren Verstandnis der Propheten', pp. 18–31; 'Prophetie und Geschichte', pp. 265–93.

Hooke, S.H., (ed.), *Myth and Ritual: Essays on the Myth and Ritual of the Hebrews in relation to the Culture Pattern of the Ancient Near East* (London, 1933).

Hooke, S. H. (ed.), *The Labyrinth: Further Studies in the relation between Myth and Ritual in the Ancient World* (London and New York, 1935).

Hooke, S. H., (ed.), *Myth, Ritual and Kingship: Essays on the Theory and Practice of Kingship in the Ancient Near East and in Israel* (Oxford, 1958).

Johnson, A. R., *Sacral Kingship in Ancient Israel* (Cardiff, 1967[2]).

Kuenen, A., *De godsdienst van Israel* (Haarlem, 1869). Translated into English by A. H. May, *The Religion of Israel*, i (London and Edinburgh, 1874).

Kuenen, A., *De propheten en de prophetie onder Israel. Historisch–dogmatische Studie*, i–ii (Leiden, 1875). Translated into English by A. Milroy, *The Prophets and Prophecy in Israel. An Historical and Critical Enquiry* (London, 1877).

Kuenen, A., *National Religions and Universal Religions*, Hibbert Lectures, 1882 (London and Edinburgh, 1882).

Livingstone, W. P., *Laws of Livingstone – A Narrative of Missionary Adventure and Achievement* (London, no date).

Maimonides, Moses, *The Guide of the Perplexed*, ii, translated by S. Pines (Chicago, 1963), pp. 360–412.

McKane, W., *Prophets and Wise Men* (London, 1965).

McKane, W., 'Prophecy and the Prophetic Literature', *Tradition and Interpretation*, edited by G. W. Anderson (Oxford, 1979), pp. 163–87.

McKane, W., 'Prophet and Institution', *ZAW* 94 (1982), pp. 251–66.

Smend, R., 'Julius Wellhausen und seine Prolegomena zur Geschichte Israels', *Epochen der Bibelkritik*, Gesammelte Studien 3 (München, 1991), pp. 168–85.

Smend, R., 'Kuenen und Wellhausen', Dirkson, P. B. and van der Kooij, A. (eds.), *Abraham Kuenen (1828–1891): His Major Contributions to the Study of the Old Testament* (Leiden, 1993), pp. 113–27.

Smith, W. R., *The Old Testament in the Jewish Church* (London, 1892[2]).

Smith, W. R., *The Prophets of Israel and their Place in History* (London, 1895[2]).

Wellhausen, J., Review of Kuenen's *De propheten en de prophetie onder Israel*, *ThLZ* 1 (1876), 203–8.

Wellhausen, J., *Sketch of the History of Israel and Judah*. This appeared as the article 'Israel' in the *Encyclopaedia Brittanica* (1881). It is identical with *Geschichte Israels. Private Druck* (1880). R. Smend (ed.), *Julius Wellhausen: Grundrisse zum Alten Testament* (München, 1965), pp. 13–64. It was reprinted in 1885 as an appendix to the English translation of the *Prolegomena* and then separately (London and Edinburgh, 1891).

Wellhausen, J., *Prolegomena zur Geschichte Israels* (Berlin, 1883[2]). Translated into English by J. S. Black and A. Menzies, *Prolegomena to the History of Israel* (Edinburgh, 1885).

Wellhausen, J., *Israelitische und Jüdische Geschichte* (Berlin, 1894).

Wellhausen, J., 'Israelitisch-Jüdische Religion', *Die Kultur der Gegenwart*, 1.4 (Berlin and Leipzig, 1905). Smend, R., *Grundrisse*, pp. 65–109.

Widengren, G., *Religionens varld* (Stockholm, 1953[2]). Translated into German, *Religionsphänomenologie* (Berlin, 1969).

6

THE CANONICAL PROPHETS: WHAT KIND OF MEN WERE THEY? (I)

The canonical prophets are sometimes called classical or writing prophets. My intention is to refer principally to the prophetic line from Amos in the eighth century BC to Jeremiah whose activity was coeval with the last years of the kingdom of Judah at the end of the seventh century and the beginning of the sixth century BC. All these prophets are writing prophets in the sense that there is an extant literature which bears their names. To what extent, if any, they were responsible for the extant books in their present form is another matter.

I

Engnell is the scourge of those whom he supposes to be guilty of modernizing these prophets by recreating them anachronistically in an image which is acceptable to our understanding of religious profundity, where the emphasis falls on rational balance and moral seriousness. Those who do this are said to be failures as practitioners of biblical science, since they turn away from the evidence and yield to the temptation of making the Old Testament prophets into the kind of persons they would like them to be. The corrective is to survey and analyse the evidence dispassionately and to allow these prophets to be themselves, to emerge as ancient men in a deep antiquity with different mental furniture from our own, with concepts which, however foreign to our way of thinking, can be organized and described objectively.

Engnell's polemic against what he supposes to be a modernizing and unscientific treatment of the prophets is directed particularly against the evolutionary account which is given of Old Testament religion in general and especially of Old Testament prophecy. Also against a view of prophetic religion which regards it as essentially anti-cultic and as dominated by an ethic which disowns cultic modes of thought (1970, pp. 137ff). He has this to say about the opinion that the canonical prophets create a new, spiritual form of religion which is anti-cultic:

> This understanding, which is still predominant (at any rate in popular expositions and text-books) is undoubtedly prompted by a Protestant tenet that cultic piety is of inferior power, a view in-

herited from the Age of the Enlightenment and Rationalism. Advocates of this position operate on the purely anachronistic assumption that the prophets propagated a 'spiritual' religion which was independent of the cult. (1970, p. 137)

Against the view that the evolution of Old Testament religion from lower to higher is a process of historical development Engnell remarks:

According to this scheme the prophets were deliberate monotheistic propagandists and educators of the people, who led their contemporaries by the hand through the jungle of popular religion or 'natural religion' to enlightened, ethical monotheistic faith which they themselves created. This reconstruction of the history of Old Testament religion, based on a pre-conceived idea of historical development throughout, will not stand the test of more recent studies into the historical and phenomenological aspects of the history of Israel's religion. (1970, p. 143)

This attitude which Engnell strikes should be contrasted with that of Gunkel. In Gunkel too there is an antithesis between a philosophical or theological concern to establish the relevance of the prophets and a purely historical interest which follows the evidence wherever it leads, untroubled about the conclusions which it may produce: 'The main question asked by the theologians is what we, with our religious and scientific world view, can gather from them. This dogmatic way of putting the question forces into the background the more rigorous historical concern about what they were like in themselves' (1917, p. 2).

But Gunkel views the development of Old Testament religion and prophecy as an evolutionary process and he is precisely the kind of scholar criticized heavily by Engnell. He supposes that there is a progress and gradual refinement of Old Testament religion, a movement from lower to higher and that this is a process of historical development or *Religionsgeschichte*: it is the emergence of new religious truth in a linear series of historical contexts. In his account of Old Testament prophecy there is a strong contrast between its primitive excitable, rhapsodical, irrational, early manifestations and the mature form of it in the canonical prophets which he describes as the high point of prophecy. Moreover, his description of this high point, though it preserves an interest in the exceptional features of prophetic states of consciousness, has, in important respects, a strong resemblance to Kuenen's understanding of the texture of the inner life of the prophet. To assume a crude supernaturalism is a bad beginning to a consideration of the activity of these prophets. There is a diversity of style in their writings, and also some conflict of thought, which shows that as human beings 'they played a large part in formulating their own words' (1917, p. 30). He attributes clarity of intellect to Isaiah and Jeremiah (1917, p. 28):

> Strange conditions of the soul recede in prophecy and the trust of the religio-ethical (*sittlich-religiosen*) personality appears in its place. The alteration in the form of the experience accompanies an alteration in content. The older prophets had received in ecstasy disclosures about particular events of the immediate future. But the more developed prophets offer more: they are able to give reasons why this must come to pass. . . . The essential aspect of this high point of prophecy is that a religious and moral character is bound up with it. The more this is so, the more the ecstatic recedes into the background. (1917, p. 29)

A general similarity to the view of Kuenen and Robertson Smith can be detected here, though a closer examination would disclose significant differences. The thought that particular predictions are subsumed under general principles, which appeared in Kuenen, should not be missed. Our main interest, for the present, is in picking up the point where Engnell and Gunkel display some agreement. Is the antithesis between the tendentious theologian and the objective student of antiquity so clear-cut as they make out? In so far as they are opposing an undisciplined manipulation of ancient men, which does violence to historical scholarship in order to secure theologically relevant prophets, no exception can be taken to the opposition which they set up.

There are, however, concealed difficulties which have to be uncovered. Gunkel refers (1917, p. 2) to the reticence of the canonical prophets about their inner states and it should not be assumed that a study which sets out to restore them as ancient men, with conceptual machinery different from our's, is not threatened by inaccessibility – by serious problems of interpretation. If they are so different from us that our assumption that we share with them a common humanity becomes almost useless as an aid to understanding them, we may find that we have been robbed of an empathy which nothing will replace. If ancient men are made into utterly strange creatures, the gulf between ourselves and them becomes a serious impediment to our entering into their human existence and may even be unbridgeable. Whatever objectivity a historical method making such investigations may claim, however precise and matter of fact its discourse, the scholar, with humanist concerns he is unwilling to surrender, is filled with a sense of irreparable loss. He is convinced that once ancient men have been made into such strangers, he has no tests which he can apply to the conceptuality which is attributed to them. They have been made as remote as Martians; the alleged objectivity is illusory and he is at the mercy of hidden assumptions more than he ever was.

II

The so-called modernizing is not necessarily wilful and irresponsible. It follows from an appreciation that there is more to our interpretation of ancient documents than the transporting of ourselves into antiquity; that to identify ourselves with those who appear in them, to grasp them and deepen our understanding of them, we have to relate them to our own quest for self-understanding in the here and now. Consequently a too absolute antithesis between historical objectivity and prejudiced modernizing should not be accepted.

In case it may be thought that this is just theological nonsense, let us take a case which has nothing to do with the Bible or theology. The book of E. R. Dodds, *The Greeks and the Irrational* (1951) is entirely humanist in its concerns. Dodds' argument is that a full appreciation of the irrational phenomena associated with prophecy in the context of Greek civilization involves two hermeneutical levels, an antique level and a modern one. In addition to a treatment of Greek irrationality in a historical context Dodds also undertakes a reinterpretation in modern terms and asks how we can achieve a better understanding and control of the irrational forces which are constituents of our humanity. The clarity of Dodds' method relieves the problems which are raised by the insistence of scholars like Engnell that the thought-forms and modes of belief of ancient men must be recovered, faithfully described and evaluated and that every tendency to modernize them should be resisted. An important perception of Dodds' book is that the account which ancient men give of themselves is not necessarily identical with the one in terms of which we can appropriate and understand them best. The two levels of interpretation are set out in the book, and the fact that there are two levels is an indication that the plea for the eradication of a quest for the modern understanding of ancient documents may not be consistent with their full interpretation.

Dodds' work is a combination of exact historical and linguistic scholarship with a concern for human problems which, he believes, are still important in a modern context and which he explores in connection with the ancient material he is studying. His method assumes the possibility of separating the irrational phenomena which he scrutinizes from the particular interpretations of them which appear in ancient Greek literature. The ancient hermeneutic is itself considered and explained, but the conviction that there is a fundamental continuity between our humanity and that of the ancients leads to the creation of a new hermeneutic. Dodds explains what is involved in the belief in 'inspiration' and 'revelation' in connection with Dionysiac ecstasy, but he is not recommending a theistic interpretation of the phenomena and his interest in them arises from his belief that they give us an insight

into the tensions between the rational and irrational in our make-up
and that they have therapeutic value: they act as a form of release or
catharsis.

Though Dodds distinguishes between enthusiasm or inspiration
(possession by a god) and 'Shamanism'(the disengagement of the soul
from its corporeal prison through Divine assistance) his special interest
in Shamanism does not arise from the powers of clairvoyance or extra-
sensory perception which are associated with it in ancient contexts, but
from the tendency towards 'Puritanism' which he discovers in it. The
portrayal of the soul separated from the body is a retrograde step, a
retreat from a frank examination of the irrational aspects of our humanity and the setting-up of a separation which has authoritarian and
repressive implications. These are detected by Dodds in Plato's pro-
posals to regulate and curb the irrational, the political expression of
which is the subjugation of the masses by a rational *élite*. This is a loss of
confidence in a truly human solution to the problem of the irrational: it
is a dehumanizing deviation from which no good can come, because it
proceeds from a wrong description of the elements of our humanity and
a misunderstanding of how it functions. According to Dodds the way
ahead lies in recognition and acceptance of the irrational side of our
humanity and in such a clarification, in terms of Freudian theory, as
will bring it to its most free and constructive expression.

My primary reason for examining Dodds' book is to show that historical faithfulness, on the one hand, and a concern to supply an interpretation which includes both ancient and modern men, on the
other, are not necessarily mutually exclusive objectives, but can be
incorporated in a single, cohesive enterprise of scholarship. It is not my
intention to assert that the form of Dodds' reductionism is successful or
that the problems of demonstrating the contemporary significance of
the canonical prophets are those with which Dodds grapples in his
account of prophecy in a Greek context. There are similarities between
the 'irrational' phenomena which Dodds discusses and the phenomena
which are attributed to the earlier manifestations of prophecy in Israel,
but it it not clear that these should bulk too large in any attempt to
grasp the essential qualities of the canonical prophets. Nevertheless,
one conclusion which should be drawn from Dodds' book is that the
explanation which canonical prophets themselves give of the nature of
their prophetic endowment ('These are the words of Yahweh') is not
necessarily the one which enables us to appropriate them most mean-
ingfully and which best serves the interests of truth.

The major difficulty which can be detected in Dodds' hermeneutic is
that he sets out from minority, exceptional psychological states and
arrives at a general view of irrationality as a universal human problem.
It appears that extraordinary patterns of irrationality which affect only

the few are being employed to construct a therapy for dealing with irrational elements embedded in us all and the question has to be asked whether the base on which the general explanation rests is not too narrow.

Whatever is thought of Dodds' particular results, the assumption of his approach, that there is a sufficient common humanity between ourselves and ancient men for us, in our modernity, to enter into their human condition is one which should be taken seriously. An antiquarianism which sunders these links and assigns to ancient men a conceptual structure alien to ours may suppose that it has discovered a method which is scientific and which removes all problems of interpretation, whereas, in reality it erects a barrier to our understanding by making them into strange creatures. It is not the Freudian character of Dodds' exposition which interests me particularly, but his assumption that, in essential respects, the humanity of ancient men is the same as our own. This is an assumption which those who criticize so-called 'modernizing' do not grant and their lack of this kind of interest results in a defective treatment of the subject-matter. What has been called 'modernizing', far from being capricious or prejudiced, is a legitimate concern to achieve fullness of understanding. Hence, while the polemic may not be entirely misplaced and may be directed against real abuses, it should not be thought to have a general validity. There is a need to assume continuity between ancient and modern men and to adopt humanity as the common factor, rather than, by attaching such a strangeness of thought and belief to the ancients, to create an impression of discontinuity.

III

Dodds dissolves the claims of the prophets to have special access to the Divine into irrational human traits, abnormal psychological states, whereas Farrar gives an account of their inspiration which diminishes their humanity to vanishing point and makes them into puppets controlled by God. Farrar's analogy of poetic inspiration and prophetic inspiration is a well-trodden path, but his exposition has fresh features and is elegantly and originally expressed. The key word is 'divination' and it is used to enrich the analogy. The mode of divination of the poet is poetry and the great prophet (Jeremiah) 'sets images moving by musical incantation' (1948, p. 125). Some prophets used external phenomena as devices of divination, even the great prophets from time to time: 'Jeremiah himself divined from the chance sight of a budding almond, and of a boiling pot. But, for the most part, the great prophets used no such methods: they simply had their minds charged with the word of God. But, in that case, what happened? Is not the answer really obvious, that poetry itself was the method of divination?' (1948, p. 128).

The poet's inspiration is creative and he is a 'maker', whereas the prophet is 'controlled' by God and speaks 'the word of God' as his 'mouthpiece'. There is no human creativeness in his poetry; God is using his poetic gifts and his vocal chords in order to declare his Word. There is a 'felt inevitability' in what the prophet says 'like that of a rhapsodical poetry which allows for no second thoughts', since the utterance does not originate in his first thoughts (1948, p. 129): 'What the prophet shares with the latter-day poet, then, is the technique of inspiration chiefly: both move an incantation of images under a control. The controls are not the same and therefore the whole nature of the two utterances go widely apart; the poet is a maker, the prophet is a mouth-piece' (1948, p. 129). Again:

> The poet is a 'maker', whereas Jeremiah is not in any sense a 'maker'. He is not stretching this way and that the elastic possi-bilities of human nature. . . . His control tells him exactly what to say, for he is not responding to the quality of human life, he is responding to the demands of eternal will on Israel as they make themselves heard in the determinate situation where he stands. . . . For greatness we may turn to Jeremiah: and there is the greatness, but it is not a 'making'. (1948, pp. 126f)

Farrar has invested the prophet, including the canonical prophet, with a kind of ghostliness which is disconcerting and which obliterates his humanity. The language employed, the statement that God is the prophet's control, is jarring and unhappy. Nor does Farrar succeed in reinforcing the analogy between the inspiration of the poet and the inspiration of the prophet. What he does is to set up an antithesis between the creativeness of poetic inspiration and the external control to which the prophet is subject: the one is a creator, the other an automaton.

Dodds, having dispensed with the claims contained in the baggage of God-possession, uses the irrationality of the Greek prophets as a model for discussing human irrationality in general. He reduces the represen-tation that the prophet speaks with the voice of God, that he has been 'enthused', to an explanation founded on the assumption that the extra-ordinary phenomena of prophecy are the consequence of irrational and abnormal psychological states. Farrar seems to glory in the weirdness of the Old Testament prophets, including the canonical prophets, and to make a virtue out of dehumanizing them, as if the more incomprehen-sible they are made, the more they confirm the transcendantal truth of theism. The greater the emphasis that they are God-possessed and that their own wits have been ejected to make room for the Divine, the

greater the enhancing of the mystery. His concept of revelation is a raw
supernaturalism which matches his 'supernatural images' (see chapter
1). The supposition that theism is made irrefragable when the prophets
are made into God's speaking-boxes is sadly wrong and the analogy of
poetic inspiration and prophetic inspiration does not stave off this
conclusion. What this resort to quasi-magical expedients does is to
destroy the humanity of the canonical prophets, the stand which they
made and the anguish which they endured; the perceptiveness of their
theism and and fineness of their moral texture are demolished. The
bond between God and man is established by displaying these human
qualities, not by devaluing them and making the canonical prophets
into automata controlled by divine programming.

IV

A programme to describe ancient men in a 'scientific' way on the
assumption that their human constitution differs profoundly from our
own may not be compatible with the conditions which have to be met to
achieve the recovery of what is recorded about them in ancient documents. It will be found that if we cannot rely on empathy, on fellow-
feeling, or if its operation is so restricted that it is reduced to insignifi-
cance, it becomes doubtful whether the documents are accessible to our
understanding or whether there are barriers to comprehension which
cannot be overcome. If we no longer have an inner human affinity with
them, we lose a means of verifying the analysis which is being used to
interpret them.

This is an experience which I have when I confront Pedersen's
account of the ancient Israelites. They become creatures of another
world and the problem of understanding them, far from being simpli-
fied, is aggravated. If we do not have a suffcent human sympathy with
ancient men, questions are raised about the accessibility of the historical knowledge contained in ancient documents: whether there are any
criteria which can be confidently used to judge the truth or falsehood of
the statements about the psychological and mental make-up of the
ancients, if this is so different from our own. These statements are
founded on an interpretation of the documents, objectivity and scientific precision are claimed for them, but they have the effect of severing
essential links between the inner lives of the ancients and our own.

What then are the outlines of Pedersen's exposition, in so far as it
relates to our understanding of the thoughts, beliefs and psychological
mechanisms of the Hebrew prophets? According to Pedersen (1926,
pp. 99–181) emphasis should be laid on psychic power or strength of
soul, and, in this connection, he employs the idea of possession or
enthusiasm, already noted in Dodds' account of prophecy in a Greek

context. Pedersen incorporates the 'Shamanism' of Dodds by attributing mobility as well as strength to the soul. The soul of a prophet which
is God-filled proves that it is so by its psychic strength and effectiveness, but it also enjoys a mobility which enables it to operate in separation from the body, so that it overcomes the limits of its corporeal
habitation. This does not amount to a complete disengagement of soul
from body: it is the capacity of part of the soul to function outside the
body. Where a concept of enthusiasm is operative and the psycho-
somatic person is thought of as God-filled, there is no awareness or
concern about the limits placed on the soul by its corporeal vesture.
Such a differentiation of body and soul is beside the point in view of the
belief that divine power inspires the person and gives him a super-
human strength, or that it is the divine voice which comes to expression
through human speech organs.

Pedersen describes prophetic endowment as psychic power and this
concept has been widely appropriated. It has influenced the interpretation of the Old Testament prophets, including the canonical prophets.
Whatever the strong soul resolves will be implemented. Psychic power
channelled into affirmations and focused on objectives secures its
effects by the influence exercised on other souls involved in the out-
comes which are determined on. In that interior and hidden sphere of
interaction between souls, the shape of events is already latently fixed
and they are always an inevitable unfolding of realities formed in secret.
The true prophet is the one who is not mistaken in his estimate of the
power of his soul, and who, because he has a divinely empowered
psychological dynamism, can turn his inner determinations or his utterances into realities.

The first thing to be said about this is that any scholar who relies on
the texture of his own humanity to annihilate great distances of time
and space and to draw near to these ancient men will suffer a sense of
defeat when he reads Pedersen's account of the conceptuality of the Old
Testament prophets. If they are so utterly different from us as he
represents, the threat of irrecoverability looms large. This is masked by
Pedersen's confident style of description, but we should not be misled
by the guise of scientific coolness and matter-of-factness. We are being
denied an immediacy of identification with the canonical prophets and
are being presented with an account of their mentality, their psychological activity and power, which affects to be objective, but which
results in a deprivation not an enrichment of our understanding. The
question is whether these men as reconstructed by Pedersen are not so
strange that we suffer an insurmountable and final alienation from
them.

The second matter is that nothing in Pedersen's treatment of the
subject touches on the truth or falsehood of what the canonical prophets

said: there is no evaluation of the quality of their perceptiveness as theists or of the profundity of their moral insights. There is no material here which could be used to construct a theology of Old Testament prophecy and infallible effectiveness and success occupy a dangerous dominance in Pedersen's unfolding of the spiritual power of a prophet. He attaches to the canonical prophets a view of inspiration which robs them of their humanity and the whole trend of his exposition is towards dehumanization. They become creatures so strange that we have no human bonds with them. We may say that scholars like Kuenen and Robertson Smith were unaware of the issues which are raised for Old Testament interpretation by Pedersen's scientific anthropology and that the modernizing of which they are guilty is a consequence of this ignorance. The charge would underestimate the ideals of humane scholarship which moved these critical pioneers and Engnell's polemic lacks any fine appreciation of this. These older scholars assumed that the Old Testament prophetic literature was a repository of humane ideas and values. It would not have occurred to them that there might be such a chasm between our humanity and that of the canonical prophets as to invalidate the assumption that these prophets had the same concern for truth and the same ethical seriousness as they themselves possessed. Whatever errors of judgement they may have made in their efforts to establish a continuity between the canonical prophets and ourselves, the main thrust of their approach does not derive from a capricious and anachronistic modernizing of ancient men, but from the humane tradition in which they stood and from their concern to inform the study of the canonical prophets with the values of this scholarship.

V

To what extent are the Old Testament prophets to be understood on the model of the Greek prophet described by Dodds or as set out in a passage of Plato's *Ion*? Socrates is engaged in a dialogue with the rhapsodist Ion who is making the point that literary inspiration has characteristics similar to those of prophetic inspiration, but is different from it. In developing this opinion he gives an account of prophetic inspiration:

> For not by art do they utter these things, but by divine influence, since, if they had fully learnt by art to speak on one kind of theme, they would know how to speak on all. And for this reason God takes away the mind of men and uses them as his ministers, just as he does with soothsayers and godly seers in order that we who hear them may know that it is not they who utter these words of great

price, when they are out of their wits, but that it is God himself who speaks and addresses us through them. (Lamb, 1925, p. 425)

References to enthusiasm and evidences of magical belief are present in narratives of Israelite prophets who are earlier than the canonical prophets, and powers of clairvoyance, associated with the separation of the soul from the body, are attributed to them. This evidence has been collected by Lindblom in *Prophecy in Ancient Israel* (1962, pp. 47–104). Even if it were supposed that these passages contain a crude, popular view of the prophet as a wonder-worker, both benevolent and malevolent, and that we do not necessarily recover the historical Samuel, Saul, Elijah and Elisha, no apologetic capital should be made out of this.

Samuel is a seer (*rô'eh* who is consulted on the matter of lost asses (1 Sam. 10.9) and who receives a fee (1 Sam. 10.7). In virtue of his powers of clairvoyance he is able to assure Saul that the asses which had strayed will be found and that he will receive reassuring news when he meets two men at the tomb of Rachel (1 Sam. 10.2). When Saul sends a force to seize David at Ramah, it is infected with the prophetic ecstasy of Samuel and his band of prophets and the contagion of this enthusiasm frustrates all Saul's attempts to arrest David (1 Sam. 19.18–21).When Saul himself comes to Ramah, he too is overcome by prophetic ecstasy and is enthused (1 Sam. 19.22–24; cf. 10.10–12). These companies of prophets engage in exercises, and perhaps employ music and dancing, in order to induce ecstasy (1 Sam. 10.5) and prophets of Baal are represented as inflicting gashes on themselves in order to acquire the desired prophetic state (1 Kgs 18.28). The statement that when Saul is possessed by the spirit of Yahweh he 'becomes another man' (1 Sam. 10.6) recalls the reference to the God-possession which is associated with prophecy in the passage from *Ion* quoted above.

Visionary experience is ascribed to Micaiah who foresees pictorially coming disaster for Israel and who hears the voice of Yahweh within his vision (1 Kgs 22.15–17). Elisha discloses to his disciple a vision of a protecting ring of horses and chariots of fire which he only was able to descry (2 Kgs 6.15–17). Elijah has the power to put an end to drought by making rain (1 Kgs 18.41–45) and thereafter, with a supernatural speed and strength, he runs before Ahab's chariot to Jezreel (1 Kgs 18.46). He raises from the dead the son of the widow of Zarepath (1 Kgs 17.17–24) for whose needs he has made miraculous provision (1 Kgs 17.14–16).

Powers of clairvoyance are associated with Elisha: he can acquire information inaccessible to him by the normal channels of perception. When he reaches Hazael in a trance-like state, he looks into the future and foresees the havoc which this man will wreak on Israel (2 Kgs

8.11f). In one case this prophetic power is associated with the 'Shaman-ism' of Dodds' account, since it is Elisha's journeying soul, separated from the body, which keeps Gehazi under scrutiny (2 Kgs 25.6). It is to Elisha, in particular, that magical powers are assigned. He engages in a ritual of sympathetic magic with Jehoash, king of Israel (2 Kgs 13.14–19); he raises the head of an axe which had sunk into the Jordan (2 Kgs 6.1–7) and he curses small boys who jeer at his bald head (tonsure?). As a consequence forty-two of them are mauled by two she-bears (2 Kgs 2.23–25). Such is the power of the bones of the dead prophet that the corpse of a Moabite raider who comes into contact with them is raised to life (2 Kgs 13.21).

It is a mistake to try to ameliorate the crudeness of these represen-tations by detecting a form of piety which somehow makes magic less magical and more respectable. Lindblom appeals to 'a more personal mode of thought which counterbalanced and overcame the magical element' (1962, p. 54), but the circumstance that 'Yahweh himself stood behind the prophets and worked for them', so that 'their results were obtained not by mysterious impersonal forces alone but through prayer and personal intercession' (1962, p. 54) does not lead to the conclusion which he recommends. He produces examples of magical acts combined with prayer to Yahweh (2 Kgs 2.13f; 6.18ff), but these do not lift magic on to a higher plane; rather they demean Yahweh by associating him with such procedures.

This leads on to a further consideration whether the psychic power which Pedersen emphasizes so strongly in his portrayal of the prophet is appropriate with regard to the words spoken by the canonical prophets and the symbolic actions performed by them. It is urged, under the influence of Pedersen, that the prophetic word once spoken, or the symbolic act once performed, is possessed of such latent power and creativeness that the future to which reference is made in a prediction or which is represented in a symbolic action will necessarily ensue: 'The prophetic word was thought of as charged with energy and power. The prophetic word was an effective and creative word. Words which to a modern mind seem to be mere predictions were in fact creative words. In the thought of ancient Israel the spoken word was also a deed' (Lindblom, 1962, p. 51). Again: 'Because the prophets not only *foretold* calamities, but also *created* calamities, it was logical enough that they were both hated and feared' (1962, p. 120). On symbolic action or 'acted parables' Lindblom has this to say:

> It is *verbum visibile*, a visible word, and shares in all the qualities which distinguish the divine word. . . . As a divine word, the word uttered by a prophet had an effective power. The same is true of the visible word, the so-called symbolic action. Such an action

served not only to represent and make evident a particular fact, but also to make this fact a reality. In this respect the prophetic actions were akin to the magical actions which are familiar in the more primitive cultures throughout the world; and the use of such actions by the prophets is no doubt an inheritance from lower stages of cultural development. (1962, p. 172)

Lindblom draws back somewhat from this statement, but his *apologia* is just as ineffective as his attempt (already noted) to mitigate magic by an appeal to piety. He contends that there are significant differences between the symbolic action of an Old Testament prophet and primitive magic:

> The power of the magical action was dependent on the inner power connected with them and their performance in connection with definite magical laws; the power of the prophetic actions, like the power of the prophetic word, was derived from Yahweh's will. The prophetic actions were never directed to occasional and merely personal ends, but always served the main end of the activity of the prophets, the fulfilment of Yahweh's plans and purposes concerning Israel. (1962, p. 172)

In *Jeremiah i–xxv* (1986) I have noticed, in connection with a case of symbolic action, the smashing of an earthenware jug by the prophet (19.1–15; pp. 443–59), that the view represented by Lindblom has attracted scholarly support. This symbolic action, it is claimed, is not simply an acted parable of a coming judgement, but a pre-determination and creation of the judgement. That Jeremiah's action has connections with sympathetic magic is assumed by Rudolph and Weiser and the supposition of Weiser that magic becomes theologically respectable when it is commanded by God recalls the expedient to which Lindblom resorted. Instead of raising the prophet above magic this makes Yahweh into a chief magician.

The connections of the prophetic word with power are also explored by A. R. Johnson in *The Cultic Prophet in Ancient Israel* (1944, 1962²). He finds in passages from the prophetic literature evidences of 'that primitive and widespread conception of the power of the spoken word which lies behind so many magical practices'. He continues: 'In fact, it is wholly in line with those magical ideas which have been rightly recognized as lying behind their so-called symbolism' (1962, p. 36). Von Rad, for his part, remarks that 'it would be an unhappy state of affairs if we had to try to make excuses for the language of the prophets, because traces of a magical use of "the word" are still to be found in it' (ii, 1965, p. 82) and he refers to the 'word of power' in 'old Babylonia and old Egypt' (1965, p. 91). His interpretation of symbolic action appears in the following: 'The symbol was a creative prefiguration of the future, which would be speedily and inevitably realised. When the prophet, by means of a symbolic act, projects a detail of the future into the present, this begins the process of realisation, and on that account the prophetic symbolic act is simply an intensified form of prophetic speech' (1965, p. 96).

Attention has been focused on these particular applications of the concept of prophetic power, because they bear crucially on the question which was asked in the title of this chapter: What kind of men were the canonical prophets from Amos to Jeremiah? If they entertained such magical views about the words which they spoke and the symbolic acts which they performed as is alleged, they have been significantly disengaged from the pattern of humane thinking which some of us supposed that we shared with them, and resort to them for a contribution to theistic truth and ethical elevation has been, more or less, put out of court. This consequence is not generally recognized or acknowledged. For example, Lindblom describes the message of the canonical prophets in these terms:

> To Amos and his successors the existence of Yahweh's people was at stake. The covenant between Israel and Yahweh was broken or was about to be broken. In sinfulness and unbelief Israel had turned away from her God. Now the task of the prophets was to arouse, rebuke, call to repentance, warn and threaten with the judgement of Yahweh, and to promise a turn of fortune in a coming age, on the condition that there were some who realised the holy will of Yahweh. (1962, p. 217)

A prophet who, when he predicts judgement is also creating it cannot be described as threatening judgement and even less as arousing, rebuking and calling to repentance. If the canonical prophets held the quasi-magical belief about the power of their words and actions attributed to them, predictions of judgement are a complete foreclosure and do not leave any room for a response to a plea for repentance which would change the course of the future. There can be no element of appeal in a prophecy of judgement and nothing which a prophet can require, if every possibility of change and amelioration has been removed once the fateful word has been spoken or the symbolic action performed.

Here then is an important respect in which a gulf has been set between our humanity and the canonical prophets and they assume the appearance of such strange beings that the affinity which we supposed ourselves to have with them is dissolved. If this conclusion is a consequence of scholarship, it must be accepted, but all that is involved in affirming it should be grasped. What cannot be accepted is the inner contradiction which is created. The result is a puzzling portrayal, a confusion, an account of them which does not hang together, and our confidence that we understood what kind of men they were is destroyed. The content of the prophetic literature indicates that they discerned profound theistic truth and that their concern for their community, allied to an extraordinary moral perceptiveness, amount to anguish, but this cannot be reconciled with the quasi-magical use of language and of symbolic action which is attached to them and the outcome of this forced marriage is a quandary. The canonical prophets have been dehumanized and we ask ourselves whether we have been deceived in our estimate of the contents of the prophetic literature.

This could be dismissed as no more than a *cri de coeur* that biblical science has reached results which disastrously devalue the theological and ethical significance of the canonical prophets. It may be urged that once the disappointment has worn off, we shall reconcile ourselves to the hard facts. We have misread the prophetic literature when we identifed ourselves so completely with it as to discover in it a search for truth and a humaneness of moral disposition which we could take with the utmost seriousness.The canonical prophets do not conform to the contours of our humanity in the way we had supposed and our grasp on them has slackened. We are much less sure that we have the qualities of human understanding and empathy which only our fellowship with them could bestow. Science, if it is science, has won a victory at the expense of humanist scholarship.

But these particular applications of prophetic power are, at least partly, founded on a lexicographical fallacy which Barr has exposed in his book *The Semantics of Biblical Language* (1961) and the Hebrew word *dābār* meaning 'word', 'thing' or 'event' is one of his examples (pp. 129–40). The nature of the fallacy is illustrated by Lindblom: 'Words which to a modern mind seem to be mere predictions were in fact creative words. In the thought of ancient Israel the spoken word was also a deed. The Hebrew word *dābār* often does duty for action as well as for word' (1962, p. 51). What is intended by 'does duty for'? Is it 'double duty'? Is Lindblom saying that in a particular context *dābār* means both 'word' and 'thing'? It is here that the fallacy lurks, because the alleged compound meaning (word- thing- event), the so-called 'word-concept', consists of the range of senses attributed to *dābār* in a dictionary. The dictionary, however, is indicating not 'word', 'thing' and 'event' as a compound meaning of *dābār*, but 'word' *or* 'thing' *or* 'event': different senses which it has *in different contexts*. In any particular context it has only *one* of these senses.

It is arguable that an author might play deliberately on these different senses of *dābār*, and that in an odd case there is ground for positing a calculated ambivalence. This is a marginal consideration and it does not significantly blunt the argument which is being conducted. What is neglected by whose who make 'word-concepts' out of a range of dictionary meanings is that, for the most part, these are mutually exclusive and that their usefulness would be greatly diminished if they were not. It is this characteristic which makes them serve as guide-lines to a translator turning Hebrew into English and searching for the English word which will capture the fine shade of meaning of the Hebrew in a particular context. The important lexicographical consideration is always to attend to the syntactical enclosure and to the context in which *dābār* occurs. It will be found that the only sense which it has is the one that gives the right translation and that a choice will have to made between 'word', 'thing' or 'event'. It is not accidental that the fashion of word-concepts has brought about the neglect of translation and exegesis. The importance of discovering the precise nuance which a word has in the semantic context where it appears is neglected and a new kind of interpretation has been substituted for an exegesis which was built on the foundation of a translation. A 'word-concept', fallaciously constructed, is superimposed on a passage and determines its meaning.

This is sometimes accompanied by the assertion that Hebrew words, which have been elaborated into concepts, are untranslatable. Such is the difference between the conceptuality of the Old Testament writers and ourselves that we can recover their mentality only after essays have been written on Hebrew words. This is another expression of the tendency to exaggerate the gulf between ourselves and the ancients. It is a serious question whether this assumption, if it were true, would not prove too much. The distance between us and them is so magnified that their mental processes become irrecoverable. We are already doing this when we say that some biblical Hebrew words are untranslatable, because the ability to translate is an acid test whether or not the foundations of intelligibility can be laid.

What is described above may be seen at work in Lindblom who says of the occurrences of *dābār*: 'There are many examples of creative words in the miracle narratives related above' (1962, p. 51). The passages in question are these. At 1 Kgs 13.32 it is said that the *dābār* proclaimed by the 'man of God' against the altar at Bethel and all the hill-shrines of Samaria will be fulfilled. The statement that a prediction will be fulfilled should not be turned into an affirmation that the prediction created the eventuation. This is what Lindblom is doing. At 1 Kgs 18.10ff Elijah delivers a word of Yahweh to a widow in which he announces that miraculous provision will be made for her needs, but there is no exegetical ground for concluding that the announcement created the miraculous provision. One could go one, but of the remaining passages collected by Lindblom (2 Kgs 1.10; 2.8, 14; 4.4ff, 40f, 42ff; 5.27; 6.5ff, 18; 13.14ff, 21), only 2 Kgs 1.10, which is a kind of curse, demands the exegetical conclusion that it is intended to create the reality to which it refers: 'If I am a man of God, may fire fall from heaven and consume you and your company.' It is indicated that the effect was immediate. In the other examples which are cited there is a strange neglect of the actual semantic content in Lindblom's handling of them, because a 'word-concept' of *dābār* is being superimposed to determine their meaning.

Von Rad says with regard to Jeremiah and Ezekiel: 'The reason why these men were hated and feared was this power inherent in their word. Their power to bring about disaster and the possibility that they might do so' (1965, ii, p. 91). He cites Jer. 5.14, a response by Jeremiah to the denial of the efficacy of Yahweh's word which I have rendered: 'Therefore this is the word of Yahweh, God of Sabaoth (to me): Because they speak this word, I shall make my word like fire in your mouth; this people will be the fuel and the fire will consume them' (1986, p. 120). A similar passage cited by von Rad (Jer. 23.29) is translated by me as: 'Is not my word like fire, says Yahweh, and like a hammer which splits rocks' (1986, p. 588). There is no doubt that these passages refer to the power of Yahweh's *dābār*, but there is nothing in the semantic content of *dābār* which is not satisfied by the conclusion that the power consists in a certainty that the judgement which has been predicted will be fulfilled, rather than in a quasi-magical *dābār* which 'creates' or 'objectifies' or 'realizes' the eventuation of judgement once it has been uttered.

VI

A second lexicographical enquiry relates particularly to the symbolic actions or the acted parables which appear in the prophetic literature and it focuses on the Hebrew word *māšāl*. At Jer. 19 (McKane, 1986, pp. 443–59) the significance of the shattering of an earthenware jar by Jeremiah is explained to him in a word of Yahweh: 'I shall shatter this people and this city as one shatters an earthenware jar so that it is beyond repair' (19.11). The shattering of the jar is a dramatic prediction of judgement, but there is nothing in the Hebrew text which requires the conclusion that it is more than an acted parable. The action of shattering and irreparably damaging the jar constitutes a 'similitude' of the destructive judgement which will ensue and is a memorable device for predicting it. The supposition that it is a magical procedure which has the power to make the judgement ineluctable, to bring it into existence, once it has been acted, has been superimposed on the text. The two interpretations are related to differing lexicographies of *māšāl*, the one 'likeness' or 'similitude' and the other 'sovereign word' or the like. The issue is whether the symbolic action of the prophet is a *māšāl* because it predicts a future judgement by acting out a similitude or parable of it, or whether it is a display of prophetic power which seals the doom of Jerusalem by making its destruction inevitable, by creating it as a reality.

The same question has been raised about the sense of *māšāl* 'proverb', 'parable' in the wisdom literature. The fundamental question is whether *māšāl* is to be derived from *mšl* 'to be like' or *mšl* 'to rule'. Eissfeldt (1913, pp. 6ff; also A. R. Johnson, 1955, p. 161) preferred the former and Bentzen (1952², pp. 167ff) and others the latter. Godbey attempted to combine the two (1922/23, p. 90). The meaning 'to rule' is confined to Hebrew and is not attested in the other Semitic languages (Aramaic, Syriac, Arabic, Accadian, Ethiopic). J. Schmidt (1936, p. 1ff) appealed to Arabic usage for the meaning 'to stand' and noted that *mṭl* in Arabic means 'to stand' and 'to cause to stand'. But when the semantic range of *mṭl* in Arabic is surveyed the meanings which are characteristic are related to 'be like' and not 'stand'. Further the sense 'to stand' is connected only with the verb and there is no evidence that *maṭal* had a meaning related to 'stand'. The attested occurrences of *maṭal* point to 'resemblance', 'similitude', 'model', 'illustration', 'example' (McKane, 1970, pp. 22–33).

The question appears to be decided for Bentzen by *a priori* considerations concerning the power of the prophetic word. A general observation to do with culture and belief in the ancient world is thought to establish a connection between *māšāl* and *mšl* 'to rule'. Even if it were true that the words of seers and poets were thought to have a magic potency, this is not a linguistic argument bearing on *māšāl* in particular and it is not clear that the verb *māšāl* 'to rule' is related to this. In so far as there is evidence of a semantic connection between *mšl* 'to rule' and *mšl* 'to be like' it comes from Arabic, but it is exiguous. It may show that the idea of perfection or excellence in *mṭl* is a development from 'exemplar' or 'model': *al-amāṭil* 'the leading men' are model or representative figures in the community. *mumaṭṭil* is the word in modern Arabic for the diplomatic representative of a state. In so far as this contains any indications, it suggests that 'to be like' is more primary than 'to rule'. It may be a mistaken enterprise to try to establish a semantic relationship between the two meanings. It is perhaps better to be content with a review of the field of usage and to say that 'to rule' is confined to Hebrew, whereas 'to be like' is distributed throughout the Semitic languages and that there is no evidence, either in Hebrew or the other Semitic languages, that *māšāl* has any connection with the meaning 'to rule'.

To sum up: we are being presented with a construction of prophetic power, applied to words and actions, which affects our over-all understanding of the endowment and vocation of the canonical prophets. It should be acknowledged that there is great difficulty in attaining certainty about how the canonical prophets understood their office and in ascertaining what were their intentions and beliefs, and there will be more about this. For the time being, it will be enough if I paraphrase what I have said elsewhere about the quasi-magical view of prophetic power. It shifts the centre of significance from the semantic content of the prophetic words to an extra-semantic aspect of wonder-working power. The opinion may be ventured that this shift is disastrous. It is the quality and profundity of the prophetic utterance, its piercing theistic vision, its exceptional moral discernment and the anguish with which it is touched (for prophets do not arrive at the truth without suffering for it), which make it a word of God. The canonical prophets are not spell-binders or practitioners of sympathetic magic (1986, p. 459).

Literature for Chapter 6 is listed at p. 153.

7

THE CANONICAL PROPHETS: WHAT KIND OF MEN WERE THEY? (II)

I

Both Gunkel and Lindblom describe and explain the extraordinary psychological phenomena associated with the canonical prophets. We can be confident that Gunkel does not intend to harness these psychological states to a theology of prophecy which presupposes a supernatural communication of truth to the prophet. He uses the term 'revelation' (*Offenbarung*), but it has a general, historical character and does not function in the context of 'special revelation' with which 'inspiration' and 'revelation' have usually been associated (Klatt, 1969, p. 76). Gunkel, as noted in the last chapter, finds a diminution of ecstasy in the canonical prophets over against the earlier Israelite prophets, but his aim is to set all ancient prophecy in a mould of ecstasy and, in this respect he uses the same framework of interpretation as Lindblom:

> There has been ecstasy as long as men have lived on the earth and it still exists in our midst. The forms in other peoples and cultures may be more striking than those described above [that is, those in Israel], but the matter is finally always the same. Religion is preeminently the sphere of ecstasy: religious thoughts and moods seize hold of men with a power in relation to which all other intellectual powers seem insignificant. (1917, p. 5)

For the canonical prophets this has to be balanced against the following: 'The essential aspect of this high point of prophecy is that a religious and moral content is bound up with it. The more this is so, the more the ecstatic has receded into the background, but it never disappears' (1917, p. 29).

This fading of ecstasy is connected particularly with the decreasing mention of visionary experience in the prophetic literature from Amos to Jeremiah and in the dominance of the representation that Yahweh speaks to his prophets ('These are the words of Yahweh' and the like). 'Word' is the medium of revelation (cf. Mowinckel, 1934, pp. 199ff) and Gunkel correlates this with an enrichment of content:

> It is significant that the literary prophets (less so Ezekiel and Zechariah) lay more emphasis on what is heard than on what is

seen. Moreover, 'word' predominates over 'vision' in the prophetic books. These prophets lay all the weight on the thoughts which they received and wish to communicate, not on the wonderful experiences by which they came to them. Thoughts are more easily and simply represented in the form of words which are heard than in a picture which is seen. The prophets are still visionaries, but they are in the process of leaving visions behind. (1917, p. 16)

The tension in Gunkel's account of the canonical prophets is created by a combination of factors: on the one hand, he is opposed to an interpretation which is monopolized by rationality, and, on the other, he has an appreciation that the appearance of Amos is a watershed: 'The literary prophets, of whom Amos was the first, have, through the greatness of their thought, put all that preceded them into the shade' (1917, p. 10) has to be balanced against 'They [the literary prophets] are understood badly if they are explained as rationalists. The style of the prophetic writings is, in large part, to be explained as a consequence of their ecstatic experiences' (1917, p. 11). Guided by the latter of these two indications we might conclude that the ecstatic state is significant only in determining the form of the prophetic expression, whether the accounts of visionary experiences or the prophetic oracles prefaced with 'These are the words of Yahweh' or the like, and that it exercises no influence on the quality of the content of the prophetic literature. In that case there is no relationship between their extraordinary psychological states and the theistic and ethical contributions which these prophets make through their literature.

Such a conclusion would underestimate the value which Gunkel attaches to ecstasy as a 'revelatory state' (cf. Lindblom, below), though 'revelatory state' has to be interpreted in a manner consistent with his account of 'revelation' (see above, p. 115) which has no implications of supernatural communication from God to the prophet. Ecstasy is defined as a psychological condition in which an intense concentration produces exceptional theistic and ethical insights, and so the products of the prophetic literature are not to be explained as the result of normal processes of ratiocination. Even when ecstatic phenomena have retired into the background and the canonical prophets reveal their thoughts rather than their psychological states, the ecstasy remains a factor which affects the content (1917, p. 31): 'The proper value of prophecy is not in the esctatic form but in its enduring content, in the great divine thoughts which were unfolded' (1917, p. 31). Yet: 'Such strange psychological conditions can be the manifestations of a deep religious understanding, of great power and high originality' (1917, p. 30). Seized by such states the canonical prophets discern an order of truth which is inaccessible to normal processes of reasoning. There is evidence of deliberation and a tendency to supply reason for attitudes which have been struck (1917, p. 29) and yet, 'The prophet is always full of a passion which overflows, full of a powerful anger or a burning enthusiasm. His spiritual roots penetrate depths to which no thinking (*Denken*) can reach' (1917, p. 29).

This 'revelatory state', which can be identified with ecstasy, is consistent with Gunkel's concept of 'revelation' (*Offenbarung*) and is not an appeal to the 'supernatural'. It is a psychological condition and nothing but a psychological condition and there is no claim that a prophet is 'inspired' in the sense which is intended when God is said to 'enthuse' a prophet, thereby filling him with supernatural truth. This theological combination of 'revelation' and 'inspiration' has been jettisoned by Gunkel. Hence he is dissociating himself from the explanation of prophetic experience given by the canonical prophets themselves and he is aware that he is doing this. The canonical prophets affirm that they have had a special encounter with Yahweh and that the words which they preface with 'These are the words of Yahweh' have been given to them directly by God. The prophetic endowment, Gunkel writes, 'is so represented that it excludes all human participation' (1917, p. 11; cf. p. 29): 'Whoever, therefore, is aware of this has the question posed to him whether he will believe their first words ["These are the words of Yahweh"] or not. If he believes such an affirmation, what follows is divine revelation; if he declines to believe, it is purely human composition' (1917, p. 11).

II

The phrase 'revelatory state', which I have interpreted above, is used by Lindblom:

> Typical of the revelatory state of mind is the feeling of being under an influence external to the self, a divine power, the consciousness of hearing words and seeing visions which do not come from the self, but from the invisible, divine world, into which, in the moment of revelation, an entrance has been granted. The feeling of being subject to an external influence is perhaps the most constant element in the revelatory state of mind. (1962, p. 173)

If we are guided by Lindblom's own statements, we should not conclude that it is his intention to make an affirmation about the God-given truth ('revealed truth') of what a canonical prophet utters in a 'revelatory state'. The detail of his exposition has to be judged in the light of his definition of the limits of his enterprise: 'I have tried to describe prophecy in ancient Israel from the psychological and social points of view. I have confined myself to describing the phenomena and have abstained from attempting either a supernatural or psycho-analytical explanation of them' (1962, p. 219). Again:

> The religious man who recognizes in the God of the prophets his own God says that the revelations of the true prophets emanated from God. They are products of true divine inspiration arising from the mysterious contact with the living God which the prophets experienced. But an analysis of the contact of a religious man with God cannot be carried through by scientific methods. The supernatural mystery of the religious experiences of the prophets is concealed from us and inaccessible to scientific enquiry. (1962, p. 219)

The implication of this is that Lindblom's phrase 'revelatory state' does not make a supernatural claim for the canonical prophets, though it establishes that they make such a claim for themselves and describes the psychological state out of which this arises. We have to interpret the following with this in mind: Lindblom is doing no more than to reproduce the claims which ecstatics give of their own experiences and to affirm their reality *qua* experiences: 'God can speak to men during a state of ecstasy as well as during a state of prayer. It is a fact that men whose awareness of the external world is temporarily inhibited can have religious experiences and receive divine revelations and spiritual impulses which by far surpass what can be given in a normal state of mind' (1962, p. 106).

The question which is raised, however, is whether Lindblom succeeds in isolating a theology of prophecy from his descriptions of psychological phenomena and this difficulty is connected with his assumption that the literary deposits which are available for our inspection can be treated largely as transcripts of inner prophetic experiences or equated with abnormal states of consciousness. The same problem is present in Gunkel who is also assured that literary accounts of visionary experiences, or the the prefacing of oracles with 'These are the words of Yahweh' or the like, enable us to make deductions about the theological convictions of the canonical prophets, that is, the claim to have access to supernatural truth which they make.

The issue is then not Gunkel's own theological position, which we know and which has been described, or Lindbom's own theological position, which, he tells us, is beyond his analysis, but the kind of supernatural belief which is attached by both scholars to the canonical prophets through their reliance on the forms of prophetic literature to give them access to the psychological phenomena of the 'revelatory state'. Lindblom chides scholars 'who are content to inquire how the prophets *themselves* regarded their visions' and who are 'neglecting the task of studying the visions scientifically in the proper sense of the word, i.e., objectively, in the light of the history and psychology of religion' (1962, p. 124), but the more fundamental question is whether it is legitimate to extract information about visionary experience or abnormal psychological states from the prophetic literature in the ways Gunkel and Lindblom do. To what degree are these transcripts of prophetic experience rather than a metamorphosis of it guided by literary conventions?

What Lindblom has to say about ecstasy in connection with the canonical prophets recalls Gunkel, and he too is convinced that an unwillingness to come to terms with evidences of the ecstatic state in them is influenced by a fear that their rationality may be compromised: 'The attempt to minimize the supernormal experiences of the great prophets arises from a desire to defend the genuine religious and moral elements in the religion of these prophets' (1962, p. 106). The canonical prophets are characterized by 'inspiration, the extreme form of which is ecstasy' (1962, p. 423; cf. pp. 173f). In view of Lindblom's definition noted above, 'inspiration' must be taken in a psychological not a theological sense and 'prophetic revelations' must be understood, not as Lindblom's own theological evaluation, but as a statement about what the prophets believed concerning the words which they spoke. This ecstasy, which is associated by Lindblom with inspiration, is named 'concentration ecstasy'; it denotes 'a mental state in which human consciousness is so concentrated on a particular idea or feeling that the normal current of thoughts and perceptions is broken off and the senses temporarily cease to function in a normal way' (1962, p. 106).

The thought that the prophetic state of consciousness is marked by a narrow focusing on brilliant points of insight, and that it is abnormal in its intensity, is a useful contribution to our understanding of the canonical prophets. It complements the approach which seizes on the anguish of the prophet, the pain of his involvement with his community and the truth which he grasps through his human suffering. But it is a far cry from this to the following conclusions: 'Thus the true prophets are conscious of being the mouthpieces of Yahweh and nothing else. They are nothing but channels for the stream of revelation. What they have to bring forth are not their own words (they would be worthless), but only the precious divine word which has been put in their mouth' (1962, p. 114). This is a view of the supernatural belief of the canonical prophets which should not be founded on the formula 'These are the words of Yahweh' or on any other features of the prophetic literature. On visionary experience accompanied by auditions Lindblom has this to say:

> By 'vision' and 'audition' we understand visual and auditory perceptions received in trance or ecstasy, or in a mental state approxi-

mating thereto. These perceptions are not caused by any object in the external world, but arise within the soul [cf. Maimonides]. He who sees and hears often says that he sees with his 'inward eye' and hears by his 'inward ear'. What appears to him is not the external world, but the invisible, the divine world, the doors of which are closed to everyday consciousness, but are open to men who are in 'the supernatural state of mind', in the holy hours when it pleases God to reveal his secrets to human beings. (1962, pp. 122f)

I again assume that Lindblom is not making any theological evaluation of these experiences and that he is affirming no more than that they are subjectively or inwardly real to those who have them. He is asserting that those who, in a state of ecstasy, see visions and hear God speaking to them are convinced that they are the subjects of special revelation. Lindblom is also establishing the same relation as Gunkel between ecstasy and a particular disposition to grasp religious truth, even it he ends up rather inconsequentially with the words: 'The value of religious preaching is not dependent on the psychological conditions associated with it, but on its content' (1962, pp. 106f).

III

The bone which I have to pick with Gunkel and Lindblom is their assumption that literary accounts of visionary experiences serve as a basis for a detailed reconstruction of these experiences. Schökel's attitude is strikingly different, because he shows the greatest reserve in using prophetic literature to recover the details of the visionary experiences of the canonical prophets or, otherwise, to reconstruct the contours of their ecstatic states. The barricades which block the way taken by Gunkel and Lindblom are formidable, even on the assumptions which most favour their enterprise. For, example, if it is allowed that the prophets (Isaiah, chapter 6) and Jeremiah (chapter 1) recorded their call visions, it is, nevertheless, evident that the writing-down of the experience, which involves recollection, is distinguishable from the experience itself. It is probable that their esctatic states had passed before the processes of recall and writing-down were undertaken and that there are elements of literary shaping in the account which was given. It is not clear that the right point of departure is to assume that a perfect recollection of all the details of a vision is embedded in a literary record of it. Schökel's tendency is to assume that there is an inchoateness which is unresolved until the literary account is fashioned. He is influenced by the general analogy of literary creativeness in his approach to the prophetic literature.

I have picked on the call narrative because both Gunkel and Lindblom refer particularly to them. On the call narratives of Isaiah, Jeremiah and Ezekiel Lindblom writes:

> 'If we have to do with a vision of an ecstatic character which contains auditory perceptions, these perceptions must be judged as ecstatic auditions. Nobody can be doubtful about the ecstatic nature of the inaugural vision of Isaiah. The visual elements are predominant, but there are several auditory perceptions, too. . . . The same is true of the initial visions of Jeremiah and Ezekiel. Auditory elements are mingled with visual elements. (1962, p. 135; cf. pp. 55f)

Gunkel, who emphasizes that visionary experience diminishes in significance with prophets like Isaiah and Jeremiah, nevertheless assigns an ecstatic foundation (*Grundlage*) to the call narratives of these prophets: 'The call as an ecstatic foundation should not be undervalued, even in the case of prophets whose stance is most elevated. Out of such experiences they derive the certainty of their deepest convictions. Such strange psychic conditions can be the manifestations of a deep religious understanding of great power and high originality' (1917, p. 30). Both Gunkel and Lindblom are assuming that, in connection with their calls, these prophets, in ecstasy, had heavenly visions and heard Yahweh speaking to them, presumably in Hebrew. This reconstruction presupposes that the literary account is a perfect recall of an ecstatic experience and that there are no details in the literary account which did not have correspondences in the ecstatic experience. There is, however, the interesting case of Isa. 21 with which both Gunkel and Lindblom deal:

> The second phase of the vision contains a feature of the greatest interest to the student of prophetic psychology. The watchman whom the prophet was ordered to station is not '*a* watchman' but '*the* watchman'. It has been questioned who this watchman was. In the light of modern psychology the watchman is identical with the visionary himself when he was transported into the other world. The prophet distinguishes between himself as ordinary man and himself when rapt away. The rapt personality is observed and spoken of by the prophet in his normal state of mind as if this rapt personality were quite another person. (1962, pp. 129f)

Whether *hmsph* (with the definite article) is correctly translated 'the watchman' (v. 6; cf. NEB, REB, 'a watchman') is a matter which can be left aside, but the implication of Lindblom's elucidation is that the 'normal state' of mind in which the prophet records his vision sets the literary account at a remove from the vision experienced in a state of ecstasy. So the prophet is self-possessed when he records what he experienced in ecstasy and this normality affects the literary shape which he gives to his vision. Once such a remove of literary version from ecstatic vision has been conceded, it becomes a matter of judgement how wide that remove should be. Gunkel discusses the same passage (1917, pp. 19–23) and remarks: 'A piece such as this has so consummate and artistic a form that it is not to be regarded as a transcript of a psychological reality. Nevertheless, one can attain to a conception of the inner life of the prophet from such a poetic flourish of prophecy' (1917, p. 23). The crucial question is whether deductions about prophetic experience should be made from prophetic literature.

IV

Up till now I have conducted the discussion about the call narratives of Isaiah and Jeremiah in the climate most favourable to the assumptions which are made by Gunkel and Lindblom. The evidences of common elements or stereotypes in the call narratives require consideration, and the effect of giving weight to these is to lessen the connection between the literary versions and the ecstatic experiences of individual prophets, or, at least to deter us from positing a precise correspondence between these experiences and the literary versions of them which are fashioned. I have gone into this elsewhere (1986, pp. 6–14) and I have expressed the view that the contents of the Jeremiah call narrative are more properly related to the final shape of the Jeremianic *corpus* than they are to the historical prophet Jeremiah. They are not connected with him in an immediate biographical way as a transcript of an ecstatic experience which constituted his call. Rather they contain stereotypes, for example, that of 'reluctance', which also occurs in the narrative of the call of Moses (Exod. 4) and in that of Isaiah (Isa. 6), and there is a pronounced *ex eventu* orientation of the narrative. It is controlled by a knowledge of the outcome of Jeremiah's career and the final shape of the Jeremianic *corpus*.

As another demonstration of the difficulty of reaching assured results on these matters, and of the dangers involved in drawing psychological conclusions from literary accounts, I consider the different interpretations of Jer. 1.11–16 which are offered by Gunkel, Lindblom and Schökel, especially vv. 11–12. For Lindblom these are 'symbolic perceptions' and he does not suppose that their initial reception by the prophet is to be enclosed in a trance-like experience or is to be attributed to a state of ecstasy: 'One day when Jeremiah was walking in a field he noticed the twig of an almond tree which captured his attention' (1962, p. 139). Again: 'The common sight of the wind blowing from the north upon a cauldron standing on its hearth was a fact from which the prophet drew a significant omen' (1962, p. 140). In both these cases

Lindblom begins at the level of an ordinary sense perception, but he then supposes an access of ecstasy in association with which the deeper significance of what has been seen is grasped, so that it acquires the form of a vision within which the prophet converses with Yahweh. This is a movement from a 'normal state' of mind to an ecstatic state – a reversing of the order which Lindblom postulated at Isa. 21.6–10. Moreover, it is the condition of ecstasy and not the normal state of mind which generates the literary version. In a prophetic reverie Jeremiah pondered over what he had seen: 'The whole had for the prophet the character of a revelation. The everyday observation was sublimated, carried over into the divine and supernatural sphere' (1962, p. 139). Since I accept Lindblom's statement that he is not making theological affirmations, I conclude that he is undertaking to recover Jeremiah's own evaluation of his experience. What should be particularly noticed for the present is that sense impressions are held to have been transformed under the influence of a 'revelatory state' and that the literary account is said to be a transcript of the content of this 'revelatory state'.

Gunkel, on the other hand, would seem to enclose passages like Amos chapters 7 and 8, and Jer. 1.11–12, entirely within the framework of a visionary experience. Of these passages he remarks (1917, pp. 15–17) that the basket of summer fruit and the almond twig are symbols of divine thoughts and that they are especially significant combinations of seeing and hearing:

> The prophet sees what is shadowy and mysterious, and the strong urge which he feels to penetrate the mystery sounds in his ears as 'What is that?' He recognizes what he sees and answers, 'A basket of ripe summer fruit' (Amos 8.2). Now he appropriates the divine word anew – the word which explains the significance of the vision: 'The time is ripe for my people Israel.' Such a vision is derived in the following manner. The fearful thought of a 'harvest' for Israel has haunted the prophet for so long, waking and sleeping, that it materializes in a vision of a basket of fruit without any conscious effort on his part. Astonished by the image which suddenly appears to him, he retraces with conscious thought the same way which he had previously unconsciously traversed and so finds the right interpretation.

Gunkel holds that the same kind of elucidation is to be applied to Jer. 1.11–12.

Gunkel's explanation is more elaborate than that of Lindblom, but they agree in important respects. Gunkel does not make a beginning with ordinary sense impressions; he enfolds the whole transaction within a visionary experience which contains auditory elements. But he then inserts an additional stage, as compared with Lindblom, by assuming that between the contents of the ecstatic vision and the literary record there is a detailed recall of these contents by the prophet after he has returned to a 'normal state' and that this is the source of the literary record. Both Lindblom and Gunkel are, however, making the same major assumption that the literary account derives from the experiences of a 'revelatory state' and is, more or less, a transcript of these experiences.

V

With Schökel the field of interpretation is a different one. There is a concentration on the prophetic literature and an unwillingness to speculate about the relation of literary accounts to psychological states: to make a detailed map of these on the foundation of the forms of the literature. How this economy and reserve work can be seen in connection with Jer. 1.11–16, where Schökel avoids completely the area of psychological speculation pursued by Gunkel and Lindblom and employs only two elements in his interpretation: sense impressions which made a powerful impact on the prophet Jeremiah and borrowed literary forms which he used to clothe his insights. On the insight generated by the almond twig Schökel has this to say:

> One morning just before Spring, a prophet was walking in the countryside and suddenly came upon a tree already in flower. The sight of it suggested its name, and the prophet said it aloud. As he pronounced the word, its obvious etymology came into his mind: the almond tree has a name in Hebrew which is derived from the word 'to watch', because it seems to be so anxiously on the watch for Spring and ready to flower early: the 'watching tree' – 'God on the watch' (*maqqel shaqed – Yahweh shoqed*). The name of the tree resounds with the echoes of a higher reality: God watching in history to make good His word. The spark of intuition contained a transcendent analogy. (1967, p. 194)

If the interpretation of the intuition as a 'transcendent analogy' and an appropriation of revealed truth is set aside for the time being, interest may be focused on the economy of the intuition: it is a point of brilliant illumination which is captured in a few words. The subsequent clothing of it in literary dress is, according to Schökel, a secondary work of craftsmanship. The model was available in Amos chapters 7 and 8: 'Jeremiah recognized the insight as a message from God, and set to work to transform it into a communicable form. For this purpose he enlisted the aid of a device already known since the time of Amos and perhaps even topical in prophetic utterances' (1967, p. 194). Schökel continues: 'As we have constructed it, the inspired process begins with a flash of insight, is followed by a movement or impulse to write, and finally is completed by the exercise of the writer's craft. The last step could hardly be called creative in this instance (Jer. 1.11–16) since it consists in "refilling" a used formula' (1967, p. 195).

The walk in the countryside is an invention of Schökel (1967, p. 196), but the most significant trend in his interpretation is his statement that 'there is no need to have recourse to extraordinary visions when we know, for instance, that Jeremiah received an oracle while watching a potter at work (18.1ff) and when here is an example of something as homespun as a boiling pot about to tip over (1.13ff), we need not imagine a preternatural occurrence' (1967, p. 196). The differences between Schökel's approach and that of Gunkel and Lindblom are clear-cut. In the first place no visionary experience is assumed, but, even if it had been, the scope of the revelatory disclosure does not correspond materially with the form of the literary presentation. If the 'inspiration' and 'revelation' had been set in the context of a visionary experience, but had consisted only of *maqqel shaqed* – *Yahweh shoqed*, it would have provided no justification for the reconstruction of an ecstatic experience containing the arrangement of visual and auditory elements which are in the literary account.

On the other hand, Schökel holds that the etymological pun (*shaqed* – *shoqed*), which he terms an 'intuition', is transformed into a 'transcendent analogy'. He is supposing as the Vulgate (*virgam vigilantem*) and a long line of scholars have done that *shaqed* has the semantic content 'wakeful branch' not simply that of 'almond branch' and that the moment of 'inspiration' and 'revelation' is when 'wakeful branch' is transformed into 'watching God' (McKane, 1986, pp. 14–16). This exegesis is reflected in the rendering of NEB ('An almond in early bloom') with which REB ('A branch of an almond tree') should be compared. The latter is the correct translation and the attempt to discern a semantic link between *shaqed* and *shoqed* should be given up. Nothing more is involved than the near homonymy of the two forms: it is a similarity of sound, and nothing more which triggers the move from the almond branch to the watching God.

Turning aside from this exegetical disagreement with Schökel, I notice that it is at the moment when *shaqed* generates *shoqed* that an 'intuition' becomes 'a transcendent analogy'. It is then that he becomes 'inspired' and receives 'revelation'. Both of these are for Schökel theological categories and he uses them to make a claim that the prophet is the recipient of supernatural truth – of special revelation. Lindblom speaks of a 'revelatory state' but he is referring to a condition of ecstasy, to abnormal psychological experiences and to the subjective interpretation which the prophet gives to them, namely, that he has had a revelation from God. Lindblom himself does not affirm that the prophets were the recipients of supernatural truth which was directly and mysteriously conveyed by God to them and Gunkel's concept of *Religionsgeschichte* dispenses with special revelation. What is striking about Schökel's attachment to *The Inspired Word* (the title of his book) is the dichotomy of prophetic experience which he creates. It is the prophet *qua* man who has the intuition (*shaqed*), but the transition from the 'intuition' to the 'transcendent analogy' (*shoqed*) involves the crossing of the great gulf between man and God: human discernment is transformed into revelation. The allocation of the first stage to Jeremiah and of the second to God is uneconomical and divisive. A theological mystery which need not have appeared has been created, since the movement from *shaqed* to *shoqed* is more convincingly explained in terms of a mental process of Jeremiah rather than as a shift from 'intuition' to 'revelation', from Jeremiah to God. The near homonymy of *shaqed* and *shoqed* and the burden of Jeremiah's concern for his people are sufficient explanations of why the sight of an almond branch should awaken the thought that Yahweh's judgement on Judah would eventuate.

The chief concern which is exercising me in all this discussion is that the humanity of the canonical prophets should be preserved and that any diminishment of that humanity, associated with a dichotomy of man and prophet, or a normal state of consciousness and a 'revelatory state', should be avoided. It may be argued that psychology and theology are watertight compartments and that descriptions of ecstatic states which are merely psychological do not impinge on a theology of prophecy. I accept that psychological phenomena do not have a theological status, but I affirm that descriptions of prophetic psychology which damage the humanity of the canonical prophets have theological implications, because I regard a docetic theology of prophecy as unacceptable and I hold that this will be the outcome if the authentic humanity of the canonical prophets *qua* prophets is not safeguarded.

VI

Visions, however, constitute only a small part of the prophetic literature from Amos to Jeremiah and attention should be focused on prophetic oracles introduced by their characteristic formula 'These are the words of Yahweh' or the like. There is not much evidence bearing on the psychological state of the prophet when he delivered such oracles and such as there is can be interpreted in more than one way. It consists chiefly of the introductory formulae which attribute the prophet's utterance to Yahweh: the circumstance that the literary form given to the oracles represents them as speech of Yahweh. Lindblom makes a statement which is gathered from this evidence and which is categorical: it is presented as if there is not a shadow of doubt about its correctness. The question which is asked is, What is the significance of the formulae and of the literary form of the oracles? Different answers could be offered to this question, but Lindblom holds that only one answer, which relates the literary form of the oracle to the special psychological state of the prophet when he utters it, faithfully represents the convictions and beliefs of the canonical prophets when they claim to speak the word of Yahweh.

In this central area of the prophetic literature the canonical prophets are dehumanized and a doctrine of 'inspiration' and 'revelation' of the crudest kind is attributed to them: 'The true prophets are conscious of being mouthpieces of Yahweh and nothing else. They are nothing but channels for the stream of revelation. What they have to bring forth is not their own words (they would be worthless), but only the precious divine word which has been put in their mouth' (1962, p. 114). We have to ask Lindblom whether he is prepared to accept all the consequences of such a view of the prophetic literature. If the prophets were merely 'mouthpieces' does this mean that their humanity, and all its resources of thought, commitment and anguish, all their power of literary expression, has been evicted; that Yahweh is agitating their vocal chords to make his voice sound through them? Does it mean that these prophets believed that 'speech of God' or 'word of God' is to be understood literally and that God spoke Hebrew?

This indication of dissent from Lindblom does not amount to a blank refusal to admit that the claim which the prophets make (if these formulae are to be assigned to them), when they identify their utterances with Yahweh's utterances, is exceptional. It may be evidence of a mental state which is extraordinarily intense and concentrated: a signal of a certitude of rightness which has to be represented as 'word of God'. Nevertheless, at the level of literary expression, the language is entirely human and, in whatever sense it is to be elucidated as 'word of God', the explanation must not have dehumanizing consequences. On this matter I am influenced by Schökel and I shall take it up again, but for the moment I shall indicate my position provisionally by re-using words which I have written elsewhere. I shall assume, without argument, that there is a transcendental dimension, an encounter of the prophet with God, though I am aware of the logical disadvantage of producing such an ultimate – an unanalysable – mystery out of the hat:

> Verbalization is a 'translation' or 'transmutation' of a prophet's meeting with God and we should not share Weiser's satisfaction with an external, talking God as the end of our understanding of 'revelation' and 'word of God'. The prophet absorbs the mysterious experience into his humanity, filtering it through human

modes of apprehension and evaluation, and causing it to issue in a linguistic form which is human and not divine. (1986, p. xcviii)

The difference between this and Schökel's analysis is that for the words 'which is human and not divine' he would substitute 'which is both entirely human and entirely divine'. That is to say, he locates both the transcendental mystery and the human reality in the linguistic deposit.

VII

Another way of expressing the opinion which I have given above is to say that it is directed against a Dr Jekyll and Mr Hyde explanation of the output of the canonical prophets. If they are thought to function as prophets *only* when they are in an abnormal or supranormal psychological condition – 'a revelatory state' – there is an implication that when they return to a state of normality they are no longer prophets but men. It is true that there is one case where Lindblom states that a prophet has returned to a normal state of mind before he records his visionary experience (Isa. 21.6–10) and that there are other passages where he prefers a purely literary explanation (Isa. 17.12; 18.4; Jer. 4.5ff – enemy from the north). These are 'fanciful expressions of a poetic nature', and Lindblom continues: 'Personally I am inclined to assume that no ecstatic experience underlies this sublime poetry' (1962, p. 136). But the dichotomy of prophet and man set up by the postulation of the 'revelatory state' holds the field, for the most part.

This view of the canonical prophets that they are, for most of the time, normal human beings whose, otherwise, uniform humaneness is punctuated by unusual psychological states in which their prophetic activities are concentrated, has led Lindblom and Gunkel to make attempts to bridge the gulf between the 'revelatory state' and the 'normality' of the prophet's humanity: 'The revelatory state of mind includes all degrees of mental exaltation, from ecstasy in the strict sense to states of mind which approximate to the normal consciousness' (1962, p. 174). Lindblom emphasizes the 'quietness' of the ecstasy of the canonical prophets: 'In addition it may be noted that, unlike their predecessors, the great prophets did not experience ecstasy of a wild and orgiastic type. Their revelatory states were of a more moral and personal character, with the tranquillity of sublime inspiration. In such an experience the content of the revelation was more important than the psychic phenomenon itself' (1962, p. 178).

Gunkel's endeavours to narrow the gulf which he has created between prophet and man are evident in the remarks which he makes about the prophet Jeremiah: 'Such a man experiences God's revelation not only on a few wonderful occasions. He receives from Him not only this or that commission. His life is full of revelation and he is always at God's service' (1917, p. 28). However, as an example of Gunkel's Jekyll and Hyde view, let us take his comment on Isa.21.6: 'The watchman is the other "I" of the prophet. For such a man, as it were, consists of two persons, the everyday person who knows his neighbours and friends, and another secret person who in the stillness of the night watches for a new revelation' (1917, p. 21).

The direction in which I am pushing and the destination in view will be clear. It may be said that since Kuenen has excluded the supernatural from his account of the canonical prophets, the way is open for him to reach the conclusion that the prophet is one, undivided human person, but this is an observation to which too much significance should not be attached. It does not support the conclusion that if a serious attempt to analyse the concept of 'revelation' is made, if it is affirmed that there was a divine-human encounter, this must inevitably lead to a Jekyll and Hyde portrayal of the canonical prophet. Schökel takes 'special revelation' seriously, but locates it, for the most part, in the prophetic literature. His quest for the 'inspired word' is disengaged from abnormal psychological states or any disjunction of prophet and man. The word which he describes as 'inspired' has a special kinship with poetry and is the product of men as fully human when they write as they are at any other time, whose product is not the outcome of an abnormal psychological state or of the experiences which it generates.

VIII

The rawest expressions of the Jekyll and Hyde interpretation of the canonical prophets have arisen out of form criticism and have been perpetrated by scholars who have confused literary forms with theological affirmations. They have supposed that a theologian's concern with 'word of God', which is a concern to establish the truth of prophetic utterances, is one for which there is beautifully simple answer. The oracles are prefaced with 'These are the words of Yahweh' or the like and Yahweh is represented as the speaker. The statement 'God speaks' is to be taken literally: wherever he is said to speak we have word of God and that is the end of the matter. The Jekyll and Hyde aspect of this appears, when, on the assumption that 'God speaks' has a literal sense, an attempt is made to separate from the divine speech elements of argument, reasoning and application which the oracle contains. These are held to be the prophet's own contribution and are separated off as 'word of man'. Such a disjunction of prophet and man within the prophetic oracles has been pursued by Wildberger (1942) and it is with this book in mind that Schökel asks the question: 'Can we discern in a prophetic oracle one part which is the direct message of God and another which is the explanation given by the prophet?' (1967, p. 71). The answer given by Schökel to the question is that such a procedure is theologically futile and the reason why this is so is given in a passage which he entitles 'Human Words'. Schökel is influenced by a Christological model, the relation between the divine and human natures in Christ, and this controls his estimate of the language of the prophetic oracle. The statement which has particular relevance for this discussion is: 'It may be that this divine abasement [the Incarnation] has left our language touched by the Godhead, raising it to a new level, giving it a new capacity of meaning. Still it will always be human language. When we speak of the language of God it is an analogous predication' (1967, p. 42).

It follows from this that von Rad's view of the canonical prophets as both messengers of God and wise men is just as much a dichotomy and falls under the same criticism. It has no point, unless 'Messenger of Yahweh' has a literal sense and the thought of God speaking Hebrew to a prophet who then relays the words to Yahweh's community is taken seriously. Von Rad has this to say about Ezek. 24.15–27: 'There is therefore a certain gulf between the divine command (vv. 15–19) and the means by which the prophet carried it out (vv. 20–27). The prophet used great freedom in interpreting the command' (1965, ii, p. 72). What principles, von Rad asks, guided the prophets in the 'human' interpretation which they gave to 'divine' words [the message]? The answer is that they were guided by the assumptions of a wisdom tradition in which they were steeped: 'They regard themselves as bound to a definite fixed order which their announcement of punishment was designed to restore' (1965, ii, p. 73).

The *lākēn* ('Therefore') with which they introduce the divine message establishes a logical connection between the human reasoning of the preceding diatribe and the content of that message:

> What the prophet applies here [in the message] is a perfectly basic piece of knowledge which is vouchsafed not only to himself, but also, in principle, to everyone who has experience of the world and of life, namely, knowledge of the fundamental God-given fixed orders to which human life is subject. This is the place where prophecy makes close and vital contact with the Wisdom literature. (1965, ii, p. 74)

IX

Another trend, comparable to this dissection of the canonical prophet into sage and divine messenger is seen in the contention that the human

desires and dispositions of these prophets were overwhelmed by Yahweh and that they were compelled – coerced – to follow the path of their
vocation. This is portrayed so starkly that obedience to a divine will
amounts to a destruction of human freedom. On Amos 3.8 Gunkel says:
'Whoever hears a lion roar has no choice whether or not to be afraid.
Similarly the prophet is compelled to prophesy. When he hears the
Divine sounding within him, his inner man is filled with a powerful
compulsion' (1917, p. 12). On the same prophet Lindblom remarks:
'He was compelled and coerced by Yahweh and then it was impossible
for him not to speak. . . . So irresistible, so overwhelming was Yahweh's
voice in the soul of Amos that he compared it with the roaring of a lion
evoking terror in everyone who hears it' (1962, p. 194). Yet, according
to Lindblom, this 'revelatory state' of mind 'did not destroy the individuality of the canonical prophets' (1962, p. 297): 'Constraint and
freedom did not exclude each other, but were synthetically combined'
(1962, p. 197). How can this be? Lindblom confesses that he does not
know: 'But to express the synthesis of freedom and constraint in a
formula is impossible' (1962, p. 197). Similarly von Rad remarks of the
prophetic vocation: 'Flesh and blood can only be forced into such
service. At all events the prophets themselves felt that that they had
been compelled by a stronger will than theirs' (1965, ii, p. 58).

Kuenen's dissociation of prophetic compulsion from extraordinary
psychological states has already been noticed (above, p. 77). According
to Kuenen such compulsion as is exercised on the canonical prophet has
an inner character: it is not a compulsion which is to be accounted for
by setting up an antithesis between natural and supernatural, between
human inclinations and irresistible divine pressure, between man and
prophet. The tension is in the opposition of duty and desire. It is the
answering of the call of duty, 'the stern Daughter of the voice of God',
which makes a man into a prophet. It is the 'ought' of prophetic duty
which forbids courses of action less sorrowful and demanding, to give
up which is a great sacrifice for a sensitive human being longing for
acceptance and friendship. 'I am full of Yahweh's wrath; I am
exhausted trying to contain it' (Jer. 6.10).These are prophecies of doom
for Jeremiah's community which fill him with horror from which the
tenderness of his humanity recoils: children, youths, families, the old,
all will be swallowed up by disaster. But his discernment of how things
are to turn out for Judah is piercing, he is convinced that he has arrived
at the truth, 'the word of God'; the force of this truth will not be denied
priority and overcomes his humane reluctance (McKane, 1986, pp.
143–8).

Along with Amos 3.8 another passage which has been prominent in
connection with 'compulsion' is Jer. 20.7–9. In examining this passage
elsewhere (1986, pp. 467–75) I have indicated my dissent from the

views of Rudolph and Weiser. I have maintained, against Weiser, that Jeremiah's deep reluctance to utter prophecies of doom is not to be understood as a resiling from prophetic responsibility or a taking offence at the demands of the prophetic vocation – a rebellion against Yahweh. The prophetic word is born out of Jeremiah's anguish and it is because there is this great tumult of inward conflict and contradiction, this accumulation of anguish, that he reaches the sorrowful truth which may not be suppressed, the deep discernment which stamps him as a prophet. Prophetic conflict is not to be identified with rebellion against Yahweh; it is not a confession of guilt by the prophet and it is not to be interpreted as a display of his human frailty. Against Rudolph I have contended that his view of 'compulsion' is unacceptable, because it is incompatible with the human freedom of the prophet: 'The prophet cannot do what he would like to do. He speaks because he must even when he does not will it' (1968, p. 131). The statement that a prophet does not will what he speaks is an unacceptable interpretation of 'compulsion'. If he speaks against his will, he is overwhelmed by an irresistible, external force and his utterance is no more his than that of a person who has been overcome by violence or torture or drugs.

The compulsion exercised by 'word of God', that is by an irrefragable conviction that truth has been grasped, does not simply impose a forced settlement on an inner human conflict. All the elements of tumult and dispeace which are at war in the prophet's soul contribute to his vision of the truth which brings him no comfort: it is not a beatific vision but a disclosure of looming disaster for his community. Hence there are special reasons for Jeremiah's recoil from speaking the truth, for he has told us that his prophetic duty had consequences for him as a human being which he could hardly bear to contemplate. The prophetic truth is a fire burning within him which is not to be endured; it is an imperative which must be obeyed and which demands a discharge of tension only to be achieved by utterance. It has destroyed his credibility and his reasonableness in the eyes of his contemporaries and has made him appear an absurd extremist whose balance of mind has been disturbed. He has become a pariah, divested of a likeable moderation and every other vestige of human attractiveness. There is no warmth in his relations with his own community, only the cold of enmity and the corrosion of scorn.

If 'compulsion' is exaggerated in the context of prophetic psychology, the activity of a prophet is made into 'compulsive behaviour' and in the modern world this has become a badge of irrationality. It is associated with loss of freedom, deliberation and the exercise of judgement in deciding between alternate courses of action. If 'compulsion' is exaggerated in the context of a theology of prophecy, it destroys the authentic humanity of a prophet and any theology which is founded on a dehumanized prophet is irretrievably flawed. Nor can any scholar hope to get away with a conclusion which consists of a junction of incompatibles, like Lindblom's statement that to express 'the synthesis of freedom and constraint in a formula is impossible' (1962, p. 197).

X

The enquiry conducted in this chapter has been an attempt to answer the question asked in the title. It is a fundamental question and those who undertake to answer it, even if they assert that they are describing only the psychological experiences of the canonical prophets and the transcendental theology which they themselves attached to these experiences, namely, that God was communicating directly with them, and are not, for their own part, making any theological affirmations, should not suppose that their conclusions are innocent of theological consequences. When we ask, What kind of men were the canonical prophets? much hangs on the kind of answer which is given and one which creates a divide between the prophet *qua* man and the prophet *qua* prophet, and which associates the latter with the onset of special psychological conditions which interrupt the normal tenor of his humanity, is entirely unacceptable. An account of prophetic activity which holds that the prophet prophesies only when he is abnormal and never when he is wholly human is a disastrous dilution of his humanity. The canonical prophet is always both man and prophet. Moreover, the descriptions which are given of the psychological states of the canonical prophets rest on the insecure basis of the accounts which appear in the prophetic literature and they tend to assume that these can be taken as transcripts of prophetic experience, whereas the relationship between the one and the other is much more complicated and problematic.

Connected with this dichotomy of man and prophet is the idea of 'compulsion': the prophets were compelled to prophesy, whether this is interpreted as psychological compulsion ('compulsive behaviour') or as coercion by God. Both are destructive of human freedom and fail to capture the inner struggle and the irreconcilable tensions with which the canonical prophet is riven when his common humanity and concern clash with his prophetic vocation. He is a man of sorrows and acquainted with grief.

When we come to Farrar, we have encountered one of the principal adversaries of the humanity of the canonical prophets. He has a zest for dehumanizing them and he takes aim at their humanity with a barrage of supernatural vocabulary. 'Word of God' receives a literal interpretation, and the existence in prophetic oracles of 'speeches of the Almighty' is thought to make it 'very difficult to humanize' the canonical prophets (1948, p. 124). He says of Jeremiah that he [the prophet] 'is not writing about a human life, but about the Lord God of Israel' (1948, p. 125) and the thought that Jeremiah is coerced by a divine compulsion, and his humanity extinguished, is given complete expression: 'There is a painful effort from time to time to obtrude Jeremiah's private hopes, fears and recalcitrances; but they are forced back, trampled, annihilated by the Word of God' (1948, p. 125). In the episode of the almond twig (Jer. 1.11–12) Jeremiah is said to be a diviner and the twig an omen, apparently an attempt to suggest a parallelism with haruspication: the insight which Jeremiah acquires from the observation of the almond twig is approximated, through the vocabulary which Farrar employs, with the divination whose method is the inspection of entrails (1948, p. 128).

But, for the most part, according to Farrar, poetry was the method of divination used. The canonical prophets are made into rhapsodists after the model set out in Plato's *Ion*, cited in chapter 6 (p. 123). The words which they utter are not chosen by them and are not rationally controlled. They have an aspect of inevitability; they are 'an incantation of shapely words' (1948, p. 128), an irresistible divine invasion:

> Whatever signs or omens set the incantation of shapely words moving in the prophet's mind, it went on moving and forming itself with a felt inevitability, like that of rhapsodical poetry which allows for no second thoughts: it formed itself under a pressure or control which the prophet experienced as no self-chosen direction of his own thinking, but as the constraint of a divine will. As the prophet speaks his own person is lost, and the person whose utterance the words express becomes the person of the Lord. (1948, pp. 128f)

What kind of men then were the canonical prophets? According to Farrar they were mouthpieces of God rather than men. When they speak only the voice is human, but otherwise they say what they must – a kind of automatic speech. They are witless men who have lost their own personalities, have been overwhelmed by a divine invasion and are God-possessed. They are overborne by a spate of supernatural, poetic eloquence over which they have no control. Farrar has done a thorough job demolishing the humanity of the canonical prophets. As the architect of a soaring supernaturalism he has worked with uncontained gusto and he has conjured up a theology of the prophets whose docetism will be difficult to surpass.

Literature for Chapters 6 and 7

Barr, J., *The Semantics of Biblical Language* (Oxford, 1962).
Bentzen, A., *Introduction to the Old Testament* (Copenhagen, 1952²).

Dodds, E. R., *The Greeks and the Irrational* (Oxford, 1951).

Eissfeldt, O., *Der Maschal im Alten Testament*, BZAW 24 (1913).

Engnell, I., 'Prophets and Prophetism in the Old Testament', *Critical Essays on the Old Testament* (London, 1970), pp. 123–79 (see bibliography for chapters 4 and 5).

Farrar, A., *The Glass of Vision* (London, 1948).

Godbey, A. H., 'The Hebrew Māšāl', *AJSL* 39/40 (1922/23), pp. 89–108.

Gunkel, H., *Die Propheten* (Göttingen, 1917).

Johnson, A. R., *The Cultic Prophet in Ancient Israel* (Cardiff, 1944, 1962[2]).

Johnson, A. R., 'Māšāl', *VTS* 3 (1955), pp. 162–9.

Klatt, W., *Hermann Gunkel: Zu seiner Theologie der Religionsgeschichte und zur Entstehung der formgeschichtlichen Methode*, FRLANT 100 (Göttingen, 1969).

Lamb, W. R. N., *Plato with an English Translation, Ion*, Loeb Classical Texts (London and New York, 1925).

Lindblom, J., *Prophecy in Ancient Israel* (Oxford, 1962).

McKane, W., *Proverbs: A New Approach*, Old Testament Library (London, 1970).

McKane, W., *A Critical and Exegetical Commentary on Jeremiah i–xxv* (Edinburgh, 1986).

Mowinckel, S., 'The Spirit and the Word in the Pre-exilic Prophets', *JBL* 53 (1934), pp. 199–227.

Pedersen, J., *Israel i–ii* (Copenhagen, 1926); *Israel iii–iv* (Copenhagen, 1940).

Pedersen, J., 'The Role played by Inspired Persons among the Israelites and Arabs', *Studies in Old Testament Prophecy*, T. H. Robinson Festschrift (Edinburgh, 1950), pp. 127–42.

Rudolph, W., *Jeremia*, HAT (Tübingen, 1968[3]).

Schmidt, J., *Studien zur Stilistik der alttestamentlichen Spruchliteratur*. Alttestamentliche Abhandlungen, 13, 1 (Münster, 1936).

Schökel, L. A., *The Inspired Word: Scripture in the Light of Language and Literature*, translated by F. Martin (London, 1967).

von Rad G., *Old Testament Theology*, ii (Edinburgh, 1965).

Weiser, A., *Das Buch Jeremia*, ATD (Göttingen, 1969[6]).

Wildberger, H., *Jahwewort und prophetische Rede bei Jeremia* (Zurich, 1942).

8

THE HERMENEUTICAL METHOD AND OLD TESTAMENT THEOLOGY

I

Why has 'hermeneutics' become such a vogue word in biblical studies? The Greek word ἑρμηνεύειν means 'to interpret' or 'to translate' and we might suppose that any sense which 'hermeneutics' conveys could be equally well represented by 'exegesis', the word which held sway for a long time. 'Hermeneutics' has become fashionable because it stands for a new emphasis in biblical exegesis, a concern to establish such a degree of openness to the future in the sense of biblical texts which belong to the past that their continuing relevance is assured. The word has been used to signify this concept of dynamic exegesis. In so far as it has been enlisted in the service of Old Testament theology, as it has been in the theology of von Rad, it is an exegetical method which seeks to demonstrate that, though the Old Testament is a collection of ancient books, it, nevertheless, has a relevance for the present and is not imprisoned in antiquity. This could be summed up, over against the kind of theological concern which was evident in the first chapter as a transference of interest from truth to relevance. It could be argued that relevance is not enough and that Old Testament theology must be concerned with truth, truth as it was conceived by those who regarded questions about revelation and inspiration as fundamental issues of a biblical theology.

It is unquestionably important to show that the Bible is not obsolescent in the modern world and that its texts have a capacity to yield new resources of significance in the face of great changes, so that they address themselves to striking and profound questions of human existence. But in order to deal with the question of truth we have to go beyond the starting-point of von Rad's hermeneutical account of Old Testament theology which has kerymatic or credal traditions as its premisses. If it is simply assumed that the traditions from which a beginning is made are true, the question of truth has not been pursued with sufficient strenuousness. If biblical truth is a principal source of dogma, biblical theology must give some consideration to the nature of such truth and not rest simply on a 'logic of obedience' (Macquarrie, 1967, p. 143).

It may be advantageous to indicate briefly the constituents of von Rad's Old Testament theology and to make some remarks on its organization. It begins with 'A History of Yahwism and the Sacral Institutions of Israel in Outline' which is Part i of the first volume (pp. 3 –102). His treatment of this before he begins theology proper is an intimation that his intention is to effect a separation between his account of the history of Old Testament religion and the constituents of his Old Testament theology. In the course of a section on the methodological presuppositions of his theology (pp. 105–28) he concludes that the correct point of departure of an Old Testament theology is the credal traditions which are the core of the Hexateuch and whose most concentrated expression is the 'little creed' of Deut. 26.5–9. The Hexateuch is a complicated and extensive elaboration of a credal core and contains what von Rad calls the old canonical salvation history which runs from the call of the patriarchs to the possession by Israel of the land of Canaan (pp. 129–305).

The Davidic traditions, focusing on the office of the Anointed king and his special covenant relationship with Yahweh (pp. 306–34) are a development from the Hexateuchal expression of the salvation history and both take on a new lease of life and are metamorphosed by the canonical prophets who push them out to fresh frontiers of significance. In the Deuteronomic account of Israel's history with Yahweh (pp. 334–47) salvation gives way to judgement: 'In the canonical saving history from the patriarchs to the entry into Canaan, it was Jahweh who made the truth of the promise good in the face of all the failure of Israel; and he did not let any part of his great plan in history, least of all the final part, be taken out of his hands. But in the Deuteronomist's history Jahweh allowed Israel to make the decision' – that is, to choose death rather than life (p. 126). Another interpretation of Israel's history is that of the Chronicler (pp. 347–54) which runs from David to Nehemiah and whose period, therefore, partly overlaps that of the Deuteronomist. The last chapter in the first volume which is entitled 'Israel before Jahweh (Israel's answer)' is a consideration of Israel's response to Yahweh's saving initiatives as this is variously articulated in the book of Psalms and the wisdom literature (pp. 355–459).

The first volume has the sub-title 'The Theology of Israel's Historical Traditions' and the second volume is described as the 'The Theology of Israel's Prophetical Traditions'. That prophecy should come last in von Rad's account of the Old Testament follows from his understanding of the nature of the proclamation of the canonical prophets which 'has its starting-point in the conviction that Israel's previous history with Yahweh has come to an end and that he will start something new with her' (i, p. 128) The conviction that 'hitherto existing saving ordinances have lost their worth' places these prophets outside the saving history 'as it

had been understood up to then by Israel' (i, p. 128). Their message
'smashed in pieces Israel's existence with God up to the present, and
rang up a curtain of history for a new action on his part with her. So
prophecy needs separate treatment in a theology of the Old Testament'
(i, p. 128).

One of the criticisms which Eichrodt makes of von Rad's theology,
and it applies especially to the credal foundations of his theology of the
Hexateuch, is that he has wrenched apart 'the theological expressions of
Israel's historical tradition and the facts of Israelite history'. The result
of this is 'the spurious factuality of salvation-history' which effects a
divorce from 'the historico-critical view of Israel's history' and it should
not be confused with historical truth, that is, historicity. There is no
adequate historical foundation for the credal affirmations which constitute von Rad's theology (i, 1961, pp. 512f). Eichrodt is reacting against
von Rad's deliberate resolve to construct a theology of credal traditions
in such a way as to separate a history of Yahwism entirely from the
subject of Old Testament theology.

There is one aspect of this, bearing on the Hexateuch, which Eichrodt notices: 'With the critical disintegration of the whole Moses tradition any conceivable historical origin for the Yahweh faith is completely lacking' (i, p. 513). Eichrodt's point is that the historical Moses
is, at best, a marginal and shadowy figure in the context of von Rad's
theology of the Hexateuch. He has a dominant position in the fully
developed Hexateuchal traditions, but virtually no connection can be
established between this Moses and the historical Moses. If it were
supposed that a historical Moses is indispensable for Old Testament
theology and that it must deal with Moses in the historical contexts in
which he was a recipient of divine truth and led Israel out of Egypt, von
Rad's theology does not meet this condition. The circumstance that von
Rad wrote a little book on Moses (1960) might appear to contradict
what has just been said, but it will be found that this is not a biography
of Moses and that in it he owes his existence not to a historical contribution but to combinations of credal traditions. 'First we shall sketch in
broad outline the picture of Moses as that has been handed down to us
by the various strands of the tradition' (*Moses*, p. 9). Further indications are given by statements which von Rad makes in the first
volume of his *Theology*:

> If it is true that the picture of the course of events given in the
> Hexateuch only arose from a confessional rearrangement of differ-
> ent complexes of tradition, then the question of the historicity of
> Moses and his functions can only be put as follows: in which of
> these groups of tradition and in which of the separate traditions is
> the figure of Moses originally rooted? (i, p. 14)

This is the question which Noth discusses in detail (pp. 156–75) in his *History of Pentateuchal Traditions* and he reaches the conclusion that the most solid piece of evidence bearing on the historical Moses is the notice about the location of his grave in Deut. 34.6. 'He was buried in a valley in Moab, oppposite Beth Peor, but to this day no one knows his burial-place.' On what does this tradition, which Noth describes as 'an original element of the Mosaic tradition' (1972, p. 172) and as 'the bed rock of historical reality' (p. 173) rest? The answer to this question is that the historical Moses belongs originally to the 'Guidance in the Wilderness' theme of the creed and was associated with 'the pre-history of the Israelite tribes that later became settled in central Palestine'. Noth continues:

> Only for these tribes was the southern part of east Jordan (where the grave is located) once significant for a period as the temporary sphere of their sojourn. It is probable that in the circle of these tribes Moses once held a leading position. ... From this standpoint it would be quite understandable that Moses as a leader figure initially gained entrance into the narrative elaboration of the theme 'Guidance in the Wilderness', and then he came to assume this role in the remaining Pentateuchal themes, with the exception, of course, of the Patriarchal theme. (p. 173)

Von Rad notices that if Noth's view of the history of the traditions of the Pentateuch is followed, the historical Moses has no connection with the deliverance from Egypt or the giving of the Law at Mount Sinai. Even those less reductionist than Noth who believe 'that the historical element can be regarded as broader and more firmly founded than this, are, for all that, far from gaining the picture of Moses as the founder of a religion so urgently sought by the modern reader' (i, p. 14). In every case they can only reach very ancient individual traditions which are difficult to reconcile with one another. The conclusion that the historical Moses can be connected only with the narrative elaboration of a single theme of the creed is one aspect of the separation between the history of Yahwism and the theology of the Old Testament in von Rad's theology and it holds a special interest.

The view that Moses occupies a pre-eminent place among the prophets is founded on Deut. 34.10 ('There has never yet arisen in Israel a prophet like Moses whom the Lord knew face to face') and it influenced both Maimonides and Aquinas when they weighed up the extent to which Hebrew prophets received a special disclosure of truth from God, in that they place Moses on a higher level than the remainder of the prophets. They interpret 'face to face' as a portrayal indicative of a more direct disclosure than that granted to the canonical prophets who had their revelations in dreams and visions and Maimonides, as we have seen, offers a special account of 'voice of God' which applies only to Moses on Sinai. Even if von Rad had been interested in the prophetic stature of Moses, he would have been precluded from carrying out an investigation of this kind, because enquiries about inspiration and revelation can only be made satisfactorily if there is an historical subject and, as we have seen, the confines of von Rad's theology are such that he does not have access to a historical Moses with prophetic status.

It was noticed that where Farrar said that supernatural images were the common property of the Church, one had a sense of dissatisfaction which arose from a demand that if supernatural images are to be invoked, individual persons with whom they originate should be found and some attention was given to Schökel's treatment of this in his chapter 'The Author and the Community' (pp. 217–33), where he rejects the idea of communal inspiration (p. 224). An objection may rise in your mind that Schökel is confusing literary creativeness ('We should first of all reject any notion of an amorphous community which is somehow creative') with 'inspiration' in a fully-fledged theological sense and that would be an interesting observation. It will be enough to say that Schökel discerns a very close relation between the creativeness of men of letters, especially poets, and the inspiration of biblical authors. What emerges for further consideration is that von Rad's Old Testament theology nowhere raises the question of inspiration and revelation in volume i and that his theology of the Hexateuch does not give him access to a historical Moses in relation to whom he could have initiated such a discussion. Everything unfolds from the core of credal traditions whose truth has to be assumed, since, thereafter, the theological thrust of the Old Testament is maintained and energized by the openness of these traditions to the future and their amenableness to reinterpretation. The theology of the Old Testament in volume i amounts to the discernment and description of exegetical processes.

The following objection might be raised: If von Rad is not interested in inspiration and revelation why do you persist in trying to hang this albatross about his neck? Perhaps it was simply that he had no appetite for flogging a dead horse, that he opted out of a somewhat tired discussion and decided to strike out in a new direction. This would not be an answer to the argument which has been conducted, for two reasons. First, the argument was that even if von Rad had desired to introduce the topics of inspiration and revelation – and perhaps he had no such desire – it would have been impossible for him to do it, because he assumed that he did not have access to historical individuals of prophetic standing, and, particularly to Moses. In the second place, there are three chapters in volume ii of von Rad's theology (pp. 50–98) which show that he was concerned with such matters and in these areas the divorce between the history of Yahwism and the theology of the Old

Testament, which he lays down as a necessary consequence of his theological method in volume i, is, at least partly, overcome. In his discussion of inspiration and revelation he assumes that he has access to the canonical prophets as historical individuals and even probes into what is special about their psychological states. His treatment of them is an admission on his part that these issues can only be discussed in connection with historical, prophetic individuals.

It would be misleading to give the impression that von Rad has resiled from his hermeneutical method in volume ii, changing horses in midstream. What he has done is to operate with two strings to his bow: the prophet is both a recipient of the revealed word and one who, relying on his own knowledge and judgement, applies it through an extraordinarily keen discernment of Yahweh's moral order or, especially, through a reinterpretation and revitalizing of old traditions.

It will be recalled that one of Eichrodt's criticisms of von Rad was that the concept of *Heilsgeschichte* (saving or salvation history) was defective. The phrase used by Eichrodt ('spurious factuality') might suggest that von Rad was unaware of the distinction between *Heilsgeschichte* and historicity or that he was obscuring it through a lack of clarity and this goes beyond a demonstration that von Rad's method rests on a divorce between theology of the Old Testament and the history of Yahwism. Von Rad is fully aware that *Heilsgeschichte* is not historiography and when he uses the term he makes no claim for the historicity of the Hexateuchal narratives which make up the *Heilsgeschichte*. It was von Rad himself in his essay on 'The Form-Critical Problem of the Hexateuch' who established that the kernel which produced the narrative growth of the Hexateuch was credal (1966, pp. 3–8; German edition, 1938) and the implications of this were fully explored in Noth's *History of Pentateuchal Traditions* (1972; second German edition, 1948).

These implications are inescapable for von Rad in the context of his theology of the Hexateuch. The narratives of the Hexateuch, though they appear to be historical, are primarily non-historical, because the *data* at their base are non-historical, often credal or cultic. The historical narrative is a secondary feature with an explanatory or aetiological intention. This may be expressed by saying that the interpretation of the Hexateuchal narrative hinges on a correct appreciation of their *genre* and that when they are handled as historiography the nature of their *genre* is misjudged. I have gone into this with special reference to the patriarchal narratives (1979, pp. 17–66). Any suggestion that von Rad was not himself fully aware of what is involved in the term *Heilsgeschichte* in connection with the Hexateuch should not be entertained.

The matter which is bothering Eichrodt is that Old Testament theology should be hitched to credal affirmations, which have been expanded into aetiological narratives with a historical form, and not to a 'historico-critical view of Israel's history' (i, p. 513). On this matter Eichrodt seems to me to be mostly wrong. No more should be conceded to him than that the opening up of too great a gap between credal affirmations and their historical foundations poses a threat to Old Testament theology. It needs a historical infrastructure and if this appears to crumble, it loses its anchorage in the world where we live out our lives and severs its connection with the sweat of human existence. Credal affirmations may constitute a particular interpretation of human events, but, if so, they must not become disengaged from these events. Otherwise they are no more than a kind of theological theorizing or invention to which the realities of our historical existence will not answer. But Eichrodt's claim is that Old Testament theology is a historical discipline, that it is a special area of the historico-critical study of the Old Testament and that it is as amenable to a critical method as any other investigation of the Old Testament. Eichrodt is mistaken in his view that the discourse of an Old Testament theology, that is, the kind of language which it uses, the affirmations which it makes and the interpretation of Israel's history which it offers, can be contained completely within the *genre* of historiography. Von Rad's use of the term *Heilsgeschichte* is a means of marking the distinction between credal discourse and historiography.

Even if there were no problems of historicity arising from von Rad's theology of the Hexateuch and it were possible to construct an entirely satisfactory historical foundation for its credal affirmations, the distinction between the two *genres* would not be dissolved. By employing the concept of *Heilsgeschichte* von Rad, in my view, does not commit himself to the affirmation that God intervenes directly in history, he does not posit a theology of a miraculous kind, a theology of theophany. Since he makes credal affirmations, which are interpretations of supposed historical experiences, the basis of his theology, we must conclude that he assumes these interpretations to possess a content of theological truth. Yet he knows that the discernment of a *Heilsgeschichte* is an exceptional response of religious faith to historical events and that a range of non-theological interpretations are available to historians in a *genre* (historiography) which describes and explains without inserting God into the events. Even where there is no difficulty of recovering the historical details out of which credal affirmations arise, the relation between creed and history remains mysterious and the distinction between the two *genres* and universes of discourse has to be maintained.

To say that God does not intervene directly in history, disturbing an intricate web of causal interactions by his personal agency, that there are no acts of God within history in this sense, and that von Rad does not intend to convey this with his concept of *Heilsgeschichte*, is not necessarily to deny that God controls the historical process by a mysterious, hidden superintendence. The pre-exilic canonical prophets proclaimed Yahweh's control of history and his ability to impose on it a moral order, but they did not think in terms of miraculous interventions. They discerned that it was accomplished by an unexplained coalescence of movements of international history with Yahweh's moral purposes. These movements were generated by the motives, the imperial ambitions, which professional historians presuppose, and which can be described in their vocabulary. These nations (Assyria and Babylonia) had no awareness of serving Yahweh's purposes and were motivated by the normal incentives of political and economic ambition, the quest for wealth and power which are recognizable ingredients of a *realpolitik*.

Another note of dissent which Eichrodt enters refers to von Rad's style of exegesis, namely, his conviction that 'the existentialist interpretation of the biblical evidence is the right one' (i, p. 515). This is directed against von Rad's assumption that Old Testament texts are open to reinterpretation and that it is this openness which gives the direction and supplies the thrust to an Old Testament theology. Eichrodt is still attached to a view of exegesis which has close associations with the historical-critical method and its premiss that there are normative interpretations of Old Testament texts with a once-for-all validity which do not admit of any rivals. These are time-bound interpretations, since they locate the text in the particular set of historical circumstances in which it is thought to have originated: they recover the intentions of the author in that context and they assume that the last word has then been said about the exegesis of the text. The original historical context is indispensable for the recovery of its meaning and the thought that it may have acquired additional meaning, or a new meaning, in a later historical context does not enter into the complex of considerations which are thought to be decisive.

This has a natural connection with a resolution of Old Testament theology into normative religious ideas held to be superior to extra-biblical religious ideas and so evidence of the distinctiveness of biblical religion. That there is something of this in Eichrodt the following quotation will show: 'It still seems to the present writer . . . that there is one task which Old Testament theology can never abandon, namely, that of pressing from Old Testament evidence to a system of faith which shall, by virtue of its unified structure and consistent fundamental attitude, present a character unique in the history of religions' (i, p. 520).

There are connections between Eichrodt and *Religionsgeschichte*, a school of thought which had special associations with Göttingen and Hermann Gunkel, and which flourished towards the end of the last

century and the beginning of the present one. The movement has been
well-treated by Klatt in his book on Gunkel (*Hermann Gunkel*, 1969),
and I have gone into it with special reference to the patriarchal narratives (1979, pp. 226f, 228f). Though the German translates simply into
'History of Religion', it is a concept with special connotations. It is not
a straightforward move from biblical religion to comparative religion.
In so far as it is connected with a new dimension of depth in biblical
exegesis, for example, the insertion of Babylonian, mythological ideas
into Gunkel's exegesis of the early chapters of Genesis, it does have
links with comparative religion. Eichrodt's connection with this school
of thought (which he probably would have denied) should not be exaggerated, since, in important respects, he was recoiling from it and such
affinities as exist are exegetical rather than theological.

Certainly not theological, because the practitioners of *Religionsgeschichte* were committed to the demolition of the ideas of inspiration and
revelation and proposed to dispense with the supernatural in their
account of biblical religion. Schökel produces a quotation whose source
he does not give, but which he attributes to Gunkel: 'The pretty myth
of inspiration has already vanished' (1967, p. 219). According to Klatt
(1969, p. 76) a resolve to dismantle the supernatural and to banish the
doctrines of inspiration and revelation from the study of the Bible may
be described as Gunkel's fundamental stance. He would have nothing
to do with an alleged *Heilsgeschichte* separable from a general history of
human culture and he refused to reckon with a special divine revelation
in Israel.

How then did biblical truth arise and acquire its distinctiveness? The
answer is given in the form of a historical judgement which makes no
appeal to inspiration and revelation. It asserts that there are certain
historical points of high religious attainment, peaks of religious and
moral insight, ideas which are normative and are to be prized for ever
afterwards. Only in this way can Gunkel accommodate a concept of the
distinctiveness of biblical religion. It is in the exegetical area, disengaged
from the discarding of inspiration and revelation, that Eichrodt's connections with the school of *Religionsgeschichte* are to be found, for he too
deals in religious ideas of a normative and unique kind which must be
expressed in relation to the historical contexts in which they emerge, and
may not be severed from them. If this is the kind of theological truth
which the Old Testament contains, it is condemned to a historical
imprisonment which creates serious problems. The school of *Religionsgeschichte* might take satisfaction in the economy of its hypothesis and
the blow it had delivered against obscuranticism. It had used Occam's
razor to dispose of the doctrines of inspiration and revelation, but it had
created a new doctrine which is difficult to believe, that at particular
historical moments religious and moral truths of such a kind emerge that

the flow of history will never leave them behind. Even though the tunnel connecting them to their antique origins gets longer and longer as time passes, obsolescence will never touch them. The circumstance that the contours of human existence are utterly different to those of the remote past, out of which they had issued and to which they are indissolubly joined, does not obscure the transparency of their relevance.

The so-called 'existential' exegesis of von Rad confronts a more serious problem of biblical theology than Eichrodt allows or discerns. It is an attempt to overcome the scandal of particularity, to close the gulf between the transience of historically-conditioned ideas and the sphere of timeless validity to which theology, including biblical theology, claims to belong. This is done by departing from a static, once-for-all exegesis of Old Testament texts – texts which cannot be severed from their original historical context – by refusing to regard them as antique encrustments and by giving to them the possibility of continued life and organic growth; by attaching to them the power to acquire new significance time and again in the future which stretches out before them. This process will not make these texts into truths of an abstract or universal kind: they will still be interpreted in a historical context and they will have particularity, but the threat of obsolescence will have been removed. They will disclose their significance in relation to the present and not in relation to a set of historical circumstances buried in the past. What has been said, however, is not to be taken as a vote of unqualified support for such a scheme of exegesis, but rather as an attempt to excavate the problems which are confronted by it. New problems are created by it, namely, an apparent weakening of objective control and a setting-aside of the criteria of the historical-critical method which have served Old Testament exegesis well.

II

The openness of the interpretation of Old Testament texts can be considered in a somewhat less exalted environment, not in the penthouse of hermeneutics but in the basement, where linguists do their work, although the matters which I intend to raise may have implications for Old Testament theology. Schökel, in particular, has focused attention in an interesting way on the literary qualities of the language of the Hebrew bible. He has described Hosea as a poet of the first rank and has submitted as evidence Hos. 11.1–9 (pp. 139f). He has described Hos. 1.2 – 3.5, where the subject is Hosea's unfaithful wife, as 'one of the most intense lyric pieces of the Old Testament' (pp. 188–91). The elaborate, acrostic organization of Ps. 119, and the manner in which it is worked out, is put down to the honest craftsmanship of a man of letters whose artistic horizons are more confined and who does not soar to great heights of creativeness (pp. 191–4). The general point made by Schökel especially concerns us: that some parts of the Hebrew bible, especially the poetry has a literary quality, that the language is of a kind which goes hand in hand with literary creativeness and that the allusiveness and expansiveness of reference possessed by the language must not be narrowed or flattened by a coarse treatment of it: 'Since this language is literary, it is not coarse or commonplace, nor can it be made commonplace in order to make it popular. Men must be lifted up and introduced to an understanding of the scriptures, so that they can appreciate the language and its message' (p. 17).

   This boils down, for the most part, to a matter of translation, since it is through translation that the great majority have access to the Hebrew bible. It also, however, touches on exegesis and it has a particular application to the proverbial or parabolic constituents of the Hebrew bible. Let us deal with translation and exegesis in turn. In a short section on 'Modern Translations' (pp. 291–3) Schökel discusses various pitfalls which must be avoided, if the process of turning the Hebrew bible into another language is to be done without unacceptable loss and debilitation. The existence of different modern translations is, he holds, an advantage rather than a source of confusion, because no translation succeeds completely and different translations complement each other. What one translation has rendered inadequately or misconstrued another will catch and the sum of their contributions to the capturing of the original will exceed the achievement of any one of them. This, however, does not absolve a translator from striving after the most adequate and sensitive translation which he can devise. The same principle was expounded in the sixteenth century by a Cambridge scholar, William Fulke in his work *A Defense of the sincere and true Translations of the holie Scriptures into the English Tong* (p. 60).

   Schökel notices the extent to which the Septuagint, in some places, transforms the 'symbols and images' of Hebrew into a more conceptual kind of discourse and he remarks: 'We may continue this process of conceptualization, provided we keep in mind the great danger of transposing a literary work into the realms of technical language. This would only serve to obstruct the actualization of the inspired work' (p. 291). Schökel discerns the fallacy of placing a 'literal translation' on a pedestal, since this almost always amounts to under-translation and may even result in non-translation. The reason for this is that the attempt to secure a one-one correspondence between the words of the original and the words of the translation takes no account of differences in word-order in different languages or of disparities in their syntactical structures. It is imaginative but disciplined transformation not mechanical reproduction which produces a translation. The flaw of the paraphrase is picked out by Schökel and paraphrase is often connected with bathetic and mediocre translation: the literary quality and allusiveness of the Hebrew are transposed into flat prose, sometimes under the influence of didactic or doctrinal concerns, and the language-field to which the original belongs is made unrecognizable. One of the assumptions of modern biblical translation which should be looked at hard is that the goal will have been reached if plainness of sense and intelligibility have been achieved. It will not have been reached if these have been achieved at a cost which is unacceptable because it involves too much loss. A plain translation which advertises its ordinariness and sinks into triviality is a failure to render those qualities of Hebrew poetry which invest it with the allusiveness and high seriousness it must possess if it is to carry the weight of the mystery.

If the openness of the Hebrew bible is to be stressed at a theological level, the maximum preservation of its full range of meaning, its nuances and its echoes, at the fundamental level of translation, is of the greatest importance. Where paraphrase converts poetry into instruction, the consequence is a narrowing, a trivializing and an imprisonment of the original. Some illustrations of this process will make it clearer. I take these from my commentary on Jeremiah 1–25 and they relate to renderings of the Hebrew in the Aramaic Targum of Jonathan. The Hebrew poetry has an allusiveness and indeterminacy which make it an inappropriate medium for pedestrian and didactic explicitness. In the Aramaic Targum the meaning is closely defined and spelled out by means of longer paraphrases which narrow the possibilities of interpretation and whose heavy prose changes poetry into instruction (pp. xxxvii–xli). I set out my translation of the Hebrew and describe the character of the Aramaic translation:

> Jer. 2.2   I remember the loyalty of your youth,
>   your love for me as a bride,
>   when you followed me in the wilderness,
>   in a land unsown.

In the Targum the marriage imagery disappears and the verse is represented as a general reference to Israel's loyalty and love. She was attached to Yahweh's word and followed his two messengers, Moses and Aaron, for forty years in the wilderness without defecting from Yahweh.

> Jer. 2.21   I planted you as a Sorek vine,
>   a strain tested for purity.
>   How is it that you have become a rogue vine,
>   a vine of unknown strain?

The Aramaic explains the vine imagery: 'I established you before me like a plant, a choice vine. All of you did what was right. But you have changed your relationship to me by your corrupt deeds! You have wandered from my worship and have become as a vine which has no usefulness in it.'

Jer. 8.22   Is there no balm in Gilead?
              Is no physician to be found there?

The Targum introduces the thought of 'intercession'. Gilead is taken as an allusion to Elijah and 'medicine' to his teaching. Even so powerful an intercessor as Elijah would avail nothing: 'Because they did not repent, healing will not overtake the wound of the community of my people.'

Jer. 14.8b, 9a   Why do you behave like an alien, resident in the land,
                  like a traveller who interrupts his journey only to find a lodging?
                  Why do you behave like a man reduced to a stupor,
                  like a hero who cannot bring help?

The Targum is influenced here by doctrinal considerations, by the unacceptability of the anthropomorphisms and anthropopathisms of the Hebrew text. The boldness of the imagery was perceived as an affront to Yahweh's majesty and the Targum has transferred to Israel the images which were applied to Yahweh. 'Why does your anger alight on us?' has no corresponding elements in the Hebrew which, otherwise, is deliberately changed: 'We are like immigrants in the land and like travellers who turn aside to find lodging for the night. Why does your anger alight on us? We are fickle and apostate, but you are a mighty man able to save. Your Shekinah is in our midst, O Lord, and we are called by your name. Do not desert us.' This is a good example of the destructive effects which doctrinal anxiety can have on translation.

I take up another related matter from a section in my Proverbs commentary entitled 'The Meaning of *Māšāl*' (pp. 22–33), where I was concerned to establish that openness of reference and an absence of foreclosure or narrowing of meaning is a special property of proverbial or parabolic elements in the Bible. Within the book of Proverbs the distinction between the Instruction *genre* which is represented by chapters 1–9 and 22.17 – 24.22, and the proverbial sentence consists not only in syntactical form, but also in respect of the differing textures of language which are brought into play. An Instruction if it is to be effective should have a pedestrian plainness; it should aim at a precision of definition which excludes ambiguity or uncertainty of any kind and narrowness of reference is a virtue in it. Ordinariness of language is what would be expected, given its function.

The case with the proverbial sentence is entirely otherwise, since its effectiveness in enhancing our understanding and penetration is associated with an intuitive leap which we make from its allusiveness and indeterminacy to the situation which it captures and illumines once we have closed the gap and perceived the character of the relationship. There is no single interpretation of a proverb or a parable. Proverbs are not limited by one interpretation of them and if they are so supplied, it is no more than one possible interpretation or application. When imagery with proverbial capabilities is supplied with a specific, limiting interpretation, a simile may result. When a parable is interpreted, this should be regarded as only one possibility, so that in the future it will be open to other applications, wherever new situations which it seizes and illumines are perceived.

I have been arguing that if hermeneutical openness is to be advanced as an important insight in the field of theology, the conservation of the widest possible range of reference at the levels of translation and literary appreciation should not be neglected. In particular, if the poetry of the Hebrew bible and its proverbial ingredients have resources of potential meaning which reach into the future, anything which would impair or destroy these at the level of translation or literary appreciation should be avoided.

Having gone thus far I am still dogged by a sharp awareness of the dubiety of the relatedness between the literary openness of the Hebrew bible, which I have been trying to describe, and the kind of transformation of meaning which is in view when a hermeneutical method serves the ends of Old Testament theology. When the exegesis of the Hebrew bible was practised in accord with a historical-critical method and was thought to be fulfilled in the recovery of the sense which the author intended in the historical context where he spoke or wrote, the task was defined with a tolerable clarity and the results were subject to a satisfactory degree of objective control. It is arguable that this control is not impaired as long as von Rad is describing hermeneutical transformations which take place within the Hebrew bible, or between the Testaments, provided that he is confining himself to Old Testament texts which are actually used by the New Testament writers and have been incorporated in the Greek New Testament. In that case all the evidence needed for a decision is available and we can make up our own minds about the worth of von Rad's arguments. The hermeneutical processes which he discerns appear in material which is available for inspection and his interpretation of this evidence is subject to independent scrutiny and judgement. Beyond this point all these checks and safeguards disappear and, where a charismatic exegesis of Old Testament texts, done 'in the freedom of the Holy Spirit', is offered as a means of exploiting the hermeneutical openness of the Old Testament, there is a feeling in one's bones of having been abandoned in a morass of subjectivity, of being left in a fearful jungle or cast adrift on uncharted seas: 'Regarding the handling of this sort of typological interpretation in the case of individual texts, no pedagogical norm may be set up; it cannot be further regulated hermeneutically, but takes place in the freedom of the Holy Spirit' (1963, p. 38).

Serious doubts are raised whether there is anything in common between the procedures by which a Christian exegesis of the Old Testament, done in the freedom of the Holy Spirit, reaches its conclusions and the kind of inexhaustibility which may be attached to biblical poetry and parables. The literary openness which I have described and the new Christian interpretations supposedly divulged by the Holy Spirit are two processes which seem to fall apart.

The second doubt about relating literary openness to theological hermeneutics is awakened by another factor of dissimilarity. It is true that von Rad is more of a conservationist than an iconoclast in his account of how the thrust of Old Testament theology is actualized and that, for the most part, he is describing the redeployment of biblical images rather than their destruction. The reinterpretation may be bold and even violent, but the assumption throughout is that the linguistic capital of the Old Testament is not expendable and that it must not be wasted or abandoned. A continuing claim is made on these resources not only to effect hermeneutical transformations within the Old Testament, but also to establish relations between the Old Testament and the New. The New Testament writers are represented as falling back on these resources in order to make their credal affirmations about Jesus and to find expression for the full significance of his coming.

A different situation is disclosed, however, when we consider the demythologizing hermeneutic of Bultmann, because, far from being founded on the inexhaustible resources of biblical imagery, it demands the destruction of that imagery as the price of hermeneutical progress. Bultmann's reinterpretation is carried out on the assumption that biblical imagery is a mythological impediment and that a restatement of the sense of New Testament passages in terms meaningful and relevant to moderns demands the sacrifice of the imagery in which they are clothed and a new framework of non-mythological interpretation. Moreover the Old Testament plays no part in this hermeneutic and von Rad's claim that the New Testament writers could not have achieved a linguistic expression for their proclamation or kerygma, for the credal status which they assigned to Jesus, without access to the resources of the Old Testament is rebutted by Bultmann. The Old Testament is not Christian Scripture and the New Testament is not a fulfilment of the Old. The Old Testament ends in shipwreck. The use of Old Testament texts in the New Testament is a secondary apologetic, a use of 'proof-texts' designed to establish that the keryma rests on the foundation of the Old

Testament, but the primary proclamation is independent of the Old
Testament (Bultmann, 1963, pp. 50–75; 1964, pp. 8–35). Here the
contact is lost between 'openness', as it applies to biblical language in a
process of literary appreciation, where the conservation of the imagery
is assumed, and the 'openness' of a theological hermeneutic.

Even in the case of von Rad one has the impression that the transformations which he describes involve more far-reaching structural
alterations than are envisaged in the descriptions of how Hebrew poetry
and proverbs can enlarge their areas of significance and the width of
their reference as they lie open to the future. It could, however, be
argued that von Rad does exploit a kind of openness on which some
light is thrown by a comparison with the possibilities of future applicability which I have attributed to the proverb or parable. For example,
von Rad's account of how the Hexateuchal Settlement Tradition, with
its leading idea of Promise (Israel's possession of the promised land)
retains its relevance and enriches its content in the changed historical
circumstances of the reign of David might be seen in this light. The old
cultic anchorage of the tradition had disappeared and the context of a
festival at Gilgal, celebrating and reliving the occupation of the land of
Canaan, had decayed, but the tradition retained its vigour, in a new and
apparently secular environment, in the new use to which the Yahwist
put it in his history:

> Doubtless the fact that the living traditions became detached from
> the localities with which they had cultic associations caused their
> content to become highly spiritualized; and it cannot be denied that
> the opportunity to grow away from the remote, stolid, materialistic
> cultic background was altogether a happy release, opening up
> unsuspected possibilities of development for the material which
> they contained. (*The Problem of the Hexateuch*, 1966, p. 49)

A chapter of Israel's history had closed, but the Promise was directed
to a new and more glorious chapter which had opened. It had been
inaugurated by David and the fulfilment of the Promise was seen in the
dignity of empire which had been achieved under his leadership. The
argument would be that just as new contexts of applicability are found
for proverbs and parable, so religious faith and insight are stirred to
insert the Promise of the Settlement Tradition into a state of affairs for
which historical explanations seem entirely adequate: the great powers
were quiescent and the time was ripe for David to fulfil his imperial
ambitions: 'Had Israel slipped from the hand of its ancient God, the
God of the patriarchs and of Moses? Had she departed from the domain
of his salvation and his leading? That was the great question' (*Genesis*,
1961, p. 28). It may have seemed that God had withdrawn from history

which was no longer a sphere of 'holiness' and divine intervention and which had become 'profane'. At this point von Rad develops his concept of a God who is hidden from view, but whose control of history though no longer manifest in a *Heilsgeschichte*, is yet completely effective and he uses this as a key in the interpretation of the Joseph narrative (*The Problem of the Hexateuch*, pp. 293–300; *Theology*, i, pp. 172f): 'For a time it must have seemed that God had withdrawn himself from history. But it was not so. His activity was only different from what had been experienced in the holy wars of former times; it was hidden and not in sacral manifestations, but almost concealed in the profane. The new experience is a background against which the Yahwist wrote his work' (*Genesis*, pp. 29f).

That there is a correlation between the literary qualities of the Hebrew bible and Old Testament theology is assumed by Schökel. He reckons with different kinds of literature in the Hebrew bible, but he remarks, 'The wise man as well as the prophet is inspired' (1967, p. 100): 'We may sum up our consideration by saying that the greater part of the Old Testament does not contain that which we call prophetic in the strict sense of the term, but rather a type of activity approximating that of the wisdom tradition. Nevertheless, we accept that the whole of the Old Testament is the word of God' (p. 102). He differentiates between three levels of language, common, literary and technical (pp. 151–73) and he urges that biblical theology because it deals with literature must follow different methods from those of dogmatic and scientific theology which are 'conceptual transpositions' of a text and are not the same as 'exegesis' (pp. 168f). 'The biblical expression is superior to the dogmatic expression of a mystery, because it is formally word of God' (p. 169). The circumstance that the Scriptures are written in literary language 'is a fact of some importance in a study of inspiration' and it has 'the greatest importance in hermeneutics, for inspiration takes upon itself and actively exploits all the rich possibilities of literary language' (p. 161).

In this connection the openness of literary language, its rich resources of meaning demands an exegesis which should not be fettered by the historical-critical method, though it should not ride rough-shod over it: 'Since the language of scripture is literary, it demands a literary interpretation and yet every interpretation leaves the text unexhausted' (p. 161). Hermeneutical openness is an acceptable principle 'in so far as it does not allow us to treat the text simply as a text, but rather sharpens our appreciation of it as a medium in and by which a subjectively experienced reality receives its new objective existence' (p. 163). The reason why there is such a necessary relation between 'inspiration' or 'word of God' and the literary qualities of Scripture is that 'is that inspiration is directed specifically to the act of language, and it is this which differentiates it from the other charisms' (p. 177). Two general consequences are the indissolubility of literature and theology in Schökel's scheme of biblical theology and the firm separation, on linguistic grounds, of biblical theology from dogmatic or scientific theology.

A. B. Davidson is a representative of an older school of Old Testament theology and his book *The Theology of the Old Testament* was published posthumously in 1904. He defines Old Testament theology as a historical science, 'the historical and genetic presentation of the religion of the Old Testament' (p. 6). But it is not an account of erratic or incompatible change, nor is the change merely 'evolutionary' in character. It is 'organic' and it maps out a cumulative thrust whose product is a body of 'doctrine' issuing from a progressive revelation: 'This means not only that Old Testament theology shows us the religion of the Old Testament *in genesi* . . . but that its progress was, so to speak, organic. It grew and that not only by the mere accretion or external addition of truth to truth. The succeeding truth grew out of the former truth' (p. 8).

Hence the characteristic of Old Testament theology which should be emphasized is its union with history and not its symbiosis with literature or language, as Schökel had contended, and there is no awareness in Davidson's theology of the different universes of discourse allocated to biblical and systematic theology respectively by Schökel, that one uses literary language and the other technical language.

Moreover, and despite what Davidson has said about the propriety of a historical method in an Old Testament theology, the circumstance that it is an 'organic' as well as a 'genetic' discipline has the effect of giving it some of the aspects of a systematic theology. Not a systematic theology in the sense that it has the non-historical, abstract character of universal truth, but because its aiming at organic status results in the introduction of systematization in its account of Old Testament theology. A glance at its organization will show that it proposes to discuss in chapters II – XII a succession of 'doctrines' beginning with 'The Doctrine of God' and ending with 'Doctrine of the Last Things – Immortality'.

Given the form of Davidson's work just described there is no place in it for the hermeneutical openness which, in different ways, was a feature of both von Rad and Schökel. If the religion of the Old Testament is a progressive revelation which is cumulative and is consolidated into a body of truth, the underlying assumption is that there is one exegesis and only one which is normative for its texts at all the different stages. Hence what has been said of Eichrodt's exegesis and its connections with the school of *Religionsgeschichte* applies also to Davidson.

Another theology which rests on the assumption of one normative exegesis for the texts of the Old Testament is Vriezen's *Outline of Old*

Testament Theology (1962; a translation of the second Dutch edition, 1954). One advances to Part II of this book (pp. 128–372) with the expectation that the lines which have been drawn in Part I (pp. 2–126) will influence his account of the content of Old Testament theology in Part II, but the promise of originality is not fulfilled in Part II. A scrutiny of its structure gives the impression that Vriezen is almost a systematizer in the old style. His lay-out recalls that of Davidson's theology. Davidson's scheme is a more elaborate one and there is more evidence that he intends to organize the Old Testament as a body of doctrine, but Vriezen has not departed from this system and there are respects in which he shares Davidson's presuppositions as to what constitutes an Old Testament theology. Thus he has a chapter on the doctrine of God (vii), the doctrine of man (viii) and a chapter on eschatology (xi). Vriezen remarks that the Old Testament cannot be reduced to a systematic theology, but he is tending, all the while, to organize it as a body of doctrine. Thus in chapter vii he gathers material from different parts of the Old Testament, organizes it and makes it coherent in order to develop a doctrine of God as holy, living, one and unique; as Creator, Saviour and Maintainer. Old Testament theology for him, as for Davidson, consists of normative doctrines which can be gathered from the Old Testament by an inductive process.

However, it has to be said that the concepts of secondary canonicity and prophetic testimony which were developed in Part I of Vriezen's theology exercise an influence on his method. In virtue of 'secondary canonicity' he is selective in his use of the Old Testament: it is only the Old Testament *qua* prophetic testimony that he needs to consult in order to formulate his theology. He is giving notice that all parts of the Old Testament are not of equal theological value. His interest in 'prophetic testimony' is an indication that he is not a detached historian examining the Old Testament critically as a source for Israel's religion, but a man who believes that it contains the word of God. Yet he supposes that acts of God can be described as historical occurrences and so belong to a *Religionsgeschichte*.

It might be thought that Eichrodt's departure from earlier Old Testament theologies, and the originality of his contribution, is greater than I have so far acknowledged. It does not seem to me to be so, though there are features of volume i in which a difference of approach from that of his predecessors can be detected. It is evident that the chapters in volume i have been organized around the concept of 'covenant', and that they draw out its significance by indicating the institutions which it generated and how it shaped the life of the Israelite community. The extent of Eichrodt's contribution is better explored in these areas rather than in connection with the preliminary theoretical contribution which he made to Old Testament theology (1929, pp. 83–91), where he argued that it was a special kind of Old Testament history and that it was entirely amenable to a historical-critical method.

The aim of volume i is to divest Old Testament theology of its anaemic, damaging theoretical appearance and to integrate what is regarded as a key concept of it with the institutions which depended on 'covenant' for their validity and vigour; and so to describe Old Testament theology in terms of the influence which it exercised in giving form and content to the life of a community and in bestowing on it a special quality of life. It was an effort to rescue Old Testament theology from disembodiment, to give it flesh and bones and to breathe vitality into it; to establish that it was not just a system of ideas or doctrine, but that it informed religious institutions and directed traffic in busier thoroughfares.

A complementary intention of volume i is to dispense with Davidson's difficult combination of 'genetic' and 'organic' as a means of creating permanency amid flux. Davidson assumes that the history of Israel's religion is indeed a progressive revelation and that as one stage succeeds another there is never a serious contradiction or confusion, so that what has originated in an evolutionary process is built up into a single body of doctrine. Eichrodt introduces in volume i the covenant concept, and the institutions which were founded on it and empowered by it, to supply elements of permanency and constancy amid change.

To turn finally to von Rad and Schökel: they are employing a new hermeneutical method and both affirm that the exegesis of texts should not be static, that their meaning is open to the future and that their hidden resources can be revealed in subsequent enrichments of meaning. But the correlation of von Rad and Schökel should not be exaggerated and their alliance terminates here. What then separates them is the union of biblical theology and language/literature which is the hallmark of Schökel and distinguishes him from all the other Old Testament theologians who have been discussed, including von Rad. The novelty of Schökel's method derives from his contrast of literary and technical language, his description of the Hebrew bible as literary language and his analysis of its characteristics. The effect of this is to entangle Old Testament theology with sensitive literary appreciation and linguistic niceties in new ways and Schökel supposes that this can be done without weakening the theological claim that the Scriptures are the 'word of God' and that they are inspired. He is describing kinds of literary inspiration in the Hebrew bible, but he also holds that it is 'inspired' in a theological sense.

The connections of von Rad's theology, on the other hand, are with advances made in Old Testament critical scholarship by himself in *The Problem of the Hexateuch* (German edition, 1938) and later by Noth in *A History of Pentateuchal Traditions* (German edition, 1948). The effect of

these advances is to modify fundamentally the kind of union between
Old Testament theology and Old Testament history which had earlier
prevailed, but the question is still one about the nature of the relationship between the two disciplines and not in any way the establishing of
a concert between Old Testament theology and Old Testament literature in the manner of Schökel.

Von Rad's work rests on a claim that Old Testament theology and
Old Testament historiography are different universes of discourse. Old
Testament theology is distilled from credal affirmations not from historiography and the historical narratives in the Hexateuch are a secondary expansion and elaboration of credal statements. Von Rad is concerned with the *genre* of the raw material of Old Testament theology
and he holds that this consists of credal statements and not historiography. His Old Testament Theology is a theology of Old Testament
traditions: as we have noted, the sub-title of the first volume is 'The
Theology of Israel's Historical Traditions' and of the second 'The Theology of Israel's Prophetical Traditions'. It is these credal traditions
which are the source of the hermeneutical thrust of von Rad's theology
of the Old Testament. That they are the seeds of exegetical enrichment
and that their meaning can be extended and transformed is (so von Rad)
already evident in the Hexateuch and they continue to supply the
linguistic capital which is further exploited by the canonical prophets.
Hence the connections of exegetical openness in von Rad are far
removed from those of Schökel. Their links are with new critical depar-
tures in Pentateuchal/Hexateuchal scholarship and not with the literary
qualities of the language of the Hebrew bible.

Literature

Bultmann, R., 'Prophecy and Fulfilment'. Translated by J. C. G. Greig from
    Probleme alttestamentlicher Hermeneutik (München, 1960), *Essays on Old
    Testament Interpretation*, edited by C. Westermann (London, 1963), pp. 50–
    75.
Bultmann, R., 'The Significance of the Old Testament for Christian Faith'.
    Translated by B. W. Anderson, *The Old Testament and Christian Faith*,
    edited by B. W. Anderson (London, 1964), pp. 8–35.
Davidson, A. B., *The Theology of the Old Testament* (Edinburgh, 1904).
Eichrodt, W., *Theology of the Old Testament*, i and ii (London, 1961 and 1967).
    Translated by J. Baker from *Theologie des Alten Testaments*, Teil i (1959⁶) and
    Teil ii–iii (1964⁵).
Eichrodt, W. 'Hat die alttestamentliche Theologie noch selbständige Bedeu-
    tung innerhalb der alttestamentlichen Wissenschaft', *ZAW* N.F. 6 (1929),
    pp. 83–91.
Fulke, W., *A Defense of the sincere and true Translations of the holie Scriptures into
    the English Tong* (London, 1583). Parker edition (Cambridge, 1843).

Klatt, W., *Hermann Gunkel. Zu seiner Theologie der Religionsgeschichte und zur Entstehung der formgeschichtlichen Methode* (Göttingen, 1969).
McKane, W., *Proverbs: A New Approach* (London, 1970).
McKane, W., *A Critical and Exegetical Commentary on Jeremiah i–xxv* (Edinburgh, 1986).
McKane, W., *Studies in the Patriarchal Narratives* (Edinburgh, 1979).
MacQuarrie, J., *God-Talk! An Examination of the Language and Logic of Theology* (London, 1967).
Noth, M., *A History of Pentateuchal Traditions* (Englewood Cliffs, 1972). Translated by B. W. Anderson from *Überlieferungsgeschichte des Pentateuch* (Stuttgart, 1948).
Schökel, L. A. *The Inspired Word* (London, 1967). Translated by F. Martin from *La Palabra Inspirada* (Barcelona, 1966).
von Rad, G., *Old Testament Theology*, i–ii (Edinburgh and London, 1962 and 1965). Translated by D. M. G. Stalker from *Theologie des Alten Testaments*, i–ii (München, 1957 and 1960).
von Rad, G., *The Problem of the Hexateuch and Other Essays* (Edinburgh and London, 1966). Translated by E. W. T. Dicken from *Gesammelte Studien zum Alten Testament* (München, 1958).
von Rad, G., 'Typological Interpretation of the Old Testament', *Essays on Old Testament Interpretation*, edited by C. Westermann (London, 1963), pp. 17–39. Translated by J. Bright from *Probleme alttestamentlicher Hermeneutik* (München, 1960).
von Rad, G., *Genesis: A Commentary* (London, 1961). Translated by J. H. Marks from *Das erste Buch Mose Genesis* (Göttingen, 1956).
von Rad, G., *Moses*, World Christian Books (London, 1960).
Vriezen, T. C., *An Outline of Old Testament Theology* (Oxford, 1962). First Dutch edition, *Hooofdlijnen der Theologie van het Oude Testament* (1949).

INDEX OF NAMES AND SUBJECTS

Fulke, W. – *cont.*
  biblical interpretation, 44–5
  Renaissance scholarship, 43–4

Gunkel, H.,
  canonical prophets and rationality, 134
  ecstasy and revelation, 133–5, 146–7
  literary form and prophetic experience,
    136, 138–40
  Religionsgeschichte, 115–16, 162
  revelatory state and the supernatural,
    134, 135
  visions and revelation, 134

Haninah, Rabbi, 1
Hooke, S. H., 67
Houtman, C., 70
Hunnius, 48

Ingold, A., 62, 63

Johnson, A. R., 67, 126–7, 131
Jülicher, A., 84

Kinsley, J., 54, 56
Klatt, W., 133, 162
Kuenen, A.,
  abnormal states, 76–8
  canonical prophets, 65–6
  canonical prophets and institution, 66,
    68–9
  canonical prophets and religious
    excellence, 80
  comparison with Maimonides, 80–3
  compulsion, 149
  ethical monotheism, 69–70
  oracular style, 76, 79
  O.T. texts in N.T., 74–5
  prophecies of hope, 73–6
  prophetic predictions, 69–73
  rationality, 76–8
  Religionsgeschichte, 73–4
  Robertson Smith, 69
  supernaturalism, 69, 77, 79–80
  theodicy, 73

Laws, R., 107
Lindblom, J.,
  compulsion, 148–51

  ecstasy and rationality, 137
  enthusiasm and magic, 124–5
  literary form and prophetic experience,
    136, 138–42
  mouth-pieces of Yahweh, 137, 144–5
  psychic power and prediction, 127
  psychic power and symbolic acts, 125–
    6
  revelatory state and the supernatural,
    135–8, 146
  the threat of inaccessibility, 127–8
  'These are the words of Yahweh', 144–
    5, 151
  word-concepts, 129–30
Louis XIV, 53, 62–3

McKane, W., 72, 77, 103, 130, 131, 149
MacQuarrie, J., 9
Maimonides, Moses,
  a prophet's regimen, 37
  anthropomorphic language, 18
  ascription of attributes to God, 1–2
  attributes of God and imaginative
    language, 4–5, 14
  defective imagination in scientists, 33–
    4, 36, 37
  defective rationality in soothsayers, 32–
    3
  denial of speech to God, 29–31, 32,
    40
  distinction between prophets and
    dreamers, 34–5
  distinction between true and false
    prophets, 35–6
  God an active intellect, 8
  God and 'overflow', 13
  imagination a source of error, 31
  language of the 'sons of man', 2, 11–13,
    17, 23–4
  language about God not literal, 7
  Moses a unique prophet, 30
  Moses heard a voice created by God,
    18–19
  'overflow' and liturgical needs, 13–14
  'overflow' and the *via negativa*, 26–9
  prophecy and the balance of reason and
    imagination, 36–8
  prophecy and 'overflow', 37–8

INDEX OF SCRIPTURE REFERENCES